ABANDONED HUSBAND . . .
OR DECEITFUL KILLER?

Detective Miller, a soft-spoken man, asked Perry March point-blank if he had killed his wife and disposed of her body. Perry adamantly denied having harmed Janet in any way. He admitted that he and Janet had argued on the night of August 15, but he said that he had not attacked her. She simply took the things that she had packed and drove away in her Volvo.

"Look at me," Perry said at one point. "On August 15, 1996, I was a respected lawyer in Nashville. I had it all. A beautiful wife. Two wonderful kids. Gorgeous home. I was a go-to guy in the business community. I was making good money. Now, my wife has left me."

Later, Perry would go on-camera on CBS News' *48 Hours* and tell a national television audience: "Janet was a wonderful mother. Very doting."

It seemed strange how he referred to her in the past tense.

Also by Gary C. King

Blood Lust: Portrait of a Serial Sex Killer

Driven to Kill

Web of Deceit

Blind Rage

An Early Grave

The Texas 7

Murder in Hollywood

Angels of Death

Stolen in the Night

LOVE, LIES, and MURDER

GARY C. KING

PINNACLE BOOKS
Kensington Publishing Corp.
http://www.kensingtonbooks.com

Some names have been changed to protect the privacy of individuals connected to this story.

PINNACLE BOOKS are published by

Kensington Publishing Corp.
850 Third Avenue
New York, NY 10022

Copyright © 2007 by Gary C. King Enterprises, Inc.

All Kensington Titles, Imprints, and Distributed Lines are available at special quantity discounts for bulk purchases for sales promotions, premiums, fund-raising, and educational or institutional use. Special book excerpts or customized printings can also be created to fit specific needs. For details, write or phone the office of the Kensington special sales manager: Kensington Publishing Corp., 850 Third Avenue, New York, NY 10022, attn: Special Sales Department, Phone: 1-800-221-2647.

Pinnacle and the P logo Reg. U.S. Pat. & TM Off.

ISBN-13: 978-0-7860-1892-5
ISBN-10: 0-7860-1892-5

First Printing: August 2007

10 9 8 7 6 5 4 3 2 1

Printed in the United States of America

For Teresita,
Always

*The heart is deceitful above all things,
and desperately wicked: Who can know it?*
                                    —Jeremiah 17:9

*Well, old man, I will tell you news of your
son. Give me your blessing: truth will come
to light; murder cannot be hid long—a man's
son may, but at the length truth will out.*
                                    —William Shakespeare,
                                    The Merchant of Venice,
                                    Act 2, Scene 2

Acknowledgments

My sincere, heartfelt gratitude is especially reserved for my immediate family. Without their full support during the writing of this book, in which they endured months of inconvenience as I isolated myself from them and forced them to virtually live on their own, this book would not have been possible. I am especially grateful to my wife, Teresita, who persuaded me to embrace this project and helped me see what a great story it really was, even though she knew it would cause us to live our own separate lives until it was finished. Thanks also to Kirsten and Sarah, who were always there when I needed them most!

A very special thank-you goes to Kevin James Bell, a very dear and close family friend who, through his love and devotion to me and my family, repeatedly came to my rescue and helped fulfill some of my duties and obligations when I was unable to do so myself, and for helping keep my family unit in top form during my self-imposed isolation. The world needs more people like Kevin!

I would also like to thank Chief Ronal Serpas, of the Metropolitan Nashville Police Department, along with his staff, for their cooperation during the writing of this book. I also want to acknowledge the dedicated work and service of Sergeant Patrick Postiglione and Detective Bill Pridemore, veteran homicide detectives who were named Metropolitan Nashville Police Department's Investigators of the Year for 2005 for their effort in bringing Perry March to justice and for providing closure to a case that, at times, seemed like it might never be solved, and to Captain Mickey Miller and Detective David Miller, retired.

I would also like to acknowledge the very fine work of the reporters at the *Tennessean* who followed this story day in and day out. It was through their great work that I was able to stay informed at a distance of the continuing developments of this fascinating case. Willy Stern also did an outstanding job in his two-part series "A Good Thing Gone Bad," which appeared in the *Nashville Scene,* and whose work actually assisted the police in locating sources that they had been unable to find. Stern's articles were instrumental in providing a basis for some of the historical aspects concerning the March family. The Nashville *City Paper,* CBS News' *48 Hours,* Court TV, and the work of a number of other news agencies, too numerous to mention here, are all worthy of acknowledgment. Attribution is provided throughout the book where information from the aforementioned sources has been used. Thanks also to Jorge Jaramillo, of the Associated Press, for his assistance with the photos used in this book.

I also want to thank my longtime literary agent, Peter Miller, of PMA Literary & Film Management, for bringing Michaela Hamilton, Executive Editor at Kensington Books, and me together again for this project. Michaela bought and edited my first book, *Blood Lust: Portrait of a Serial Sex Killer,* in 1992, when she was at Penguin USA, and was instrumental in making it a great success. Michaela's integrity, professionalism, and business savvy in the publishing industry are without reproach, and I couldn't be happier working with her again.

Last, but definitely not least, I would like to gratefully acknowledge Stephanie Finnegan for the exceptional and thorough job she did copyediting the manuscript. I'm sure that it was no easy task, but Stephanie's effort and attention to detail served to greatly improve the final product. Thanks, Stephanie!

Author's Note

The book that you are now reading is a true crime story. It is not the typical true crime story that attempts to titillate the reader with gruesome or overly sensational details, because a body was never found. There was, nonetheless, a murder that was committed—according to the victim's family, the police, a prosecutor, and a jury—as well as a host of other alleged serious crimes, including a kidnapping, con artist schemes, shady real estate deals in which elderly women were charmed and duped into turning over their life savings to an unscrupulous sociopath, and a murder-for-hire plot that made this story one of the most compelling that I have ever told. It is my hope, my intention, really, that this book will transcend the typical true crime genre and move the reader into the realm of a gripping and captivating human interest story involving two wealthy professionals who seemed to have everything, and the numerous lives that were destroyed due to the unfortunate chain of events that were set in motion following a purposeless homicide—an ultimate tragedy if ever there was one.

The characters in this real-life drama include former Nashville, Tennessee, attorney Perry March, whose wife, Janet, literally disappeared without a trace. According to all accounts, she did not leave a note behind, nor did she instruct anyone to convey a message from her to anyone—not even an attorney to deliver divorce papers to her husband on her behalf. She simply vanished, leaving Perry and her children amid an unusual turn of events that would eventually find the lawyer living an entirely new life in Mexico, presumably to be able to make a living and evade public scrutiny in the United States.

Portions of this story were related to me by residents of La Manzanilla, Mexico, who were knowledgeable about certain aspects of the bizarre case surrounding Perry March. The story will follow Perry March as he attempted to assimilate into his new environment, his various alleged schemes that revolved around shady real estate deals made with retired expatriate women, and how he became involved, along with two other attorneys that he retained, in getting his children returned to him after the children's maternal grandparents, armed with a visitation order and the cooperation and assistance of a Mexican judge, who had the children picked up at their school, whisked them out of Mexico and brought them back to the United States without March's knowledge or approval.

This story first came to my attention in 2002, as it was still developing, and due to prior contractual commitments on other book projects, I could not get involved at that time. However, by the time the case broke in 2005, the timing for my involvement was just right. I was just finishing up the manuscript for *Stolen in the Night,* my book about the Joseph Edward Duncan III case, and I was actively looking for a story that was markedly different from anything that I had ever written before. The Perry March case fit that bill perfectly.

Though at times the story might seem like fiction—how could a story like this have really happened?—I want to take this opportunity to assure my readers that all of the incidents portrayed herein are indeed factual and all of the characters depicted are real people. The research needed to bring this story to fruition included hundreds of hours of research, and interviews with people who were close to the case and the investigations. I have attempted to present the facts of the case as they are known and as they have been presented to the public in various media formats, including newspapers, magazines, tabloids, television and radio news and entertainment programs, as well as what happened in the courtroom at the various stages that this case has gone through. Some of the dialogue that appears herein is based on statements that were made in the various news media mentioned above, as well as from my own interviews with certain individuals. The dialogue quoted from news sources includes, but is not limited to, the following: the *Tennessean*, the *City Paper*, Court TV, *Nashville Scene*, CBS News' *48 Hours*, CNN, MSNBC, ABC News, the *National Enquirer*, and a host of other sources, including police documents, transcripts of taped conversations, and trial documents. I have made every possible effort to present the story as historically accurate as possible. Because of the story's complexity, I elected to tell it in more or less chronological order for the sake of clarity and to enable the reader to relive it, if you will, in the order that it occurred.

—G.C.K.

Part 1
NASHVILLE

Chapter 1

The road to Nashville wealth, affluence, and fame is not an easy road to traverse, and is one that is often filled with broken deals, hardship, disappointment, and outright failure. Those who are able to scratch and claw their way out of the ranks of the masses to realize their dreams are few. To the average tourist, the social class divisions in Nashville are not readily apparent; quite the contrary, however, to those who reside there and are trying to make it to the top of the ranks by attempting to break out of the mold of the common folk. It is one thing to make it in Nashville—quite another to make it only to be literally chased out of town—like the Native Americans of the Mississippian culture, there one day and gone the next. But that is precisely what happened to financial attorney and self-proclaimed genius Perry Avram March.

Nashville, by and large, is a charming, friendly city, where people smile at each other and occasionally greet each other on the street, as is somewhat common among Southerners. Most of the lifelong residents have more than a bit of a Southern twang in their voices, and it is relatively easy to spot the more recent transplants because, unless they are from the South, they lack the telltale accent. In the past decade Nashville has attracted a lot of "Northerners." Nashville's former mayor and the state's current governor, Phil Bredesen, moved to Tennessee from Massachusetts in 1975. Homes are still moderately priced, and the cost of living is considered reasonable. Although it can be hot and humid, the weather, overall, is typically mild. Nashville is home to several major colleges and universities, including Vanderbilt, Meharry Medical School, Fisk, and Tennessee State. Although Nashville has become very cosmopolitan over the years and boasts a relatively low crime rate, compared to other cities of its population, it is, nonetheless, a metropolis that is not unlike many other cities of its size—busy with traffic and tourists, the usual hustle and bustle of the rush hours, gang activity, graffiti and tagging, drive-by shootings, disappearances, and murders. In short, the unfriendly side of Nashville can easily chew you up and spit you out, and often does.

As with most tourist-intensive cities, the darker side of Nashville is glossed over and nearly hidden by the neon lights of the many nightclubs, performance stages, bars, and restaurants. In The District, located in the downtown area along Second Avenue and the historic Broadway area, disco à la the 1970s and 1980s can be found at Graham Central Station; additionally, numerous restaurants, chic boutiques, and microbreweries are located there. The District is known as the liveliest entertainment area of the city. Music Row is a colorful area with its aspiring musicians, singers, songwriters, twenty-nine major record labels, 150 recording studios, and other diversions, and many who live there contend that it is the music industry that really drives the city and makes it interesting. Most people can be easily taken in by Nashville's Southern charm, scenic beauty, great food, and the warmth of many of its people.

As residents of Nashville awoke on Thursday, August 15, 1996, the mercury was in the low 60s, and the humidity a comfortable 50 percent as its inhabitants sat down for their morning coffees and breakfasts. Although a light breeze stirred the sometimes stagnant air quality, the local weather reporters were predicting a high temperature of around 90 for later in the afternoon, with humidity levels reaching near 100 percent—it would be sticky and miserable as the day wore on.

On that same day, Perry March, thirty-five, was still a successful Nashville lawyer employed at his father-in-law's firm, Levine, Mattson, Orr & Geracioti, and his beautiful, dark-haired wife, Janet Gail Levine March, thirty-three, an accomplished artist and children's book illustrator, was still alive. They lived together in their mansion dream home, which Janet herself designed, situated on four acres on Blackberry Road, in the posh, upscale community of Forest Hills, located a few miles southwest of Nashville, sandwiched midway between Interstate 40 and Interstate 65. They resided there with their two beautiful children, five-year-old Samson, affectionately known as "Sammy," and two-year-old Tzipora, named after her paternal grandmother, Zipora, and known as "Tzipi." By all appearances, the children seemed happy, healthy, and contented, and enjoyed the companionship provided by their part-time Russian nanny, Ella Goldshmid, who adored them. When they weren't with Ella, Sammy and Tzipi were often with their maternal grandparents, Lawrence "Larry" and Carolyn Levine, which allowed Perry and Janet the freedom they desired to get out and socialize with a circle of friends and acquaintances that included some of West Nashville's most

high-flying young Jewish couples. To those looking in from
the outside, the Marches appeared to be a near-perfect
family that had everything going for them and, materially
at least, everything they could possibly want. That all
changed, however, on that fateful day when Janet disappeared without a trace.

Whenever Perry and Janet March had a beef with each
other, which had become more and more frequent as they
neared the end of their nine years of marriage, it was their
custom to always take their arguments outside onto the
deck of their French-style house so that Sammy and Tzipi
would not have to be subjected to their parents' shouting
matches. Perry was described by associates as a bright, aggressive, and tenacious financial attorney who sometimes
had a short fuse. Financial attorneys are typically involved
in commercial litigation, real estate, and business organi-
zations, transactions and contracts, and their area of the
legal world is often a stressful one. While it was not certain that Perry's stress at work had been unleashed and
transmuted into yet another fight with Janet on Thursday
evening, August 15, 1996, at home, it remained a distinct
possibility. Janet, too, could be hot-tempered and easy to
set off, and was known to be able to escalate a mere squab-
ble into a heated argument as quickly as Perry. Whatever
they fought about that evening was known only to Perry
and Janet, and it would be some time yet before the pieces
to their jigsaw puzzle could be sorted out and put together.

What was known about that fateful day was that Janet
spent much of it at home overseeing the work of two cabinetmakers, John McAlister and John Richie. Perry, who had
come home from work a little early that afternoon, had

announced himself by greeting Janet and the cabinetmakers, and then entertained himself and the children outside. The two cabinetmakers were employed by Classic Interior and Design, and had been summoned to the Marches' $650,000 home on Blackberry Road to complete warranty work on wooden countertops that they had installed on an earlier date.

Janet's demands were sometimes considered unreasonable, and they were perceived as such by the two tradesmen that afternoon as she supervised the countertop repairs, according to McAlister's and Richie's recollections. She had become so vocal, it was later recalled, that Perry had to come inside to calm her down. McAlister and Richie, unsettled by her behavior, finished their work as quickly as possible and packed up their tools and left the March residence at approximately 5:00 P.M. Besides Perry and the children, McAlister and Richie were the last people to see Janet March alive.

After the cabinetmakers left, according to what Perry later told the police and others, he and Janet sat down to a "nice, quiet dinner" with the kids. Afterward, Janet went into her studio to work on an art project. Sometime between 7:00 and 7:30 P.M., Perry put the children to bed in their rooms upstairs—first Sammy and then Tzipi. When he returned to the downstairs area of the house, Perry noticed that Janet had packed three bags, and had placed them and other items in the deck area. It was then, according to Perry, that he and Janet had become embroiled in an argument. Sometime around 8:30 P.M., Janet said "see ya" to Perry, placed her things in her gray 1996 Volvo 850, and left. He said that she also took between $4,000 and $5,000 in cash with her, along with her passport and a plastic bag of marijuana. Perry would later tell his in-laws, family friends, and the news media that he had asked Janet where she was going, and she had responded that it was none of his business. She purportedly told him that she would return in a few days. That, Perry said, was the last time he had seen Janet. Unfortunately, there was no one to corroborate Perry's account of what had occurred inside their house that evening—not even the children. They had spent the evening asleep.

Perry, by his own account and as reported by the *Nashville Scene,* called his brother, Ron, at 9:11 P.M., at his home in Illinois, to tell him that Janet had left him and the kids. Ron, also an attorney, and his wife, Amy, had been preparing for bed when Perry called. Perry only talked to Ron for three minutes at most, because he called his sister, Kathy, who was living in New Buffalo, Michigan, at 9:14 P.M. The conversation with Kathy ended after only four minutes.

The next call that Perry made was around midnight when he called Janet's parents, Larry and Carolyn Levine, to inform them of their fight and Janet's departure. Perry would later say that he did not call his in-laws immediately because he and Janet had promised each other that they would not involve them in their marital issues. He had also waited to call the Levines because he first called several Nashville hotels to see if she had checked in somewhere. When he couldn't locate her, he said, he decided to call her parents because he felt that she might have gone to their home to spend the night and cool off. Perry said that he had told the Levines that he should call the police and report Janet missing, but, he insisted, the Levines suggested that he wait and give her a chance to come home. Perry said that Janet's parents didn't want to get the police involved because it could prove embarrassing. Everyone reasoned, perhaps convinced by Perry, that Janet would return home soon.

Janet's mother, Carolyn, later said that she had initially believed what Perry had told her and Larry about Janet's sudden departure, but she was suspicious. Janet's disappearance was so out of character, in part because her life revolved around her marriage, her home and family, and her art career, according to her mother and her friends. If she had left Perry, for whatever reason, she would never have left her children behind.

Janet apparently had not told Perry that she had invited one of her friends to drop off her son to play with Sammy the next day. She apparently had not told him of the plans for Sammy's sixth birthday party, either, only a few days away. Both were critical factors that would weigh heavily on the credibility of Perry's account of what had happened to Janet.

Chapter 2

The following morning, Friday, August 16, one of Janet's many acquaintances, Marissa Moody, arrived on Blackberry Road with her six-year-old son. Marissa never really liked going to visit Janet and Perry, but her son and Sammy were friends and she did not want to deny the children their friendship because of her own feelings. Marissa, a divorced mother with two children, wasn't sure why she felt uncomfortable around the Marches, but she, at one point, told *Nashville Scene* writer Willy Stern that she had never felt accepted by Perry and Janet, which was one possible explanation. They had slighted her on prior occasions, for reasons that were not made clear. Nonetheless, she had made arrangements with Janet a day earlier to bring her son over to their home that Friday so that he and Sammy could play for part of the day. Whatever problems that existed between the adults, Marissa didn't want them to come between the children. It was about 10:00 A.M. when she turned off Blackberry Road, pulled into the driveway, and parked. When she got out of her car with her son in tow, she noticed that Tzipi was playing in the yard that ran along the side of the house with her nanny, Ella. She smiled and waved as she and her son walked up the stairs and through an outer archway and into the short vestibule that led to the front door.

From the outside, the appearance of the multilevel A-frame-designed house was awe-inspiring, intense, and somewhat foreboding, with its grayish stone and mortar facade, two elevated outside decks—one on each side of the front of the house—and an arched front window. Tall, mature trees surrounded the gargantuan dwelling in the rear and on each side, giving it an even more ominous effect. In the neighborhood of estatelike homes, the houses were set back a significant distance from the road and spaced acres away from each other, affording much privacy to the residents.

Sammy eagerly greeted Marissa and her son at the door and led them inside the house, with Ella following close behind. They walked down a short hallway toward the kitchen, across highly polished hardwood floors. The house's interior seemed like it was made almost entirely of a light hardwood—wood was all that caught a visitor's eye: wooden floors, wooden railings, wooden doors—wood everywhere. The interior was plain and austere, with no carpeting and few rugs, yet the wood provided the house a luxurious look and feel. The 5,300-square-foot house was so extremely clean and orderly that it appeared to shine. Deneane Beard, a housecleaner hired by the Marches, had already been there for two or more hours following her usual routine by the time that Marissa had arrived that morning. The only thing that seemed even remotely out of place was a large dark rug, rolled up, lying near Perry's closed-door study and near where the children's playroom opened into the hallway. From Marissa's vantage point, it

could have been an Oriental rug, but because it was rolled
up, it was difficult to tell for certain. Ella told her that
Janet was not at home.

While Marissa waited for Perry to come out of his study,
she talked with Sammy, who, by this time, was sitting atop
the rolled-up rug, occasionally bouncing up and down on
it as any child his age would do. Sammy explained to
Marissa that his mother was not at home, and said that he
and his father were planning to visit Perry's office later in
the day. During the time that Marissa was there, however,
Perry never did come out to greet her—he stayed inside his
study and told Sammy to tell Marissa that it was okay for
her to leave her son to play for a few hours. Perry had
always treated her that way. Aside from feeling disre-
spected yet again, Marissa thought little of Perry's behavior at the time. She told her son that she would be back to
get him later, said good-bye to Sammy, went outside, and
got into her car and left. She had no idea whether she
would see Perry when she returned. Based on his previous
behavior, it was doubtful.

When Marissa Moody returned a few hours later to pick
up her son, she noticed that the rolled-up rug, which she
had seen earlier, was gone. She wasn't sure why at the
time, but it was a small detail that she would not forget.

After Marissa left the March home with her son, Perry
took Sammy and Tzipi to their grandparents' house, located near Edwin Warner Park, a few miles southwest of
Perry and Janet's Forest Hills house. He met with his in-
laws and discussed Janet's sudden and out-of-character departure, explaining that he and Janet had been having
marital problems. They also talked about plans that Janet

purportedly had made to visit her brother, Mark, in Los Angeles. She had apparently told Mark that she was flying out for a visit, but she did not show up. At one point he may have alluded to a "to do" list that, he said, Janet had left him to complete while she was gone. As the discussion about what steps they should take continued, Perry suggested that they search for Janet's car. After confirming that she had not shown up in Los Angeles to visit her brother, Lawrence Levine agreed, and he and Perry drove together to Nashville International Airport, located several miles northeast of the Levines' home. They drove through parking garage after parking garage, looking for Janet's gray Volvo, to no avail. It just wasn't there. If it was there, they had missed it. Because Janet was fond of going to Chicago on extended shopping trips, they also considered the possibility that she may have gone off to the "Windy City" and would return home soon, or at least contact someone. But she had done neither.

Perry and the Levines also began calling many of Janet's friends, but none of them had seen her. Even though Perry had said that he had already contacted several local hotels, where he thought Janet may have gone, her parents nonetheless systematically called many of the area's hotels as well in their efforts to find their daughter. None of them, however, could confirm that Janet had checked in.

Despite the fact that Janet had not contacted anyone that she knew, no one—yet—would report her to the police as a missing person. Later, when confronted with the question of why, Janet's parents would claim that it was Perry who did not want to contact the police. Perry, on the other hand, would continue to contend that it was Janet's parents who did not want to call the authorities out of fear that it would cause trouble for their daughter.

Perry left the children with their grandparents for much of the weekend following Janet's disappearance, and it was during that time frame that he began talking more about a list of twenty-three things that he was supposed to do while Janet was away for, what he claimed was, a twelve-day vacation. He told a number of people, including the Levines, that Janet planned to return home within twelve days so that she would not miss Sammy's sixth birthday party on August 27. According to Perry, Janet had typed the list on their home computer prior to her leaving on the evening of August 15. He said that she had made him agree to do the things on the itemized list, and insisted that he sign it on a line above the date of August 15, moments before she walked out of the house that night. "Janet's" list contained a centered heading that read: "Perry's Turn For Janet's 12 Day Vacation." The list was numbered, and read as follows:

1. Feed the Children nutritious food—3 meals per day
2. Coordinate Deneane and Ella
3. Pay Deneane and Ella
4. Buy Raffi's Birthday present
5. Get Sam to and from Raffi's party on Sunday
6. Do Children's laundry
7. Be with Children all day—don't pawn off on Mom and Dad
8. Keep list of Sammy's Birthday party RSVP
9. Go through Bill Drawer and pay bills
10. Call Shaun Orange $$$$ and dead trees
11. Bell South Mobility
12. Video Place
13. Make sure Children have bath everyday

14. Read to Tzipi
15. Do educational activities with Sam
16. Spend quantity and quality time with your Children—not your guitar or computer or clients
17. Pay Dr. Campbell
18. Get OPEs back
19. Cancel credit card charges for computer crap
20. Change burned out light bulbs
21. Clean-up garbage area—children will get sick
22. Clean-up your closet
23. Call Steve Ward about driveway

> I agree to do all of the above before Janet's Vacation (in response to Perry's cowardly, rash and confused vacation) is over.

Perry signed it, and it would later be noted that the computer file was saved at 8:17 P.M. on August 15, 1996.

When taken at face value, it could be argued that Perry and the Levines did not call the police right away to report Janet as missing because they had the expectation that she would return in a few days, if what Perry had been saying was true. On the other hand, why had Perry and the Levines taken steps so soon after Janet's departure to look for Janet's car at the airport, call her friends, and check with local hotels to see if she had checked in, if Perry had shared the existence of the "to do" list with her parents? If Janet had demanded that he sign it prior to her leaving the house that night, reason dictated that he could have initially deliberately withheld information about the list's existence from them. Why? If Janet were truly taking a vacation from Perry and the kids and had promised to return in twelve days, what would have been Perry's purpose in calling everyone the night she left, worrying everyone, particularly the Levines at midnight, needlessly? Was it possible that the list was Perry's "ace in the hole," a resource that he kept in reserve until it was needed to perhaps convince Janet's parents, as they became anxious and more concerned over not hearing from their daughter, that it was not necessary to go to the police yet? If that is what he had thought, wouldn't he have realized that it would quickly bring suspicion upon him for initially withholding the information about the list's existence? Or was the list, if Perry had written it himself, merely for the benefit of the police when they did eventually begin investigating Janet's disappearance? It seemed possible, from the manner that the chain of events unfolded, that Perry may not have told anyone about the list's existence immediately. If he had, it was also possible that everyone moved to action and began looking for Janet because she had not shown up in Los Angeles. In any case, it would not be until the police began investigating Janet's disappearance that an actual theory would be applied toward the list.

As that first weekend without Janet drew to a close, Perry called his father, Arthur March, at his home in the Lake Chapala area of Mexico, on Sunday evening, August 18, at 5:11 P.M. They spoke to each other for about four minutes—Perry informed his father that Janet had left him and the kids. Perry called his father a second time that evening, at 10:18 P.M., during which the father and son discussed the possibility of Arthur driving to Nashville to help Perry take care of the kids while Janet was away—at least that was the account that the father and son would agree upon when discussing the situation with others. Lake Chapala, located near Guadalajara, was about fifteen hundred miles from Nashville and was about a four-day drive under normal driving conditions.

At the time that Janet March disappeared, Perry March, with a nearly full head of curly brown hair, looked very youthful in appearance at thirty-five, and was in great physical shape. At five feet eight inches, he was of small stature, was lean, and neither smoked, drank, nor used illicit drugs. He also claimed that he did not take any prescription medication, according to Perry's father, Arthur. Perry has also claimed that he was trained in karate and holds a black belt, was very much into conditioning, and liked mountain biking. Except for the various-sized moles on his face and forehead, Perry was characterized as a handsome devil at that time of his life, and was known to be able to easily attract women.

That would all change over the next ten years, however, as the ordeal over his wife's disappearance took its toll on him.

Chapter 3

Perry March was born to Arthur and Zipora March, the first of three children, in East Chicago, Indiana, on January 14, 1961. Situated along the southern edge of Lake Michigan, the city is home to a diverse mix of Caucasian, African American, and Hispanic inhabitants, with nearly one-quarter of its citizenry living below the poverty line. In recent years East Chicago is known for its corrupt government officials, some of whom have been involved in vote buying and "electioneering" schemes. In days of old, when Perry March's ancestors first settled there, it was known as an industrial center.

In 1961, astronaut Alan Shepard made the first U.S. space flight, and "Moon River" and "Love Makes the World Go Round" were both popular songs heard on radios and record players everywhere. John F. Kennedy was inaugurated as the thirty-fifth and youngest president six days after Perry's birth, the Berlin Wall was constructed, Adolf Eichmann was found guilty, *Judgment at Nuremberg* hit the theaters, and Harold Robbins published *The Carpetbaggers*. The year 1961 also recorded the notable deaths of

Carl Jung, Dashiell Hammett, and Dag Hammarskjold, among others. Little could anyone know how such a seemingly insignificant date, such as a birthday, would create, years later, such an array of legal entanglements, a murder, and family destructions.

The March family came about when Perry's grandfather, Paul Marcovich, on his father's side of the family, immigrated to the United States from Eastern Europe sometime shortly after 1900—the exact year is uncertain. For whatever reason, he decided to settle in East Chicago. Marcovich married Pearl Cohen, a native Chicagoan, with whom he had two boys, Arthur and Martin. Arthur was born first, and attended Ohio Northern University, in part because his father insisted that his two sons should learn a trade. Arthur became a pharmacist and Martin, however, became a football player. He excelled in the sport right out of high school—he attended Exeter and, later, Princeton, reaching great heights playing on each school's football team. The boys' father, being the hard worker that he was, became very wealthy, in part through real estate deals. Truly an entrepreneur, Marcovich went on to own several businesses, including a pharmacy, a travel agency, and a bank. At one time the Marcoviches were one of the wealthiest families in East Chicago.

After he graduated from college, Arthur March joined the U.S. Army and served three years in Japan, from 1950 to 1953, where he performed his military service as a pharmacist and as a laboratory officer in a military hospital. Upon his discharge he returned to East Chicago and worked at his father's pharmacy, all the while maintaining his military service in the U.S. Army Reserves.

While in the reserves, according to records at the U.S. Army Reserve Personnel Center in St. Louis, Missouri, Arthur took several correspondence courses in guerilla warfare and would later brag to anyone who would listen that he had been in the Green Berets, served in the Special Forces, and had been sent on a number of missions to Israel. He was also fond of handing out business cards that identified him as a retired colonel in the Army Reserves, but much of the information that he had been disseminating about army status turned out to be either bogus or only partially accurate. In reality, according to army records, Arthur had retired from the reserves as a lieutenant colonel, the step of rank just below that of a full colonel.

"If he thinks he's a colonel," said an army spokesperson, "he's never complained about the fact that his pension payments reflect lieutenant colonel status." The army spokesperson contended that Arthur March's identification card was either a forgery or the result of an error by the clerk who issued it.

Art, as he prefers to be called, changed his surname from Marcovich to March in 1956, according to an article in the *Nashville Scene*. He told the *Nashville Scene* that he changed his name so that it would be easier for others to pronounce and to spell, not because he wanted to mask the fact that he was Jewish.

In the late 1950s, Art March, now using his new name, made an actual trip to Israel, apparently as a civilian. While there, he met Zipora Elyson, daughter of a working-class man employed by a Tel Aviv bus company and whose mother had immigrated to Israel from the Ukraine. The two fell in love almost immediately—it seemed like love at first sight. Art and Zipora married quickly, and together they returned to East Chicago. Within a couple of years Zipora was pregnant with Perry—and in what seemed like rapid succession she and Art gave Perry a brother, Ron, and then a sister, Kathy.

Like Perry and Janet, Art and Zipora seemed like a happy younger couple raising a happy family of young children, aged closely to one another. While not well-off, they were financially secure, despite Art going from one job to another, purportedly due to his not-much-desired rough etiquette. Nonetheless, they were able to afford to purchase a vacation home in Michiana, Michigan, situated along the shore of Lake Michigan, approximately forty miles from East Chicago. It was a popular vacation destination, particularly for residents of Chicago and its suburbs. Arthur, Zipora, and the children spent a great deal of time there.

In 1970, when Perry was nine years old, his world, and that of his immediate family, was met with tragedy when his mother died of an apparent overdose of barbiturates. According to Arthur's version of the events leading up to her death, Zipora had apparently sustained a head injury, for which her doctor had prescribed Darvon, a much-prescribed painkiller. Arthur believes that Zipora succumbed to anaphylactic shock after experiencing an allergic reaction to Darvon. But her death certificate shows that she died of "barbiturate overdose," and indicated that a "partially empty bottle" of Darvon capsules were recovered from her bedroom. It was generally believed that Arthur had latched onto the anaphylactic shock explanation of his wife's death because he may have been attempting to shield the stigma of suicide from his children.

Following Zipora's death, Arthur decided to leave East Chicago. He sold their house, packed up the kids, and moved to the Michiana vacation house. Although he liked to spend a lot of time on the weekends with friends, some of whom dated to his army days, Arthur was very devoted to each of his kids and would literally do anything for them.

Years later, his degree of involvement with Perry and his schemes would serve as a testament of sorts to how much he would do for one of his children. Perry became a lawyer specializing in taxation. His other son, Ron, became a lawyer who works in Chicago, and his daughter, Kathy, graduated from dental school and has a practice in Michigan. All of his kids did well for themselves. It would be Perry, however, who would take a wrong turn later in life.

Even though he is Jewish, Perry March went to the Catholic college preparatory high school, La Lumiere School. La Lumiere is a coeducational lay Catholic boarding school situated on an estate in La Porte, Indiana, about sixty miles east of Chicago. Actor-comedian Chris Farley attended La Lumiere for a short time, and the school produced a chief justice of the United States, John Roberts. It was clear that Arthur wanted nothing but the best for his kids, and got it. Perry always achieved high marks at La Lumiere, and took part in many extracurricular activities, such as tennis, wrestling, soccer, and karate. He earned a first-degree black belt while still in high school. He graduated with several varsity letters in wrestling and in soccer, and could have had his pick of many universities to attend. He also liked to ski, and he enjoyed mountain biking. He also played guitar—at times it didn't seem like there was much that he could not do.

Of the many offers of acceptance that he received, Perry decided on the University of Michigan because, he said, the lower rate of tuition for being an in-state student would help out his father financially. He also chose the University of Michigan because of his interest in learning the Chinese language—that school, according to Perry, offered an excellent program in Chinese. Perry, majoring in Asian studies, went on to become fluent in the language. He also served on the University of Michigan's Honors Student Council.

It was at the University of Michigan that Perry met Janet. They were introduced by Janet's roommate, and like his father had been attracted to his mother, Perry and Janet hit it off almost instantly. Although Janet missed their first date because she overslept, she and Perry were always together after they finally went out on a date. Janet was capricious and creative, and she was beautiful—all attributes that attracted Perry to her. She could be quirky at times, but she always had a sense of humor, which Perry liked. When Perry graduated in 1983, he had made plans to relocate to Chicago, where he had obtained work as a brokerage house manager trainee. Janet joined him in Chicago approximately six months later, toward the end of the year.

They lived together in the Windy City for about two years, before deciding to move to Nashville, where Janet's parents lived. Perry, at one point, decided that he wanted to be a lawyer. He subsequently applied to and was accepted at Vanderbilt University Law School, one of the top-twenty law schools in the United States. Janet's father, himself a lawyer and fond of Perry, offered to pay Perry's tuition and expenses while he was at Vanderbilt, even though he and Janet were not yet married. Perry was, of course, ecstatic at such an opportunity and he eagerly accepted the Levines' generosity.

It wouldn't be until 1987, however, that Perry and Janet would wed. Janet had been hoping for years that Perry would propose to her, but when he never did, she took matters into her own hands and proposed to *him*. They had gone on an outing to Percy Warner Park, not far from the Levines' home and near to the location of Janet's future dream house on Blackberry Road. While at the park, Janet knelt on the ground and asked Perry to marry her. He, of course, accepted, and Janet became, in a manner of speaking, Perry's "golden goose." What more could he ask for? It was a dream come true, especially on the financial side of things.

Now that Perry and Janet were finally married, Lawrence and Carolyn Levine wanted to do everything in their power to assist their only daughter as much as possible. According to family friends, Perry had developed a close relationship with Janet's mother, Carolyn, because of his desire for a mother figure in his life, since his own mother had died when he was only nine. As a result, the Levines gave Janet and Perry money so that they could purchase a house that they both wanted. They wanted so much, they would later say, to help make their daughter happy. At that time they also wanted to help Perry so that he could make a good life with their daughter and provide for her in the manner to which she was accustomed. The house, located on a hill on Thirty-second Avenue, helped a great deal in that regard.

Perry, by this time, had begun to worry about his father's financial situation. Arthur's finances had suddenly put him on a track with hard times ahead. The mortgage company had foreclosed on his Michiana home a year earlier, due to his inability to keep up the payments, and Lawrence Levine, upon hearing of the foreclosure, purchased the property from the mortgage company for $115,000 and allowed Arthur to live in the house, presumably until he could get back on his feet. Records show that Levine terminated Arthur's lease on the property in early 1987 when Arthur was unable to keep up with the rent payments. Levine sold the house the following year for $144,500, which was $29,500 more than what he paid for it.

After vacating the Michiana house, where he had lived for years, Arthur moved to Nashville in order to be nearer Perry and Janet. When he first got into town, Arthur stayed with the Levines at their home and they loaned him money to help him get established in his new locale. However, despite his efforts, Arthur would file for bankruptcy in 1991, the same year that his grandson, Sammy, was born. Upon his discharge from bankruptcy court, he would begin making plans for his move to Mexico, where he would eventually reside in a caretaker's cottage on a Lake Chapala estate. The Lake Chapala area is a beautiful setting where many American retirees relocate so that they can live for significantly less money than it would take to retire in the United States.

Meanwhile, Perry excelled at Vanderbilt, just as everyone had expected he would. He made Vanderbilt's prestigious Law Review and, upon graduation, claimed that he had received a number of lucrative offers from some of the country's most prestigious law firms, including two in New York. However, Perry decided to accept an offer as an associate from the prominent Nashville firm of Bass, Berry & Sims at a starting salary of $42,500 annually. In 1988, Perry became the first Jew ever hired as an attorney for Bass, Berry & Sims, the same year the firm hired its first African American attorney.

One of Perry's former professors at Vanderbilt characterized him as being personable and extremely bright.

"Perry wanted very much to be a good lawyer," said Vanderbilt law professor Donald Langevoort. "He was quite committed and hardworking in pursuit of just about everything he did."

Several of his coworkers thought that Perry was on the fast track to becoming a partner at the firm. Little did anyone know at that time that Perry would be asked to leave the firm three years later in disgrace after an internal investigation indicated that he had written a series of sexually explicit letters to a young female paralegal. The incident would mark the first of many problems that would affect his personal, as well as his professional, life.

After being forced to leave Bass, Berry & Sims, Perry landed a position practicing corporate law at the firm where his father-in-law was a senior partner. Levine, Mattson, Orr & Geracioti was a much smaller firm than Bass, Berry & Sims, and Perry justified his move there by telling people that he desired more freedom to pursue his own legal interests. Others would say that he landed there because he had nowhere else to go at that juncture in his life. Nonetheless, Perry proved that he could be successful at his father-in-law's firm. While employed there, he represented several local businesses, including Music City Mix Factory, a strip club, and several prominent and wealthy individuals.

Perry and Janet's second child, Tzipi, was born in 1994, and it was during that time frame that they were making plans to build the 5,300-square-foot Forest Hills French-style dream house, which Janet had designed. Even though they had known that it had been several years since Janet had been truly happy in her marriage, Janet's parents once again put up the money to finance the deal for the house. At the time of Janet's disappearance they continued to hold the note for the approximately $650,000 home. Janet had purportedly confided to her parents that she no longer trusted Perry, and alleged that he had "badly mismanaged their money." In part, because her father was an attorney, the Levines thought it prudent that Janet keep all of her assets in her own name, and so advised her as such, just in case she decided to file for divorce at some point in the future.

Chapter 4

Arthur March didn't recall for certain the exact date that he arrived in Nashville, following Perry's telephone call to him after Janet disappeared, but he believed he arrived on either August 21 or August 22. Since Perry had called him on the evening of August 18, a Sunday, the time frame of his recollection would fit. Even if he had left the very next day, it is an approximate four-day drive from the Lake Chapala area of Mexico to Nashville. At any rate, Perry and his father were seen driving around Nashville in Arthur's Ford Escort station wagon during that time frame. Arthur had purportedly come to help Perry take care of the children, until Perry and his in-laws could decide what to do about reporting Janet's disappearance to the police. Perry still insisted that he had recommended that the police should be informed, all the while claiming that the Levines did not wish to take that route just yet.

Meanwhile, Perry had been telling everyone that Janet had planned to return home so that she would not miss her son's sixth birthday party on August 27. What Perry may have overlooked before the RSVPs for the birthday party started coming back was the fact that Janet had planned Sammy's birthday party for Sunday, August 25, not for Tuesday, August 27, as Perry had been telling everyone. If Janet had planned to come back from her "vacation" in time for Sammy's birthday party, she should have told Perry that she would be back in ten days, not twelve.

Nonetheless, Janet had planned Sammy's birthday party for August 25, and Perry and the Levines were forced to deal with it. It was scheduled to be held at Fannie Mae Dees Park, located on Blakemore Avenue, and referred to by Vanderbilt area residents as the so-called "Dragon Park," because of a sea serpent built there twenty years ago by Pedro Silva. The *Sea Serpent* is a structure that the children can climb on, and it depicts hundreds of various designs, such as birds, faces, aliens, flowers, and so forth, each made out of chipped tiles that were painted by area artists. Dolly Parton's image can be found on one of the dragon's tiles, as can local civic leader Fannie Mae Dees, the park's namesake. Janet apparently chose that park because it was clean and suitable for children, and because it was not far from their Forest Hills home.

Due to the fact that many of Sammy's friends, as well as their parents, had been invited, and the fact that so many had responded that they would attend, Perry and Janet's parents knew that it would be difficult to call it off on such short notice. Instead, they agreed to tell everyone that Janet had remained in California visiting her brother, Mark, due to an ear infection that could cause her problems on the flight home. It was better, they said, if Janet waited until the infection had completely cleared up before attempting the flight back to Nashville. The invented story to explain away Janet's absence apparently was believed by everyone in attendance that day, and the party went off without a hitch.

Finally, on Thursday, August 29, exactly two weeks to the day from when Janet disappeared, Perry and Janet's parents went to the Metropolitan Nashville Police Department (MNPD) and reported that Janet Levine March was missing. Perry told the police officer who took the report basically the same account of the events of August 15 that he had been telling everyone else. He also provided details of Janet's gray four-door 1996 Volvo 850, with Tennessee license plates numbered 844-CBD, which, he said, Janet had driven away on the night she left their home for her supposed twelve-day vacation.

David Miller, Metro's veteran homicide/missing person detective, caught the assignment. Miller investigated 1,244 missing-person cases in all of Davidson County in 1996, and he solved all of them, except for that of Janet March. He didn't know it at the time, of course, but he would be only one of several investigators who would work the Janet March case. Detective Tim Mason, of homicide, and forensic specialist Sergeant Johnny Hunter would assist him at the outset.

Among the first things that Miller did as he began his investigation of Janet March's disappearance was to obtain her bank and credit card information. He needed it to determine whether Janet had withdrawn cash, written checks, or had made any charge card purchases during the two weeks that she had been missing. He learned within a short time that there had been no activity on any of Janet's accounts—certainly not a good sign from a homicide investigator's perspective.

As Miller and his coinvestigators began talking to Janet and Perry's friends, of whom there were several, a picture of two highly intelligent—but very different—people began to emerge. Perry was described as a practical man who brimmed with self-confidence and possessed strong common sense. He was also arrogant and, at times, seemed boastful of his intelligence. Janet, on the other hand, was regarded as somewhat flighty, often late for appointments because she had either forgotten about them or had overslept—her attitude seemed to be "oh, well," but her friends seemed to accept her quirks. They both enjoyed their work—Janet, with her paintings and sketches, and the jobs she took on as illustrator for children's books; and Perry, with his legal work and his active involvement as a board member of the Jewish Community Center, for which he sometimes did legal favors pro bono. Janet could be enjoying the pool at the Jewish Community Center with her kids one moment, then dashing off to Chicago for a spur-of-the-moment shopping trip the next.

Janet had also been exhibiting traits that indicated to her friends that she might have been depressed in the weeks prior to her disappearance. Even though she had most everything that a person could want—a beautiful home that she designed, two beautiful children—Sammy had many of Perry's features and Tzipi had Janet's—her friends suggested that she may have felt that something was missing in her life. But no one really knew for sure what was bothering Janet. Even though she had a close circle of friends, she did not confide in them with many details about her personal life. Their friends suggested to the police that Perry had been spending more and more time away from home in recent months, and it seemed, at times, that he had become bored with Janet. Employees at the Jewish Community Center told *Nashville Scene* reporter Willy Stern that Perry had been showing up so often to take part in aerobic workouts and weight lifting that they thought he was single.

Several people told the police investigators that Perry had been seen around town with other women in the months prior to Janet's disappearance. One person claimed to have seen him leaving a local cinema with an attractive blond woman, walking arm in arm. Another person reported seeing him enjoying dinner in an intimate setting at Bound'ry restaurant, on Twentieth Avenue, near Broadway and Division, with an attractive brunette. The Bound'ry has an alfresco setting when weather permits, and offers an unusually large menu that ranges from crayfish-stuffed trout to Australian ostrich marinated in sweet pomegranate molasses. It was a restaurant that both Perry and Janet favored—Janet was seen there in the company of several of her girlfriends two nights before she disappeared. Perry explained his sightings with other women as business-related socialization and that he was acting no differently than anyone else in his profession would behave.

In the early part of August, barely two weeks before Janet disappeared, Perry had begun spending nights away from home, without Janet. He had asked one of his clients if he could rent a spare condominium, which he knew the client owned, but it was not available for when he needed it. As a result, Perry ended up staying for a few nights at a Hampton Inn, located near Vanderbilt University, and a few nights at a Budgetel Inn, on Lenox Avenue. Detectives Miller and Mason questioned employees at the hotels, and even though Perry admitted to them that he had spent several nights at each of the hotels, they issued subpoenas to obtain the records from both hotels. Perry told the police that he did not leave home on the nights in question until after Sammy and Tzipi had gone to bed, and he always made sure that he returned home by 7:00 A.M. Because of the fact that Perry had been spending nights away from home, it seemed to the detectives that his relationship with Janet had become worse. Perry explained that he was often unable to sleep at home, presumably because of his by-now poor relationship with Janet, and that he had gone to the hotels merely to be able to get some much-needed sleep.

Had Perry and Janet talked about getting a divorce? The detectives wanted to know.

Perry acknowledged their marital problems, and the fact that he and Janet had been seeing a local psychiatrist— occasionally together and sometimes separately—in an attempt to work out their problems. He also said that they had mentioned divorce as a possible solution, but that they had not talked about it seriously. A number of people, mostly friends, claimed that Perry and Janet had been working on a list of issues through the psychiatrist. According to the friends, Perry resented Janet for pressure that he received from her and others to change so that Janet would be happier. Janet had told friends that Perry had never fully gotten over his mother's untimely death and that he had carried that issue into their marriage and it had caused problems for them. She had also complained that she had taken the greater share of responsibility for their children while Perry went out and wined and dined his clients. It was never clear, however, whether or not they had taken the subject of divorce to the next level; but one person, Deneane Beard, who cleaned the house for Perry and Janet two to three times per week, told the police that she had seen a book on the subject of divorce lying on Janet's nightstand a few months before she disappeared.

Did Perry March have a propensity toward violence? It was a question that the detectives wanted an answer to as they delved into Perry's past. As a result of their probing, they found a woman who claimed that Perry had assaulted her when they were both undergraduates at the University of Michigan. She claimed that he had struck her in the face with his fist during a sudden and unexpected moment of jealousy. The *Nashville Scene* interviewed the woman, as well as many other people during their search to learn the truth about Perry March. They interviewed Perry as well, and published his account of that situation.

"She was a slut," Perry told the *Scene*. He denied that the incident had occurred. "I fucked her for a few months. Then she came back from vacation, told me she had the crabs, and I dumped her. . . . If anybody else had been subjected to the kind of scrutiny I've received . . . you'd find people to say unpleasant things about them as well." The woman told Willy Stern that she and Perry had never had sex, and she had not reported the incident to the police or to campus security. She apparently had felt that it was important to come forward when news about Janet's mysterious disappearance began hitting all of the area newspapers. Perry, on the other hand, told the reporter that he was contemplating suing the woman for slander.

Detective Miller, a soft-spoken man, asked Perry point-blank if he had killed his wife and disposed of her body. Perry adamantly denied having harmed Janet in any way. He admitted that he and Janet had argued on the night of August 15, but he said that he had not attacked her. She simply took the things that she had packed and drove away in her Volvo.

"Look at me," Perry said at one point. "On August 15, 1996, I was a respected Jewish lawyer in Nashville. I had it all. A beautiful wife. Two wonderful kids. Gorgeous home. I was a go-to guy in the Jewish community and the business community. I was making good money. Now, my wife has left me."

Later, Perry would go on-camera on CBS News' *48 Hours* and tell a national television audience: "Janet was a wonderful mother. Very doting."

It seemed strange how he referred to her in the past tense.

Chapter 5

On Saturday, September 7, 1996, just as the investigation into Janet March's disappearance seemed like it wasn't going anywhere fast, residents at Brixworth Apartments, after seeing news reports about the missing woman and her car, reported that Janet's Volvo had been discovered in the parking lot at the large apartment complex. Brixworth Apartments is located on Brixworth Lane and Harding Road in the prestigious Belle Meade area of Nashville, not far from Vanderbilt and Belmont universities. The complex, only minutes from downtown, consisted of one- and two-bedroom apartments and townhomes, and was 6.6 miles from Perry and Janet's Forest Hills home. The police later estimated that it was about a thirteen-minute drive from Blackberry Road to the location where Janet's car had been found.

Detectives David Miller and Tim Mason wasted little time getting to the apartment complex. They brought along Sergeant Johnny Hunter for his forensic expertise, which would be needed as they began to process the car for possible clues that might shed some light on what had happened to Janet. It was obvious from the accumulation of weather-induced dirt on and around the car that it had not been moved recently. It actually looked abandoned, like it had been there for weeks.

Although there was no sign of thirty-three-year-old Janet March at the scene, several of her personal effects, including her purse, passport, and wallet with credit cards, were found inside the car. The investigators also found several articles of clothing that a person might take with them if they were going on a vacation: a bikini swimming suit, three sundresses, and two pairs of white socks. There didn't appear to be anything, however, to positively indicate her fate.

It wasn't so much what they found inside the car that interested them—it was the essential personal effects that should have been packed as part of the vacation scenario that were missing that bothered them. Janet's toothbrush, her hairbrush, and even an extra bra were missing from her things. It didn't take a sharp detective to know that these kinds of items would be essential to pack and bring along for an extended vacation. A person planning a trip just wouldn't have left home without them, they reasoned. But what bothered the investigators most was a pair of Janet's sandals they found in the front of the car. They were on the driver's-side floorboard, lined up and neatly placed there, rather than simply dropped. It didn't seem likely that a person who had taken off their shoes would go to the trouble of placing them there so neatly—they would instead likely have just kicked them off and let them fall where they may. The positioning of Janet's sandals seemed like an important clue, and the detectives noted it as such. Miller ordered that the vehicle be impounded and towed to a secure location, where it could be gone over more thoroughly for clues.

Meanwhile, Miller and the other investigators became even more skeptical of why Perry and the Levines would wait so long before reporting Janet missing. Captain Mickey Miller, no relation to Detective David Miller, voiced his skepticism publicly at one point.

"Within two weeks, you got a lot of time to get rid of a body," Captain Miller said. "A lot of crucial evidence is gone [by that time]."

At the investigation's outset Perry remained cooperative and allowed Detectives Miller and Mason, as well as Sergeant Hunter, into his house so that they could search it, to perform at least a cursory examination of the house's interior. They went through the labyrinth of concealed closets, cubbyholes, every nook and cranny that Janet had carefully designed that way for reasons that could only be explained by her quirkiness, but the house appeared spotless and there weren't any obvious signs that an act of foul play had occurred there. The only clue seemed to be that there were no clues. Even the cleaning lady, Deneane Beard, told the police that the house seemed particularly spotless when she came to clean after Janet disappeared.

"It was almost as if somebody had already scrubbed the place and emptied the trash," she said.

In a moment of idle speculation Detective Miller opined that there was not much of a chance that Janet's body would ever be recovered. He stated that if her corpse had been placed inside a Dumpster two weeks before she was reported missing, it would have already been taken to a landfill by the time the detectives began their investigation. Spokespersons for the local garbage services confirmed what Miller had said, that many area Dumpsters, particularly those at restaurants and at construction sites, are emptied regularly, often daily, and that the chances of recovering a body after it had been deposited in a landfill, where refuse is sometimes burned, were practically nonexistent.

Approximately one week later, a group of construction workers that had been completing a project called Crater Hill, located in close proximity to the March residence, contacted Detective Miller to report that they had noticed a strong, foul odor in the area during the week of September 8. It was a very distinctive odor, like that of something or someone that had died and was decomposing. By that time they, like the residents at the Brixworth Apartments, had seen news reports about Janet March's disappearance, and—given that the odor was in the area of her home—they had felt compelled to contact the police about it.

When the detectives returned and asked Perry if they could search his house and property again, he refused. They also asked him if he would be willing to take a polygraph examination and answer questions about his wife's disappearance. On the advice of an attorney that he had retained, Perry refused that request as well. He stated through his attorney that his psychiatrist had prescribed Xanax and Zoloft for him to help relieve anxiety and that a polygraph examination wouldn't be advisable under those conditions. Because any antianxiety medication had the potential to affect his heart rate, one of the measures used in a lie-detector test to determine whether a person is being truthful or not, the results of any such test would be invalidated. Again the investigators were skeptical. They didn't know when Perry had started the regimen of medication, whether it coincided with him being scrutinized as a possible suspect in Janet's disappearance or whether he had been taking the medications for some time. They also knew that because of doctor and patient confidentiality rules, it might be difficult to find out unless Perry was willing to tell them himself. It seemed plausible at that time that Perry had been taking the medication for a while, and they had no choice but to give him the benefit of the doubt. They didn't know at that time, of course, that he would later tell other people that he did not take prescription medication.

It was at about that point in the investigation that detectives began scrutinizing the "to do" list that Perry had said that Janet left for him. They obtained written materials that Janet had typed, and compared them with the list that she purportedly left for Perry. The list, they immediately noticed, was written using a combination of uppercase and lower-case letters, like a person would normally write a document that required a capital letter at the beginning of a sentence. It was in a style that was not consistent with the way Janet typed—she normally used only lowercase letters, even at the start of a new sentence, like many people use when sending an e-mail. Janet's "to do" list, on the other hand, was very consistent with the style that Perry used when he wrote out lists or correspondence. The detectives also noted that Perry normally dated his written material at the bottom of the page, like Janet's "to do" list had been dated, whereas Janet normally dated her written material at the top of the page.

By this point in their investigation, Detective Miller and Detective Mason had learned about Marissa Moody's visit to the March residence on the morning of August 16 to drop off her son to play with Sammy. In part, because Janet's "to do" list had made no mention of the fact that she had made plans with Marissa that particular day, it was decided that Detective Mason would interview her. Mason conducted his interview with her on Saturday, September 14, 1996.

Marissa told the detective the details of her Friday-morning visit, and said that she had spoken to Janet the night before to make the plans—the night that Janet supposedly left after leaving the list for Perry.

Perry, on the other hand, claimed that it was he, not Janet, who had made the plans with Marissa to bring her son over to his house to play with Sammy, a statement that obviously conflicted with Marissa's.

She reiterated the events that transpired that morning—how she spoke with Ella, the nanny, and had come inside the house to speak with Perry, but ended up only talking to Sammy as he bounced up and down on the dark-colored Oriental rug that was rolled up and lying in an area near Perry's study and the children's playroom. She stated that she didn't think the rug seemed to belong there, and that when she returned to pick up her son a few hours later, the rug was gone.

It was a chilling thought, but after speaking with Marissa, the homicide detectives suspected that Janet's 104-pound body might have been concealed inside the rolled-up rug, and that her five-year-old son may have been bouncing up and down on his mother's corpse! They couldn't prove it, but it seemed a distinct possibility based on what they were hearing.

Perry told the police investigators and a number of other people that the rug Marissa Moody claimed that she saw never existed. Perry said that she was mistaken, that she never even came inside the house that day. Similarly, Ella, the children's nanny, said that she did not recall ever seeing the rug in question. Deneane Beard, who had come by to do her routine cleaning on the morning of Marissa's visit, told the police that she was there for two hours doing her work and that she had not seen the rug, either. But Perry, she said, had told her not to clean the children's playroom that morning, which was just behind the area where Marissa claimed that she had seen the rug. Since Deneane had left prior to Marissa's arrival, the detectives considered that it was possible that the rug had been inside the children's playroom all along and that Perry had moved it from there into the hallway prior to Marissa's arrival. After all, according to Janet's "to do" list, Perry hadn't known that Marissa was coming over that day.

At one point the *National Enquirer* would report that it had learned of a secret witness who came forward with information claiming that she believed that she had seen Perry March disposing of his wife's body. According to the article, the witness said that she believed she had seen Perry March "place a rolled-up rug with something inside it into a Dumpster." The witness was purportedly told by the man to "leave it alone. My dead collie is inside. You will get sick."

Astonishingly, the language that the secret witness had claimed that the man used was similar in nature to item number twenty-one on Janet's "to do" list, which read: "Clean-up garbage area—children will get sick."

Perry would later tell *48 Hours* that the only rug he owned that even remotely resembled an Oriental rug was a long, thin runner. He said on national television that if Janet's body had been rolled up inside the runner, she would have looked like a small sausage or wiener, the type that can be found rolled up inside a wrapper on an appetizer tray.

Somebody was obviously lying about the rolled-up rug, but Miller, Mason, and Hunter didn't believe it was Marissa Moody.

Chapter 6

Because Perry March's cooperation with the police had dwindled to the point that it appeared that it would soon be nonexistent, Detective David Miller, wanting to search the March residence again, wrote up an affidavit in support of a search warrant. They still had much work to do, and because Perry, with each passing day, looked more and more like a viable suspect in Janet's disappearance, Miller needed to get back inside the house so that it could be gone over more thoroughly than it had been processed earlier. In preparing his affidavit, Miller went over the facts of the case as they were known at that time. He included information surrounding Detective Mason's interview with Marissa Moody, Perry's contention that Janet had taken an extended vacation because he and Janet were having marital problems, the fact that Janet had missed her son's sixth birthday party, details about the construction workers reporting the foul odor in the March's neighborhood after Janet disappeared, and details regarding the discovery of Janet's Volvo. He also cited the fact that it appeared that Perry had been untruthful with him and his colleagues as they attempted to investigate the case, and that he had refused to take a polygraph examination and had become uncooperative.

Of course the fact that Perry had refused the polygraph examination was not proof that he was guilty of any wrongdoing. Refusing to take a lie-detector test is a common practice, according to longtime Nashville criminal defense attorney Charles Ray.

"Any criminal defense attorney worth his salt would not allow his client to take a polygraph exam," Ray said, because it would require a suspect "to give full statements that could come back later to haunt him."

Miller also stated in his affidavit that it was important from an evidentiary standpoint that the police be allowed to examine the personal computer inside Perry's house.

As Miller prepared the affidavit, word got out from the district attorney's office that a search warrant was forthcoming and imminent. As a result, at least in part, of the impending search warrant, Miller, along with an attorney representing the district attorney's office, held a closed-door meeting with attorney Lionel Barrett, whom Perry had retained to represent him during the early stages of the investigation. At that meeting, according to what Perry would later tell the *Nashville Scene,* someone said that Perry might consider pleading guilty to charges of voluntary manslaughter. Such an agreement would have netted Perry a three-to-six-year term, with the possibility of parole after serving 30 percent of the sentence. When he learned of the purported plea-bargaining discussion, Perry claimed that his response was: "Fuck them. I didn't do anything."

The district attorney's office declined to comment about the purported plea bargain meeting, and Perry's attorney, Barrett, claimed in a prepared statement that no such agreement had been attempted.

The following day, Tuesday, September 17, Detective Miller presented his affidavit in support of a search warrant to a Davidson County judge, who promptly approved it. The search warrant was served and executed promptly, and a more thorough search of March's house, outbuildings, and four acres was begun. This time several dozen police officers and trainees converged on the house, accompanied by forensic experts, as well as a computer specialist.

Inside the house evidence technicians processed the hardwood floors for traces of blood and searched for palm prints, perhaps in blood, on the floor's shiny surface. They also collected ashes from the fireplace for examination, and scoured the bathrooms, attic, and basement for anything that might lead them one step closer to discovering what had become of Janet. However, the house appeared devoid of any clues.

Outside, the police cadets carefully probed the ground with sharp stakes, while heavy equipment operators used a bulldozer and a backhoe to remove layers of earth in designated areas. While all the activity was occurring around him, Perry sat on the back porch with his brother, Ron. They talked quietly and smoked cigars, and didn't appear to be too concerned about all of the police activity.

Since there were no traces of blood found inside the house, and not much of a motive for murder, the detectives found themselves wondering where the investigation would lead them, if it led them anywhere at all. The search of the outbuildings and the surrounding grounds had failed to yield any evidence of a body. Without a body, there wasn't any proof that Janet was actually dead.

As they tried to piece the case together with what little they knew, the homicide detectives could only theorize about what might have happened. In one such scenario they speculated that Perry, in the heat of the argument that he admitted having with Janet on the night in question, might have killed Janet by accident with a karate blow. Holding a black belt in karate, he would have known how to deliver a deathblow that could kill a person in a matter of seconds without spilling a drop of blood. If her death had been deliberate, a karate expert would also know how to kill a person with a choke hold or, perhaps, a blow to the sternum. In either case there likely wouldn't be any bloodshed. If Perry had killed Janet in such a scenario, the cops theorized, he could have temporarily hidden her body in the woods that surround their house, only to retrieve it the next day, wrap it up in the rug, which Marissa Moody had described, and then haul it away to dispose of it, likely inside a Dumpster. The detectives believed that Perry delayed calling his in-laws until midnight because that would have given him plenty of time to temporarily hide Janet's body, write Janet's "to do" list, drive her car to the Brixworth Apartments, and perhaps ride a mountain bike back to their home. He was fond of mountain biking, and the detectives learned from a Volvo dealership that Janet's car was equipped to carry a mountain bike.

The detectives also considered that Perry may have enlisted the aid of his father to help him dispose of Janet's body, and may have kept her body hidden until Arthur March arrived from Mexico. They also suggested that Perry and his father used Arthur's Ford Escort station wagon to transport Janet's body. Both Perry and his father denied being involved in such a scenario, and the elder March even told the detectives that they could search his car for clues if they so desired. The truth of the matter was the detectives just didn't know what had occurred and could only guess at that point about what *may* have happened.

Perry referred to all of their theories as "bullshit."

When the investigators finally got around to examining Perry and Janet's Ambra home computer, they made another interesting discovery: the computer's hard drive had been removed. When Miller and his colleagues had searched Perry's home on prior occasions at a time when they had his permission, they had asked Perry to print a file—presumably Janet's "to do" list—for them and he had complied. The hard drive, they knew, was still with the computer at that time.

Why had the hard drive been removed? The detectives wondered. And who had removed it? Furthermore, when had it been removed?

Perry was out of town on the weekend of September 14 and 15, just prior to the execution of the search warrant. He had taken Sammy and Tzipi, he said, to Chicago to celebrate Rosh Hashanah, the Jewish New Year, and had left his father at his house, alone. When the detectives suggested that perhaps Perry's father had removed the hard drive without Perry's knowledge, Arthur denied the allegation. Instead, Arthur told the police that the burglar alarm for the house had been turned off during part of the time that he stayed there. The cops felt like he was alluding to the possibility that someone else had come into the house without his knowledge when the burglar alarm was turned off and removed the hard drive. Similarly, Perry said that he had no idea what had happened to the hard drive.

"I didn't take it out," Perry said. "I had nothing to hide on my hard drive. If someone thought they were helping me [by removing the hard drive], they didn't. It hurt me."

Chapter 7

Unbeknownst to his in-laws or anyone else, except his closest relatives, when Perry March was in Chicago in mid-September celebrating Rosh Hashanah with his children, he was also making plans to relocate there in the near future. Suspecting Perry's plans, Lawrence and Carolyn Levine immediately filed documents to obtain an emergency court order that barred Perry from taking Sammy and Tzipi out of Tennessee. However, they were too late. Fearing that the Levines would try to obtain custody of his children, Perry had already sent them to live with his brother, Ron, in suburban Chicago. When news of the court proceedings became public knowledge, a reporter asked him why the Levines would suddenly turn against him after treating him like their own son for many years.

"That's the thousand-dollar question," Perry replied. "I'm being treated like a murderer and they (his in-laws) are taking away all our property."

On Tuesday, September 24, the homicide detectives continued their effort to find Janet's body. They used specially trained cadaver-sniffing dogs to search the acreage in the vicinity of Perry and Janet's home, where the foul odor was reported a few weeks after she disappeared. They also brought in an army helicopter that was equipped with a heat-sensitive device to scan for any sign of Janet's remains. Divers searched nearby lakes, paying particular attention to Radnor Lake, located a few miles east of their Forest Hills home. They also examined freshly poured concrete foundations in the area, but their efforts, when all was said and done, had not yielded any results.

Two days later, on September 26, Lawrence and Carolyn Levine appeared in Nashville Juvenile Court and asked Judge Andy Shookhoff to order that Perry allow them to visit their grandchildren every weekend, beginning on October 4. However, by that time Perry had also relocated to Chicago, and Nashville authorities were unable to immediately serve him with the visitation orders.

As a result of continued legal actions by the Levines in their effort to be granted visitation rights to see their grandchildren, Perry March was subpoenaed and ordered to provide a deposition in a civil proceeding on October 15 about his wife's disappearance, his financial affairs, and his current state of mental health. During the videotaped deposition Perry invoked his Fifth Amendment right against self-incrimination at least fifteen times. He did so, of course, on the advice of his attorney. Because he had by then been named by the Metropolitan Nashville Police Department as the prime suspect in his wife's disappearance and probable death, it was sound advice according to legal experts.

"They beat the shit out of me," Perry said, referring to the deposition.

One of the questions that he had been asked and to which he had invoked his Fifth Amendment rights was whether he had killed his wife. The next day, the *Tennessean* front-page headline read: MARCH TAKES THE FIFTH. WON'T ANSWER ON HOW WIFE DISAPPEARED. If he hadn't already been convicted in the court of public opinion, the newspaper headline had certainly accomplished it. Perry March, for all intents and purposes, was finished in Nashville—even if he hadn't killed his wife. Even though he had been ostracized by all of his former friends and associates, he had intended to return to Nashville in the not-too-distant future to practice law so that he could gain "the future respect of his children." He wouldn't be able to do that now.

"The sad thing is, I had thought I wanted to go through life with these people," Perry said of his former friends and associates, all of whom had literally turned their backs on him. "But when it's all said and done, they are nothing but small-minded, petty little people."

As Detective Miller continued his search for answers to the mysterious puzzle that he was handed, the subject of Perry's employment with Bass, Berry & Sims—more appropriately his swift departure from that firm—surfaced again. He decided that he would look into it further, to see if he could use any of the information to help him in his search for a possible motive if Perry had indeed killed his wife, either accidentally or deliberately.

Among the things that Miller eventually learned as he ran down the potential lead was that on July 19, 1991, a Friday, an attractive blond paralegal employed at the firm found a letter on her chair when she arrived at work that morning. Leigh Reames was highly regarded by most everyone at Bass, Berry & Sims, and was recognized as a hard worker. When she opened the sealed letter, she noticed that it had been typed, single-spaced, and was three pages in length. It didn't take long for Leigh to realize that the letter was a sexually explicit offer for her to have oral sex with the as-yet-unknown writer, who stated that he was a married man.

"I want to inhale the essence of you," the letter said. "I want to taste your arms. The pure animal sexiness of your body grips me and embarrasses me. . . . I want to make love to you because I am attracted to you, all of you. . . . The thought of my tongue buried within you excites me more than anything else in the world. . . ." The letter included the writer's notion of wanting to have "hours and hours" of oral sex with Leigh, and talked about "licking and sucking . . . kissing and caressing (your) soft belly and thighs."

The letter included details of the writer's marriage, including that "marriage has a way of making sex boring at times, routine and old. I do not mean that it loses its pleasure. We still climax. We still love passionately. We still love our partners and aim to please. . . . I want you to cry because you never knew how good it could be."

The letter included somewhat complex instructions for Leigh to follow if she wanted to communicate with the letter writer: "This is an indication, if you ever should consider or wish to communicate, check out of the library the Tax Management Estates, Gifts and Trusts Portfolio No. 134-4th, titled 'Annuities' located near the Westlaw terminal on the 25th floor in the library. When you check it out, insert a library checkout card signed by you in its place. I will periodically notice if it is gone. If so, I will contact you to let you know how to reach me anonymously."

Leigh, being a moral, upstanding woman, was disgusted by the letter. She wanted no part of it, and she immediately took the letter and showed it to her supervisor. Following a meeting with the firm's upper management, it was decided that if the anonymous letter writer had placed one letter on Leigh's chair, he would likely leave her another one, especially if she agreed to play along. She agreed, and with that thought in mind, the firm hired an outside security service, Business Risk International, to learn the identity of the mysterious letter writer.

The security firm promptly installed two inconspicuous closed-circuit video cameras and focused them on Leigh's workstation, located on the twenty-fifth floor of the First American Center. They also set up surveillance in the library and waited. Leigh followed the instructions laid out in the letter and removed the annuities portfolio. She also signed a checkout card and left it in the space where the volume had been located. Just as they had suspected, Leigh received an additional letter from the anonymous writer.

By this time it was August 14, and the new letter began: "I can barely type this. My hands are unsteady and my thoughts are whirling in a maelstrom of emotions. . . . I feel as if my heart stopped beating. . . . My world is far less grey [sic] today than it has ever been in my life. I feel like the lucky leprechaun who has seen the rainbow and knows what lays [sic] beyond. And like the leprechaun, I wonder if I'll ever find it. . . . Say what you will, my dearest, you will forever be my truest longing."

The thing that was different this time was that the letter writer was no longer anonymous. Perry March, thirty years old at the time, had been captured on video as he removed Leigh's checkout card from the shelf that had been designated in the letter, and he was subsequently named by Business Risk International as the mysterious letter writer. Perry's office was also on the building's twenty-fifth floor, not far from Leigh's work area.

Perry's son, Sammy, Miller reflected as he pondered the information, was only eleven months old when Leigh had received the letters.

Miller learned that upper management, upon learning of the letter writer's identity, called Perry into a closed-door meeting during which they gave him two options. He could resign, or they would fire him. If he chose to accept the offer to resign, the firm required that he would obtain counseling for his sexual issues. Perry agreed, and the firm sent Leigh on a paid vacation.

However, when Leigh returned from her vacation, she saw that Perry was still there, working at the firm. She ran into him everywhere, despite her best efforts to avoid him. She couldn't even go to the bathroom or get coffee without seeing him. Finally she'd had enough and resigned from the firm, and in the process retained a lawyer to represent her in a possible sexual harassment suit. Perry March left Bass, Berry & Sims two weeks later.

Miller learned that Perry had reached an out-of-court settlement with Leigh Reames for $25,000 over the letter-writing incidents in order to avoid a full-blown sexual harassment lawsuit. However, he had been slow in paying off the settlement, and by the summer of 1996, he had only paid half of it. Apparently, Janet had learned of the settlement, possibly through her father, Miller learned, or possibly by somehow getting hold of a letter that Perry had written to Leigh on August 13, two days before Janet disappeared, in which he had explained that he was having difficulty coming up with the remainder of the money that he owed her. Miller theorized that if Janet had learned of the letter, it could have been the cause for their argument on the evening of August 15. Miller theorized that Janet may have confronted Perry about the letter, perhaps even threatening him with divorce and the bleak prospect of cutting him off financially, and that the argument had been enough to send Perry over the edge.

It was only a theory, however, one of many that Miller and his colleagues would explore. By this point in time, however, there was little doubt in anyone's mind that Perry March, if not a murderer, was a scoundrel.

Chapter 8

On Wednesday, November 20, 1996, Perry March appeared in Davidson County Probate Court on behalf of
himself and his children in which he provided a lengthy
and often interesting deposition that, at times, revealed significant details about his character. Janet's parents, along
with their attorneys, were present. Perry's brother, Ronald
March, was present, along with Perry's attorney, Lionel R.
Barrett Jr. Jon E. Jones, attorney for the Levines, began the
questioning after Perry had been sworn in. His deposition
was, in part, a result of litigation that he had filed in a legal
battle between himself and the Levines over Janet's assets.

"Your brother, Ron March, is here today sitting beside
you," said Jones. "Is that correct?"

"That is correct," Perry responded.

"In what capacity is he here?"

"He is my attorney."

"Did he help you at any time move personal property
from the residence at Blackberry Lane?"

"No."

"Have you transferred any funds to him since August 15, 1996?"

"No."

And so the questioning went. Jones wanted to know if Perry had given his brother any funds to hold for him for any period of time, and Perry responded that he had not.

"Have you deposited any checks written to you into his account since August 15, 1996?" Jones asked.

"No. Not to the best of my recollection," Perry replied.

"Did you contact him on August 15, 1996?"

"Yes."

"At what time?"

"To the best of my recollection, it was sometime around nine [P.M.]."

"Why did you contact him?"

"To let him know that my wife, Janet, had left."

"When had you last talked to your brother before that conversation?"

"I do not remember. I speak to my brother daily, once or twice."

"Had you told your brother that you and your wife had separated?"

"We hadn't separated."

"During the days before August 15, 1996, did you tell your brother, or had you told your brother, that you were not living in the house, were not staying there overnight?"

"I had not moved out of my house," Perry responded. "I had stayed in hotels a few nights."

"Was your brother aware of that before August 15, 1996?" Jones asked.

"I don't remember."

Jones asked Perry whether he had spoken to his brother during the two weeks prior to Janet's disappearance to inform him that he and Janet were having marital problems at that time, and Perry told him that he had. In response to Jones's questioning, Perry described their marital problems simply as routine, and that they had had such difficulties on and off throughout their marriage. Jones asked if their marital problems had become worse.

"There had been times in our marriage where they were equal degrees," Perry responded.

"Had you spent other nights in a hotel rather than stay at home?" Jones asked. "Because of your marital difficulties."

"Not at all."

"Sir?"

"No."

"So, immediately before August 15, 1996, is the first occasion where the problems in your marriage caused you to stay in local hotels, is that correct, rather than stay at home?"

"Correct."

"Tell me what happened on August fifteenth leading up to your claim that Janet walked out or disappeared," Jones asked.

Perry explained that he had arrived home from work at approximately 4:00 or 4:30 P.M. that day, and that Janet was at home with their two children while the cabinet workers were completing the repair work that Janet had requested. Jones then wanted to know what Janet had been wearing when Perry arrived home that day.

"I don't remember," Perry responded.

"Was she wearing blue jeans? Was she wearing a dress? Was she dressed up?" Jones asked.

"Mr. Jones, I don't remember."

"Okay. You have no idea at all. Is that what you're claiming?"

"That's correct," Perry responded. "As of today I don't remember."

"Did she ever change clothes before you claim she left on August fifteenth? From the time you arrived home that day."

"I believe she did. I do remember that I noted that there was a change, but I don't remember exactly what it was," Perry said.

"So you don't remember if she changed from a dress to casual clothes or from casual clothes to a dress? That's just blocked out of your mind. Is that correct?"

"I don't remember. I think she was wearing shorts and then—and then jeans or vice versa. But that's about as good as I can remember at this time."

"When do you think she changed clothes?"

"Prior to her leaving."

"Immediately before she left?"

"I think pretty close to when she left, yes."

"What time do you say she left?"

"Again, approximately, based on my recollection right now, sometime between eight-thirty and nine."

"How long after she left was it until you called your brother?"

"Again, I know I called my brother sometime around the nine o'clock hour. It could have been nine-thirty, it could have been a quarter to nine. I don't remember exactly."

"Do you have a sense that she had been gone an hour or more before you called him?"

"I think she had been gone a relatively short period of time, but I don't remember exactly."

"What do you mean by 'a relatively short period of time'?"

"I don't have any way to give you an estimation of that—of that time period."

"Okay. Was it dark when she left?"

"I don't recall. I think it was dusky, or it could have been dark. I just—I don't remember. I was inside. I wasn't outside at all."

"You didn't follow her out?"

"No."

"All right. You arrived home, you say, around four to four-thirty P.M."

"Sometime in that time period."

"Where did you arrive home from?"

"My office."

"Did you go straight home from the office to your house?"

"I don't remember."

"In other words, you don't know if you stopped somewhere for an hour or so before you went home?"

"That's correct. I simply do not remember that day. A lot of things happened since then. I do not remember if I came directly home. It was a routine day to me."

"Mr. March, how could you not remember the last day you saw your wife?"

"My testimony is I do not remember, Mr. Jones."

"Well, do you have any explanation for your lapse of memory?"

"Yes. Lots of things have occurred since then and now, and it was not logged in my memory what happened."

"What was the last thing Janet said to you?"

"Something to the effect, 'It's your turn. See ya.'"

"Do you have a memory of that?"

"Yeah, I definitely remember that."

When Jones asked him what had happened after he came home, Perry responded that it was difficult to recall because it had been more than three months since the evening of August 15. He said that he had taken care of the children while Janet stayed with the cabinetmakers and oversaw their work. He explained how he had played with the kids outside, and later had prepared their dinner and gave them baths before putting them to bed. Afterward, he said that he had helped the workmen replace the faucet in the kitchen and later went out to a grocery store.

"Why did you go to the grocery store?" Jones asked.

"Pick up some dinner," Perry replied in his sometimes fragmented manner of speaking.

"Who cooked dinner?"

"I did."

"What did you cook?"

"I don't remember. I've been trying to remember what I cooked. I have no idea."

"What store did you go to?"

"I'm sure I went to the Com—Steven's. That's it. I'm sorry. Steven's. Steven's grocery store—near the split of highway one hundred and [highway] seventy."

"You remember going."

"Absolutely. Because I never go to the grocery store."

"All right. What did you drive to the store?"

"I don't remember. Probably my Jeep, but maybe her car. I just don't remember what the situation was with the cars."

Jones changed the course of his interrogation with his next question.

"Why did you have a roll of carpet in the house, or a partial roll?" Jones asked.

"Mr. Jones, I have no idea what you're talking about. What roll of carpeting?"

"Was there any rolled-up carpet at any time in your house on August fifteenth?"

"Mr. Jones, I have no idea. My house is full of things. I have no idea if I had rolls of carpeting in my house. We have three rooms of carpeting. I have no idea what extra carpeting is in my house. None. My wife was completely in charge of the construction of that house. Whatever extra materials or excess materials were, she was in charge of putting wherever she put them."

"When you lived in the house, did you see rolls of carpet or any rolled-up carpet anywhere in the living area of the house?"

"I don't recall any rolled-up carpeting in the living area of the house. I'm certain it wouldn't have been in the living areas of the house. Although it could have been. I just don't recall it."

"In other words, it might have been there and it might have been something that was there every day you were in the house or it might have been brought in just shortly before August fifteenth, but your mind's completely blank about that; is that right?"

"No, sir. I think that you're putting words in my mouth. My testimony here and my answer to you, my truthful answer to you, is I don't recall any rolled-up carpeting in any living section of the house whatsoever. There may have been remnants of rolled-up carpeting somewhere in my house, either stored in my basement or in some closet, but certainly not in a traffic living area. That I can recall."

Perry explained during the lengthy questioning that Janet had requested him to come home early that day. She had called him sometime during the day at the office, which she had often done. When asked if he had ever recorded Janet's telephone conversations with him, Perry responded that he had, on two or three separate occasions when she had become hysterical or had been in a very upset frame of mind.

"I would record those conversations to—I would just record them," Perry said.

"When you said you did them 'to,' and then you stopped. To do what?" Jones asked.

"At the time I did them, it was to play them back to her to analyze them and go over what it was that she was upset with. Or to—I think on one occasion when Janet was hysterical and I taped it, I gave that tape to Carolyn and Larry Levine to have them listen to it to see if they could help and shed some light on what was the font of her anger. But really that—it was only—I can only recall two occasions I have taped Janet at my office. Both of them for that purpose."

"All right. Tell me about those two occasions."

"I honestly don't remember the significance, the substance, or the purpose of the times when Janet was upset on the phone on the two occasions that I taped her. Now, I will say to you it may have been three times, it may have been one time, but I do know that I did tape her on, I think, two occasions with my Dictaphone, standing like this in my office with my eyes rolled up because she was being hysterical on the phone with me."

"Have you ever taped Larry Levine?"

"Never."

"Have you ever taped anybody besides Janet?"

"To the best of my recollection, I have not taped anybody else."

"All right. You got home. You said you gave the children a bath. You said you went out shopping. You cooked supper."

"I think you have the order reversed, Mr. Jones. I said that I came home and I played with the children and I puttered around. I believe I had some conversations with the cabinet people. And then I went out to the grocery store. I made the children dinner, I gave them baths, and I put them to sleep."

"Did Janet eat with you and the children that evening?"

"No, she did not."

"Why?"

"She was working."

"Where was she working?"

"In her studio."

"What was she working on?"

"A painting."

"Did you have any conversation with her about your marriage that evening?"

"Not until after the children were asleep."

Jones grilled Perry repeatedly regarding the time of day that Perry claimed to have put the children to bed, and Perry responded that it was sometime around 7:00 P.M. Jones continued to push Perry into being specific about the time on the evening of August 15, and Perry eventually told him that he took offense at Jones trying to find out the specific time periods of that evening.

"Why do you take offense to my trying to find out specific times?" Jones asked.

"I misspoke," Perry responded. "I do not take offense, but I will correct you because it was not specific in my mind."

"Okay. And you want to, in your testimony, keep time general. Is that correct?"

"No, I want it to be truthful. And I want to tell you that I do not have specific testimony about specific times. And it would be untruthful to do that."

"So no time during the evening of August fifteenth did you look at the clock, or do you have any reliable time estimates? Is that correct?"

"That's not correct."

"What's incorrect about that?"

Perry explained that he had a "reliable feel" regarding the time that Janet had left the house the evening she disappeared because he could remember that he had called his brother shortly after she had left. That had been sometime around the "nine-ish hour," he said. Perry's telephone records, according to the police, had shown that he had called his brother in Wilmette, Illinois, at 9:11 P.M. Even though Perry's time estimate of when he had called his brother was reasonable based on the telephone records, Jones kept hammering away at him about being more specific regarding time that evening. He wanted to know whether Perry looked at his watch that evening; whether he watched television; and if he had watched television, which shows had he watched. When Perry said that he didn't recollect, Jones asked him if he had changed clothes anytime that evening.

"I have no recollection of that," Perry responded. "I'm sure I changed into my sleeping clothes."

"When you came home wearing a coat and tie—"

"Oh, I certainly changed out of my suit. I would never have taken care of the kids and given them baths that evening—in my suit."

"What did you change into?"

"No idea. That was the middle of summer. I don't know what I put on."

"Did you ever hit Janet?" The question seemed to have come out of nowhere, and took Perry somewhat by surprise, even though he knew that such a question would eventually be posed to him.

"No. I never struck Janet," Perry responded.

"With a fist or open hand, you never struck Janet at any time in your life. Is that your testimony?"

"Mr. Jones, to the best of my recollection, I have never struck my wife. It has always been something that I am proud of. I have never struck my wife."

"You said that to the best of your recollection you had never struck her. That's not something that you could possibly forget, is it?"

"Mr. Jones, I don't believe I ever struck my wife."

"Do you know that?"

"As I sit here today, I tell you that my testimony is that I do not believe I ever struck my wife."

"I didn't ask you if you believed it. I asked you if you did. Do you know that you never struck her?"

"Yes, I think I believe I do know I never struck her."

"Did you ever choke her?"

"No."

"Did you ever physically hurt her or attempt to physically hurt Janet?"

"I'm just—I'm thinking because I'm just trying to separate—I can't—I don't know, but there is certainly a possibility that at times I grabbed Janet's arm and moved her out of the way or I took something from her, which she was holding back from me, or where I, you know, held her harm—arm in a firm manner, which might be construed by some to be twisting. But certainly never with the intent of inflicting bodily harm on my wife."

"Did you ever pull her hair?"

"Not to my recollection."

"Is that something you have any question about?"

"Does that mean did I pull her hair in lovemaking?"

"Did you normally pull her hair in lovemaking?"

"No. What does that mean, 'pull her hair'? Does that mean if I'm sitting on a chair and her hair is underneath my arm and she sits up and her hair is pulled, did I pull her hair? No, the answer is I never intentionally grabbed my wife's head, pulled her hair with the intent of inflicting bodily harm on her."

"Did Janet ever complain that during sexual relationships you would choke her or pull her hair?"

"Not to me."

Chapter 9

As Perry March's November 20, 1996, deposition continued, the questioning turned toward whether Perry was aware of anyone who might want to harm or kill Janet. Janet was known to have an unpleasant side to her personality, and it had surfaced regularly during the construction of her and Perry's house. No less than seven subcontractors, who worked primarily on high-end-type projects, had said that she was difficult to work with and was never pleased until some of their work was redone, whether it was needed or not. Some of the subcontractors recalled that Perry often had to enter the picture to help smooth things out when Janet would become unreasonable in her demands. It didn't seem likely that any of the subcontractors would want to harm Janet simply because of her occasional nasty disposition, but it did seem to be where Perry was trying to lead his inquisitor during questioning.

"Do you know of anybody who might have any motive to kill Janet?" Jones asked.

"Yes," Perry responded.

"Who?"

"I believe there are a number of people involved with the construction of our house that carry extreme animosity and feelings of hate toward Janet."

"Have any of those people ever threatened to kill her or do her bodily harm?"

"I have heard of intimations of such."

"All right. Let's go down the list, if you would. Give me their names and what you've heard."

Perry responded that he believed the general contractor, as well as others, seemed to have extreme levels of "hate and animosity" toward Janet. Perry also mentioned a painter who did not particularly like Janet because he had not met Janet's standards regarding the painting of their house. He said that the painter and Janet were battling constantly about what he should do and what he shouldn't do. He said that Janet was often very demeaning to many of the workmen, and explained that he didn't really remember all of them because of the enormous size of the job.

"You have to remember, Mr. Jones, this is a large construction job," Perry stated. "I was on the site two, sometimes three, times a day talking to various people who had contact with various other subs who had contact with my wife who had contact with numerous people. It was a project that lasted over a year. . . . I know for a fact that I warned Janet on a number of occasions to attempt to modify her behavior and to attempt to modify her statements and interactions with the various subcontractors and contractors working on our job because she was creating a great degree of animosity, and it was counterproductive to the job. It was also dangerous to her."

"How long has it been since you have seen the contractor . . . or the painter?" Jones asked.

"Over a year. Year and a half maybe."

"During the year or year and a half, did they ever make any attempts to physically harm Janet or have any contact with her?"

"Certainly not to my knowledge, Mr. Jones."

Perry said that Janet had apparently caught an employee of one of her subcontractors stealing chairs from their house, and she had apparently confronted him about it. She had also caught another employee stealing materials for his own personal use.

"I know that Janet caught a trim carpenter on our job one afternoon on a beautiful day making a birdhouse out of our materials, on our time, and she took the birdhouse away from him," Perry said. "So, again, this is a process that lasted over a year. There were a great number of people flowing in and out that my wife had personal contact with. . . . So, I guess, I'm just trying to be honest with you. . . . There must have been over a hundred people in some aspect of [the] work, flowing in and out of our project that Janet had day-to-day contact with. Sometimes one shot and sometimes over a protracted period of time."

"Do you think any of these people might have killed her?" Jones asked.

"Mr. Jones, I play with theories constantly about where my wife is," Perry responded. "It is my fixation. It is all I think about. So, nothing is beyond the realm of speculation for me. My own situation is so bizarre that nothing appears bizarre to me."

"My question was, do you think any of these people killed her?"

"I don't know."

A little later in the questioning, Jones again asked Perry if he and Janet argued on the night of August 15.

"It's a matter of semantics, Mr. Jones," Perry replied. "The answer to the question is Janet was upset. I did not argue, but I believe she was upset with me and she did argue."

Jones wanted to know what the argument or confrontation had been about, and how it began.

"Janet wanted to discuss her continuing issues with our marriage," Perry responded.

"Okay. You said that's what she wanted. I'm asking what was said. How did the discussion or the argument get started?"

"Again, Mr. Jones, I don't specifically recollect. My wife had—it was routine that Janet had lists of issues, things she wanted to discuss, recurrent themes, and she wanted to bring them up and talk about them. I sat at the kitchen table. She talked for a while, asked me what I was going to do, and left."

"Did you ever tell the Levines that you had an argument with Janet on August fifteenth?"

"I—you know, I may have—matter of degree, Mr. Jones. And a matter of when I told the Levines that. You have to understand I was in an extremely upset frame of mind after my wife ran off. I could not find her. I did not know where she was. I missed her terribly and I was concerned for her safety. So, the specific time frames and what I said and who I said them to immediately following Janet's leaving, very difficult for me to recollect."

"Now, my question is, did you tell the Levines that you and Janet had an argument on August fifteenth?"

"Again, Mr. Jones, I don't specifically recollect the statement, but I'm certain that it could have been said because I know that Janet was upset and I was not withholding anything."

"Did you tell the police that you had an argument on August fifteenth?"

"Again, certainly a strong possibility."

"Was that the truth?"

"Absolut—well, again, Mr. Jones, it's a matter of degree of what you consider to be an argument. . . . The truth is that I did not have an argument. The truth is that Janet did, but it's hard to dance with only one person. So, someone observing it may say it was an argument between a husband and a wife, but I can tell you that my demeanor was the exact same as it is here today with you, sir. If Janet was upset . . . she grew emotional and passionate. That was her nature. . . ."

"And it was your demeanor that night not to become upset and you didn't become upset on August fifteenth. Is that correct?"

"That is absolutely correct."

"You never lost your temper on August fifteenth. Is that correct?"

"Correct."

"You never went into a rage or became emotionally upset and angry and lost control of yourself on August fifteenth. Is that correct?"

"Correct."

"You did not do anything on August fifteenth in the heat of passion. Is that correct?"

"Correct."

"Anything you did on August fifteenth in regard to Janet—"

"Let me say this to you, Mr. Jones."

"Let me finish—you did with full control of your emotions and with full insight and knowledge into what you were doing. Is that correct?"

"That is actually not correct, Mr. Jones. As the evening wore on, and I became more and more concerned for my wife's safety and her emotional stability, I did become ever increasingly distraught and I did become ever increasingly emotional in concern—in relation to her safety. . . . I started to call hotels. I called my brother. I called my sister. I became worried."

"Before she left, at all times on August fifteenth . . . anything you did with her that evening was done by you with full control of your emotions and full insight and understanding of your actions and your thought processes and what was going on. Is that correct?"

"I—you know, I believe so," Perry responded with much difficulty at finding what it was he was trying to say. "I mean, I don't know if I—if—I can't—I don't—I think the only—I mean, we obviously were upset with each other during our conversation before she left. And I'm not sure if I was upset with her or she was upset with me about other issues when I came home. . . . But correct me if I'm wrong, the tenor of your question is was I upset or angry or was there anything of that nature going on that evening, and the answer is we were—we had a general disquiet, a general sense of upsetness between the two of us. Things weren't right in our marriage, Mr. Jones."

"Okay. . . . Would you read the question back, please?" Jones asked the court reporter. "And I'll try to move on from this, but I really need an answer."

"Before she left," responded the court reporter as she read back the original question, "at all times on August fifteenth before Janet left, anything you did with her that evening was done by you with full control of your emotions and full insight and understanding of your actions and your thought process and what was going on. Is that correct?"

"I guess the only way I can answer that truthfully," Perry

responded, "is I don't recollect. I don't recollect every moment of the time when I came home. It was a routine day for me. It did not become unroutine until I started becoming worried about my wife's safety."

"After she left," Jones added.

"After she left."

"Up until the time she left, you had not become angry with her. Is that correct?"

"Well, again, I'm modifying my answer to make it more truthful, which is I probably was upset to some degree with her from the moment I even came home. But it was a general issue in our marriage at that time that we both had unresolved tensions with each other."

"Before she left that night, had you become angry with her?"

"Again, a matter of degree of what someone would call angry and what someone else would call angry."

"I'm asking you about what you would call it. Would you say, 'I was angry with her,' the way you use that term?"

"I don't recollect. I may have been."

"In other words, you can't remember one way or the other?"

"That's absolutely true. I cannot remember one way or the other."

"Did you ever lose any consciousness that night or have any blackouts that night?"

"No."

"Are you on any medications today?"

"No."

"Is there anything going on that affects your memory here today or impairs your ability to give rational answers?"

"Not at all. Other than the fact I just had the flu. But I've recovered, I think."

"You don't have any illness and you're not under any medications that keep you from having normal ability and thought process[es]. Is that correct?"

"That is correct."

"Now, because you've modified your answers as we've gone along, to use your words, I want to know where we are. Because where Janet is, or what happened to her, or what you know about it, may be affected by your view that night of what happened. . . . Do you claim at any time before Janet left, you did anything in any passionate state, or in any heat of passion, or in any emotional state, where your normal judgment and ability and control of your actions was impaired?"

"To the best of my recollection, no."

"Can you remember one way or the other?"

"To the best of my recollection, no, sir. I say to the best of my recollection."

"Could your recollection be wrong about that?"

"I don't believe it is. I've given you an answer."

"Okay. What were you and Janet arguing about that night? I used the term, 'argument.' Now, we've gone back and forth about it. Is it your position that you and Janet had an argument on August fifteenth or that you did not have an argument on August fifteenth?"

"Again, Mr. Jones, truly it's a matter of degree. And I think that it's fair to characterize it as an argument, but it's also fair to characterize it as really not an argument. I don't—I don't know how to answer your question, but I think that a rational person listening would be able to answer it and understand what I'm talking about."

"Did she yell at you?" Jones's inflection displayed a

degree of sudden irritation, and at times the interaction between Perry and Jones was almost comical—not unlike a scene from a Three Stooges short film in which the bailiff repeatedly tried to swear in Curly, who did not understand the question that was being asked of him.

"Yes."

"Did you yell at her?"

"No, I did not yell back."

"Did you throw anything at her?"

"Not at all."

"Did she throw anything at you?"

"No, not that night."

"Did she talk about divorce?"

"No. That night I don't believe she did."

"What was the subject of this discussion, which some people might fairly call an argument and what some people might not call an argument?"

"Again, I believe—the general tenor was how was I going to make up to her for the period of time that she claimed I had deserted my duties to the household."

"Did you talk about money that night?"

"Not at all. I don't believe so."

"Were you under any financial pressure as of August 15, 1996?"

"No, I wasn't."

"Did you have any outstanding unpaid bill or debts at that time? Other than just routine monthly bills?"

"I had a ten-thousand-dollar payment due at some point in the near future, but I had planned on moving my offices, so it wasn't—I mean, I don't know what you want me to say about that. . . ."

"What was the ten-thousand-dollar payment for?"

"In settlement for a disputed claim of harassment when I was at Bass, Berry, and Sims."

"Who was the debt to?"

"Leigh Biggs Reames."

"Was that a pressing matter as of August 15, 1996?"

"I didn't believe it was."

"Well, tell me what was going on as of August fifteenth with regard to that debt, if anything."

"That I owed the debt . . . but I had sent a letter off explaining that I was moving my office. I would get the payment made sometime in the next couple of months, unless I heard otherwise, and I hadn't heard otherwise."

"Was that payment overdue?"

"Yes, but disputed as well."

"What do you mean 'disputed'?"

"Means that I had a legitimate claim, I believe, and I still believe to this day that I may not pay that debt based on breaches of confidentiality."

"As of August fifteenth, were you still promising to pay the debt?"

"I believe so, yes."

"Had you been pressed shortly before August 15, 1996, for payment of that debt?"

"I may have received a letter saying pay, but I wrote back a letter saying, 'I'm not paying it till this next time period,' so, you know, legally I didn't feel pressed."

"What do you mean, the 'next time period'?"

"Sometime in September or October."

"Did you tell your wife about that debt?"

"Yes."

"When?"

"I don't recollect. On a number of occasions."

"Tell me about those occasions in telling her about that debt."

"Again, I don't recollect, but sometime early in the process I told her about the situation. Couple years ago. And then I know specifically she and I discussed it at length when we were on our last trip to Quebec together, and that was sometime in February or March of this year."

Perry said that he had discussed his debt to Leigh Reames with Janet again in June or July 1996, to explain to her that he owed his final payment and that he was going to try and clear up the debt after he moved his office. He explained that he had established a separate bank account that he utilized to pay the debt to Leigh Reames.

"Why didn't you just pay it out of your joint account?" Jones asked.

"Because my understanding with my wife was that money had to come out of my extra money. It was not to impact our household finances at all."

Perry said that anytime he had extra money to spare, it was easier to keep it separate by placing it into the special account he had set up.

"So, you talked to your wife about that before you established that account. Is that correct?" Jones asked.

"I'm not sure if I—I—I have to be truthful. I don't know if I established that account before I told—talked to Janet about it or after I talked to Janet about it. But certainly she—she knew about it."

"Well, if you established it after you talked to Janet about it, what you said about why you established it would be totally just untruthful and a lie. Isn't that correct?"

"I don't know how you're characterizing it. Why don't you explain that or ask me a question."

"Did you or did you not establish that account to keep these payments to Mrs. Reames and her husband a secret?"

"Yes. No. No. No. No. No, I'm sorry. Not to keep it a secret. I established the account to pay the Reameses."

"If you didn't want to keep that secret—those payments secret from your wife, was there any reason to establish a separate account to make payment to the Reameses?"

"Yes. It was easier for me to monitor it. It wouldn't impact my household finances at all. I could—I knew exactly what the balance was in the account. I could monitor the account easily. And it had—my wife would move in and out and take money out of my checking account, put money into my checking account, move funds freely amongst all of our moneys. She was in charge of our moneys. And that account was one that I could easily maintain because I had a contractual obligation to do so, Mr. Jones."

"When did you mail the letter that bore the date August 13, 1996, to the Reameses asking for more time, saying you couldn't pay them right then?"

"I don't know."

"Did you have that letter with you when you came home, unsent and unmailed, on August 15, 1996?"

"I don't know."

"Did you mail a letter to the Reameses on August 16, 1996?"

"I don't know."

"Is that something you could possibly forget, Mr. March?"

"Yes."

"So, on August sixteenth, after your wife was—had disappeared the night before, you might have mailed a letter asking for more time on this ten-thousand-dollar or twelve-thousand-five-hundred-dollar debt to the Reameses that you just forgot about doing. Is that correct?"

"Absolutely. Correct."

"Because you were so distraught on August 16, 1996, you just can't remember what you did that day. Is that fair?"

"Well—well, Mr.—Mr. Jones, I—your characterizations are your—you're speaking from my testimony, sir."

Jones had become brutal in his questioning, and it was obvious that Perry March had been rattled by his approach.

"Well, how do you characterize them?"

"On August sixteenth, I wasn't totally distraught," Perry responded. "I was upset. I thought she had packed her bags and she was gone for a few days. I honestly, on August sixteenth, believed my wife would be home when I came back from the office. I was slightly upset with her. I was slightly miffed that she would have left that night without calling anybody, letting us know where she was, what—whether she was safe or not safe. And then not calling the next morning even."

"And you're telling us that this matter with the Reameses and this debt to the Reameses was of so little concern to you that you don't know if you were essentially begging them for more time, as of August 15 or 16, 1996. Is that correct?"

"I don't understand your question."

"You just can't understand those words. Is that correct?"

"You're—you're speaking an answer. Why don't you just—why don't you just rephrase your question, Mr. Jones?"

"Are you telling us that you don't understand that question?"

"Again, Mr. Jones, I reiterate. I'm seriously not attempting to be difficult with you. I approached this deposition fully cooperative. I want to find my wife. This is a tragic situation. I simply want to answer the questions truthfully without you putting words in my mouth."

"Well, you know, I have a right to cross-examine you. I intend to cross-examine you. That's part of my job here today."

"Absolutely, sir."

"What was your wife wearing the day she—at the time she left?"

"I believe you answered that—asked me that question."

"What was she wearing?" Jones was being insistent, and seemed intent on catching Perry in a lie.

"Again, I don't specifically recall. Could be shorts, could have been jeans. It was summertime. Over three months ago. I don't remember."

"What did she take with her?"

"I don't know."

"What do you believe she took with her?"

"I have no idea what was in her car. But I know that when she left the house, she was carrying, I believe, three bags."

"Okay. Describe those bags."

"Her standard overnight bag, which is a small gray valise. I believe she was carrying with her a backpack, like a leather backpack that she carries on airplanes with her. That's really the only time she uses it, when she—when she gets on an airplane. And she was carrying a canvas tote that she used for her pool bag, but she had used it—it looked like it was full of her toiletries and things of that nature. I just—I don't know. I didn't take a close look inside of it. I was a little stunned when she came down-stairs with her bags."

"How long had she been upstairs before she came down with her bags?"

"I don't know, Mr. Jones."

"An hour? Thirty minutes?"

"It was a short period of time."

"How long had it been since this discussion that might have been an argument ended and she went upstairs?"

"All within the hour."

"So there might have been as much as an hour's time lapse between the time the discussion or the argument ended and the time she came back downstairs with her bags. Is that correct?"

"You're confusing me. I don't really remember."

"How did the argument end?"

"With her being upset. My staying calm. Sitting at the kitchen table. With her asking me to leave for the evening. My answering her, 'Are you sure you want me to leave?' Her response was 'Yes. I want you to go to a hotel.' I got up, I went to the phone. I called the Hampton Inn. I made a reservation. I hung up the phone.

"She got up," Perry continued, "she said, 'You're not going again on my time and my money.' And she took my credit card from me. She took my wallet from me. She grabbed the stuff. She ripped up the card. She handed me back my driver's license and my cash. And she walked into my study, where she was there for a short period of time. I heard her. I sat at the kitchen table."

Jones seemed somewhat stunned as he listened to Perry. It was, after all, the first time that so many details had come straight from his mouth regarding the night of August 15.

"You want me to—should I continue?" Perry asked. "I mean, want me to continue? Are you asking me to continue? I don't—I forgot what the question was. I'm sorry."

"Just go ahead. Continue." It was obvious that Jones wanted to hear what came out of Perry's mouth next.

"I heard the printer," Perry said. "She walked out of my study. She walked upstairs. I don't know how long she was upstairs, but it was a relatively short period of time. I stayed at the kitchen table. She came downstairs. She had the bags. She handed me the note that she had typed and asked me to read it and sign it. I did so. She turned around. She said something to the effect of, 'It's your turn. See ya.' She left. That was the last time I saw my wife."

"And she had these three bags with her?"

"Yes, sir."

"Any idea what was in the bags?"

"No, sir."

"Any idea what was in her purse?"

"No, sir. Well—well, that's—that's an unfair statement. I do know subsequently that—I have an idea, as I told you, that there were some toiletries in the bags. And I do know she took some CDs with her because I do remember her making a little sidestep to the CD—where our stereo is, and she took some CDs with her, which gave me an indication I thought that she was going to be driving somewhere.

"And I subsequently learned," Perry continued, "that she took cash and her passport and a small bag of marijuana that she keeps in a cabinet. I could not locate that small bag. I think it's—I think it's a better way for me to characterize it now is I assume that she took the cash, the passport, and the small bag of marijuana. Because they're not there. And they weren't there a day or two after she left."

"Did you know that small bag of marijuana was in a particular place before she left?"

"She never really told me where it was and she kept it hidden. . . . I knew it was in her desk, built-in desk cabinet area. And I don't know exactly what drawer it was, but I do know specifically where the money was and where the passport was. And both were gone, Mr. Jones."

"You know, I really would like an answer to my last question." Jones asked the court reporter to read it back.

"Did you know that small bag of marijuana was in a particular place before she left?"

"No. I knew a general locality of where I thought it was."

"Well, then, why did you say she took it with her?"

"Because subsequently I searched for it and I could not find it."

"You knew it was in a general area. Is that correct?"

"Yeah. I knew that she kept it in her desk area."

"When did you last see it before she left?"

"I don't know. She smoked marijuana pretty much on a weekly basis."

"The question is, when did you last see this small bag?"

"I don't remember."

"Within a month of her leaving, would you say?"

"Absolutely within a month of her leaving, yes."

"Within a week before she left, did you see it?"

"Again, I can't be any more specific than that."

"Than what? Than a month?"

"Yeah. Because sometimes she'd come out with a particular joint. And sometimes she'd come out with the whole bag. Sometimes she would roll a new one. Sometimes she would come out with a butt. I don't know how familiar you are with parlance of marijuana. I'm not too familiar with it."

"Have you ever used marijuana?"

"My wife attempted to get me to smoke it on a couple

occasions. I did the proverbial Bill Clinton thing. I pulled it into my mouth and I spit it out. Simply to appease her because she wanted me to try."

"So the answer is yes, you used marijuana. Is that correct?"

"No, sir. That's not the answer. The answer is I never inhaled marijuana. I know it sounds crazy, but I tell you it's the truth. I've never smoked a cigarette and I've never inhaled marijuana."

"Did you ever use cocaine?"

"Never."

"Now, let me see if I understand. You claim that a month or so before your wife left, you were aware that there was a small bag of marijuana somewhere in a general locality."

"No, sir, that's not correct. That's not a correct statement."

"What's incorrect about that?"

"I'm telling you that I believed up until the day she left that there was a bag of marijuana in the house that she purchased . . . that she shared with her friends."

"You said that you last saw it, as best you can characterize it, a month before she left. Now, was that testimony true?"

"No, sir. That's not what my testimony was. . . . You asked me had I seen the bag within the month. And my answer is yes, I had seen it within a month."

"Had you seen it within a week?"

"Again, I can't be more specific. I may have."

"Had you seen it within two weeks?"

"I may have."

"Had you seen it within a month?"

"Mr. Jones, we're talking about four months ago? Five months ago? Three months ago? The answer is I can't be specific the last time I saw Janet's bag of marijuana."

"Other than the fact that you had seen it sometime, as best you can characterize it, within a month of August fifteenth, and the fact that you looked for it later and you didn't find it, do you have any other reason to believe that she took it with her?"

"Yes."

"What?"

"That anytime Janet was upset and wanted to get away—anytime Janet left on a vacation or a weekend or a day, she would take her marijuana with her. It was an important part of her relaxation."

"Did she take it to Canada?"

"I know Janet took it to Canada with her."

"How do you know that?"

"She smoked it in Canada. Sat in the Hotel Frontenac room being late for dinner because she wanted to finish her joint. I have a specific recollection of that, Mr. Jones. And, actually, it's a fond one."

"Do you love Janet?"

"Yes."

"At the time she disappeared, are you claiming you were still in love with her?"

"Yes."

"You want to do everything you can to protect her and cherish her and cherish her memory if she's gone and dead. Is that correct?"

"Mr. Jones, I don't believe my wife is dead, but if she is dead, I will do everything I can to cherish her memory."

Chapter 10

Moments after Perry March told Jon Jones, the deposition questioner, how much he would do to cherish Janet's memory, if it turned out that she was dead, by explaining in great detail—in front of her parents—that she smoked marijuana on somewhat of a regular basis, Jones continued his questioning, but turned the subject toward Perry and Janet's computer.

"What happened to the computer?" Jones asked.

"I do not know," Perry replied.

"Computer would tell, if somebody had the hard drive, whether—the sequence of when this alleged note that you say she typed and gave to you, when that was prepared. Isn't that correct?"

"There's no question about it," Perry replied. "I can be very truthful with you. I know that—I know this. That the word-processing program that Janet and I used on our home computer has a file stamp of the last time it has been saved on the computer. I know that the note that Janet typed and printed and gave to me on the night that she ran away's file stamp time was eight-seventeen. Eight-seventeen at night.

"Once the computer hard drive was determined to be missing," Perry continued, "which I know nothing about, I also made inquiry as to whether or not there would be some separate corroboration of that time period. To know whether or not I had been put in a compromising position by its being missing. And based upon my understanding, no. Other than the file stamp copy time period on the actual word-processing program, there is no other memory log in the operating system or anything else which would corroborate or not corroborate that time period."

"Who did you make that inquiry to?" Jones asked.

"I stopped in personally to a—I think it was a Comp-USA," Perry responded, "and went up to the desk and asked a person who was—software person, and I was informed that unless you have a specific DOS-based or Windows-based utility program, which records the time periods of all the files, that the regular Windows 95 operating system does not record the time periods for all the respective files that are generated or discarded in a computer."

"Where was this store?"

"I don't remember. I think it was the one in Nashville that I went to. The CompUSA out, like, on Hickory Hollow or something."

"When did you do that?"

"Probably sometime after they effected the search warrant and I found out my hard drive was gone. I was trying to figure out what the heck does that mean. Why would it be gone?"

"When did you find out the hard drive was gone?"

"When Detective David Miller came storming out at me on the day that they effected the search warrant, screaming, 'Where's the hard drive, Perry?' like out of some B-rated detective movie."

"Did you know he was coming?"

"I had no certain knowledge that Detective Miller was—" Perry tried to answer. However, Jones cut him off.

"I didn't ask you if you had certain knowledge," Jones said, staring intently at Perry.

"No, I didn't know that Detective Miller was coming," Perry clarified.

"Did you have any information that the police were coming with a search warrant?"

"My attorney had informed me that unless I allowed the police to come out and effect a third voluntary search on my house, they were going to issue a warrant."

"Did you have any information that one of the things the police wanted to look at or search was your computer?"

"I will answer this question, the specific question, which is that Mr. Barrett informed me the day before that the police wanted to come out again and make a third voluntary search of my house. But this time they had informed my counsel that I was the prime suspect in my wife's disappearance."

"So, shortly before the police came out and searched the computer, found out somebody had ripped out the hard drive, you had been told that the police intended to come to your house and search the computer—is that correct?"

"Actually, Mr. Jones, I knew before then because the police had come out once before then, saying they wanted to inspect my computer, and they did."

"Who do you say tore the hard drive out of your computer?" Jones asked.

"I don't say anybody," Perry replied. "I have no idea, Mr. Jones."

In response to further questioning, Perry said that he did not have an opinion regarding who may have removed the hard drive. He explained that the computer was used primarily for "home stuff."

"I did a lot of work on it at home," Perry said. "I'd do documents for clients . . . office work. I used it quite a bit to access Internet. Databases, things of that nature. Janet used the computer for the construction of the house. All of her house budgets and Excel spreadsheets were on the computer. And then there was—clearly, Janet used it for her personal word processing as well, when she needed to type somebody a letter or send some correspondence. . . . And then I used it probably mostly for education for my kids, for Sammy."

"Who owned the computer?"

"We did. My wife and I."

"Where was it located?"

"In my study."

"After August fifteenth, did you use the computer?"

"You know, Mr. Jones, I don't have any recollection of specifically using the computer after August fifteenth. I don't think I did. . . . I may have used it once for some office-related issue . . . and I did turn it on for the police when they came and inspected it."

Over the next few minutes, Perry and Mr. Jones moved into the area of differentiating between using a computer and programming one. Perry—in his typical manner of playing his game of semantics with his questioner—quibbled at length over the use of the word "programming" with regard to how it pertained to computers and their use.

"Mr. Jones," Perry said, "I've never written a program."

"Have you ever attempted to do any programming of the computer?"

"I don't understand your question," Perry responded. "I just think it's because you're probably just not using the correct vocabulary with me. When you say that, are you asking if I wrote software programs? I'm not . . . trying to be truculent here, I'm just trying to understand what you're saying."

"Have you ever modified a program?" Jones asked.

"Modify a program," Perry repeated. "Every time you save a file, you modify a program or data. That is part of a program. So the answer is every time you save, you modify. That's the truth."

"Other than just saving, have you ever modified a program?"

"Sure, I have. I've installed pieces of programs where you don't fully install the program (when initially loading it into the computer). You take pieces of it out. You put pieces of the program in as part of the installation process. I've deleted programs. I mean, again, I just think it's imprecision in language. I'm not being evasive. I just don't understand what you're trying to ask me."

"When did you last use or attempt to use the computer before the police came and found that the hard drive had been ripped out?"

"I don't remember, but I do know—wait. I'm sorry," Perry said. "That—I did not answer your question properly. The last time I used the computer—that I turned it on physically before the police executed a search warrant on my house and I learned that the hard drive was gone—was in the presence of Detective David Miller and one other police officer."

"Was that, to the best of your memory, within a week of . . . your discovery of the hard drive being ripped out?"

"I think so," Perry responded. "I think that I discovered that the hard drive was missing. I don't know the exact date

they executed the search warrant of my house. It was the fifteenth or the seventeenth of September. I can't remember."

Jones offered the date as the fifteenth of September.

"That was like . . . a Wednesday?" Perry asked.

September 15, 1996, was actually a Sunday, but neither
Perry nor the questioner, Jones, seemed to know that. In
actuality, the search warrant in question had been executed
on September 17, 1996, a Tuesday.

"Anyway, if the police executed, assuming that it was
Tuesday—I don't remember the date," Perry said. "But if
they . . . came to my house with their corps of paramilitary
boot-camp folks . . . and executed their first search warrant
on Tuesday, then I think that Detective Miller—inspected
my computer Wednesday of the week prior, because I left
for the Rosh Hashanah holiday on Thursday. So I was gone
Thursday, Friday, Saturday, and Sunday. I was back in town
on Monday."

Even though Perry's testimony had been inconsistent
and had wavered back and forth with regard to the date of
the search warrant having been served, and had conflicted
with whether the warrant had been served before or after
his trip to Chicago for the Rosh Hashanah holiday, Jones's
incessant questioning was eventually able to show that the
warrant had, in fact, been served upon Perry's return. It
had been at that time that Detective Miller had discovered
that the hard drive was missing from Perry and Janet's
computer.

After getting the dates of the sequence of events somewhat straightened out, Jones wanted to know whether or
not Perry's house had been burglarized prior to the police
arriving and discovering that the computer's hard drive had
been removed and taken from the residence. Perry responded that the house had not been burglarized, at least

not to his knowledge, either before he left for Rosh Hashanah or while he was gone. He had not noticed any signs of a break-in, nor had he been aware of anything missing from his house. When he was asked whether he left his house unattended at any time in the days leading up to the point where he discovered that the computer hard drive was missing, Perry responded that he had not. He said that his father, Arthur March, had stayed at the house on Blackberry Road while he was in Chicago with the children.

"Did you leave your house unattended when you went to Chicago for the holy day?" Jones asked.

"No. My father was there," Perry responded, "but I'm not sure he was there the whole time."

"Why was your father there?"

"Because he couldn't afford to come up for Rosh Hashanah holiday."

"Well, why did he stay at your house?"

"Because it was more comfortable."

"More comfortable than what?"

"Than the condominium that I had rented."

"What had you rented a condominium for?"

"I rented the condominium so that when Janet came back, I'd have a place to go."

Perry explained that his father could have stayed with friends that he knew in Nashville rather than at his house or at the condominium, or he could have stayed at a hotel, like he normally did when he came to visit.

"Did your father stay at your house . . . to watch it?" Jones asked.

"Sure," Perry replied. "He was there because it was comfortable, free, and he would also be able to take care of it. It's a large place. Things go wrong. Things happen."

"Did your father have any motive to tear out the hard drive?"

"Not to my knowledge."

"Have you asked your father if he tore out the hard drive?"

"I believe I did."

"What did he say?"

"No."

"You believe him?"

"Absolute one hundred percent."

"When did you ask your father if he tore out the hard drive?"

"That I can't remember," Perry said. "I was relatively shocked when it happened. I don't remember when next I saw my father."

"Was your father there when the police executed the search warrant?" Jones asked.

"I'm sure, yes," Perry responded. "I believe he was in town."

"Was he at your house when they exercised it?"

"No."

"Did your father chase people away from the house, the press away from the house that week?"

"I don't know," Perry replied. "He may have. I think I heard a story. My father is a character. He may have chased away people who tried to trespass on my property. I didn't—I know that when I left for Rosh Hashanah, I had him put up No Trespassing signs."

"Okay. You had him put up No Trespassing signs and you asked him and told him to keep people away from the house and out of the house; is that correct?"

"I can't say that I explicitly told him to keep people out of the house or away from the house. My dad's a big old cuddly bear; and if he was there to watch the house, I promise you, no one would get in my house."

"And he was there to watch the house; is that right?"

"No, he was there because it was a comfortable place and it also served another purpose that he could keep an eye on it."

"I'm sorry, sir," Jones responded. "You just said if he was there to watch the house, he would keep people away. Is that what you said?"

"I said if he was there, yeah, to watch the house."

"Oh, you were just speaking hypothetically, Mr. March?"

"Absolutely, sir."

"Because he was not there to watch the house; is that your sworn position?"

"No, Mr. Jones," Perry responded. "It's not my sworn position. My sworn position is that my father was at my house because it was comfortable, because he couldn't afford to travel with us, because he was not invited to Rosh Hashanah at any other place in town, and that he also served another very good purpose of keeping an eye on the house, making sure that things were okay. And at that time it had already become a media circus, so keeping reporters and press people off my property was important. And my father was there and I'm sure he would have chased people away, as you put it."

"Well, the words 'to watch the house' were your words," Jones said. "Was he there to watch the house?"

"As another—as one of the many reasons my father was there, I'm sure it can be construed that he was there to watch the house."

"Well, now, Mr. March—" Jones began, but was abruptly cut off when Perry interrupted.

"Mr. Jones," Perry said, "if you would have walked up

to my house during Rosh Hashanah, my father probably would have chased you off."

"Okay. And that's one of the reasons he was there; is that correct?"

"I'm sure that's—okay. One of the reasons."

"And when you found out that the police had come and the hard drive was ripped out, and as you told channel four in an interview, that was just an enigma to you."

"Yeah."

"Just a real mystery."

"Yeah."

"Surely, you asked your father, 'Has anybody been in the house this weekend?'"

"Right."

"You did that, didn't you?"

"Yeah."

"What did he say?"

"Said, 'Not to my knowledge.' But he wasn't there the whole time."

"Did he tell you that?" Jones asked.

"Yeah, he said, 'Not to my knowledge.'"

"Did he tell you he had not been there the whole time?"

"Yeah."

"Did he tell you when he was gone?"

"Not all the times," Perry responded. "I didn't inquire as to every hour that he was gone. My dad can't remember twenty minutes ago, let alone where he was on Saturday if you ask him on Thursday."

"Well, look," Jones interjected. "You knew when this computer was broken into and the hard drive was ripped out, that there was a serious issue, didn't you?"

"Yeah."

"And did it occur to you that whoever ripped out the

computer might have had something to do with Janet's murder or her disappearance?"

"Possible inference," Perry replied. "One of many."

"Well, did that occur to you when you first learned the computer had been torn out?"

"Absolutely."

"So you went into detail with your father about who might have gotten into the house while he was there to watch it; is that correct?"

"The answer to your question, Mr. Jones, again, I'm really not trying to be evasive, is that my—when I learned that the hard drive was gone, it was at the time that I had a loud and bellowing police detective in my face with approximately seventy to a hundred paramilitary types swarming all over my house. It was certainly an enigma to me. When it all calmed down, things were very, very different in my life and there was a profound change. And I asked my father, I'm sure, 'What's going on?' And I'm sure the answer was, 'No idea.'"

"What did he say?" Jones persisted.

"Said, 'I was here the whole time, except I wasn't,'" Perry replied. "'I went out to have coffee with the guys at synagogue. I went to the grocery store.' I know he said he went off one evening to watch a ball game and had a beer at a bar. I mean, my dad was not consigned to the house. He was not shackled to the house. He was doing me a favor by staying there to keep an eye on things as well as doing me a favor by not costing me money to have to bring him up to Chicago for a time that he really didn't need to go up there for. So, my father came and went freely."

"Did he tell you he left the house locked?" Jones asked.

"I didn't even ask him."

"Well, if he's there because you're concerned about the

safety of the house, among other reasons, did your father leave the house locked when he wasn't there?"

"Mr. Jones, I don't know the answer to that question."

"It just never occurred to you to ask him that?"

"No, it always occurred to me that he would have left the house locked."

"Do you believe he left the house locked?"

"I think that it's very easy that my father could have left that house unlocked. Very easy. My dad very easily could have just—it's a very secluded spot. Have you ever been to my house?"

"Go ahead and answer the question."

"I am. You asked me, do I believe he could have left the house unlocked? My father could have easily left the house unlocked."

"Did you tell your father how to work the alarm system on the house?"

"I don't recollect."

"Who had keys to your house?"

"Lawrence Levine, Carolyn Levine, my dad, me, Janet. That's probably it."

Jones moved on with his line of inquiry into the matter of Perry's telephone call to his brother on the night that Janet disappeared.

"What did you tell your brother when you talked to him on August fifteenth at about nine o'clock at night? Now, do you understand my question?"

"Yes, sir."

"It's real simple."

"Yes, sir. I understand your question."

"It's the third time. Answer it. You know, you don't have

to look at your lawyer. Answer the question. He'll say something if he wants to."

"Mr. Jones, he's my lawyer. I'll look at him if I want to. I'll be happy to answer your question—I called my brother up on the phone and I said, 'Ronnie, she's done it. She's pissed off. She's packed her bags and she's left.' My brother responded, 'Perry, just don't worry about it. Don't worry about it at all. Whenever she comes back, she'll come back. If she's not back, call me in the morning.' I felt he was a little brusque with me, kind of hung up the phone on me, and that was it. That was the tenor of the conversation. May have lasted a minute. May have lasted three minutes. But it was a short conversation. 'Ronnie, Janet's gone. She's pissed. She's taken her bags. She's driven off. And I'm worried. What should I do?'"

"Why were you worried?"

"Because my wife had never packed her bags and driven off before. She's stormed out of the house and driven off before. Squealing tires and all kind of stuff, but she's never packed her bag. And she also handed me a note that said 'twelve-day vacation' on the top, Mr. Jones. So, I was a little bit worried this time than normal."

"And you have related everything—you've told us everything you can remember you told him or he told you in that conversation," Jones asked.

"To the best of my recollection, Mr. Jones, it was a very brief conversation," Perry responded. "My brother just told me to calm down and relax and don't be worried about it, and if she wasn't back, call him in the morning. The same thing that my sister told me and the same thing that Lawrence and Carolyn Levine told me around midnight."

"Did you leave home that night at all?"

"No, sir. I had two children upstairs asleep."

"And you never left the house between the time that you claim your wife left and the next morning; is that right?"

"That's correct. I did not leave that house again until ten or ten-thirty the next morning, when Ella Goldshmid came."

"And this was not a fifteen- or twenty-minute conversation you had with your brother."

"No, sir. I don't believe it was."

"Okay. You've told us it was a one- to three-minute conversation; is that right?"

"It was a short conversation, Mr. Jones."

"And you didn't tell your brother anything to the effect that 'Janet and I had an argument and I've killed her, and what should I do?'"

"Mr. Jones, your question is offensive and the answer to it is no."

"When did you talk to your sister?"

"Almost immediately thereafter."

"Tell me what you said to your sister."

"Almost the exact same thing, Mr. Jones."

"What did she say to you?"

"Almost the exact same thing as my brother. Well, you know, she has a little bit different feel for Janet. She's not as charitable toward Janet. Her response was 'Good. Maybe she'll, you know, go off and have a nice weekend and get her head together, come back. But don't worry about it. Talk to you tomorrow.'"

"Another minute, or two, conversation," Jones said matter-of-factly.

"No, Mr. Jones. Again, my conversation with my brother is not a minute or two. It is, I don't know how long it was, Mr. Jones, but it was a short conversation."

"With your sister, was it a conversation more than a minute or two?"

"Again, Mr. Jones, I don't specifically recollect, but it was a short conversation."

"Do you possess any expertise in martial arts?" Jones changed the subject again.

"Currently, no," Perry responded. "Historically, yes. I probably can't lift my leg past my hip as we sit here today."

"Are you a black belt?"

"Yes, sir."

"What degree?"

"Third-degree provisional."

"What system?"

"Sor Yukan."

Chapter 11

A deposition is, without question, a useful device that is used by our legal system as a method of discovery. To be effective, the expectation that the person being deposed will be truthful in their statements must exist, and that the results of the deposition will yield the truth about the subject matter being investigated. Even when a person being deposed provides untruthful and inconsistent responses repeatedly, the truth can still be arrived at—although it may take longer to get there, through a careful reading of between the lines. In addition to the fact that much can often be learned about a person's character through the process, a deposition can preserve the testimony of a witness who might become unavailable for trial and can sometimes be used to impeach the testimony of a witness at trial.

"What did you do on August sixteenth?" Jones asked as the deposition continued.

"I woke up about six, five-thirty, six, six-thirty, whenever my kids woke up," March responded. "They had a fitful night. I took care of them. I got dressed. I sat around, steaming at Janet. I took care of the kids. Then I calmed down. I said, 'Fine. To heck with it.' I waited for Ella to come. I actually called her and had her come a half—she got to my house a half an hour early. And as soon as Ella got there, I went to my office."

August 16 was a Friday, and it had been determined earlier that Marissa Moody had dropped off her son to play with Sammy at around ten o'clock that morning. Marissa Moody had also told people, including the police, that she had heard Perry talking to Sammy through the door of his office—the office that he kept at home. Had Perry gone to the office that was not a part of his home *after* Marissa had left? Or had he gone to it *before*? If he had left his house, as he had stated, "as soon as Ella got there," Moody wouldn't have heard the conversation that she claimed she had heard between Sammy and his father inside the house, which indicated that he hadn't left the house "as soon as Ella got there." So, did he leave the house later in the day? Perry's statement did not seem consistent with what Marissa had recounted, an indication that someone's information was incorrect.

"I sat around," Perry continued. "I did my work. I checked at home to see if Janet had come back. I checked with Carolyn to see if she had heard from Janet. I checked with Larry to see if he had heard from Janet. I called Vanderbilt Plaza. I called the Hampton Inn. I called the Union Station Hotel. Just to see if she had checked in somewhere to chill out. I did work for clients. I came home early."

"Did you do anything else other than you've just told me?" Jones asked.

"I don't recall. I think it was a relatively routine day."

"Did you meet with any decorator?"

"I may have met with Laurie Rommel," Perry responded. "I don't remember. I could look at my planner."

"What planner?"

"I've got a planner—at home in Chicago. I think I've got it. I don't remember. I don't even know if I have that planner. That planner was in my office. Larry must have stolen it. I don't know if I've got it or not. I have no idea what I've got in my office."

"Okay. You said you took it to Chicago. Now you said Larry may have stolen it. Did you take it to Chicago?"

"Mr. Jones, I've got a couple planners. Different ones. I had an electronic organizer that I was trying to transition to, I had a daytime planner, and I had a calendar from my desk. I don't know exactly where and when I had different things. It is very possible that on Friday, the sixteenth, I may have met with Laurie Rommel, and maybe I even met with Herb Seloff—I can't even remember—about looking at space next door for me to move into."

"Where did you have these meetings?"

"I may have met with Laurie. I don't know where I met with Laurie on that day. I mean, I met with Laurie at the space a couple times, next door. I met her at her home a couple times. I met her at a carpet place. I met her at a furniture place. I had a number of meetings with Laurie."

At one point in Perry March's two-day deposition, Jon Jones turned his questioning toward the reason why Perry's father came to visit him after Janet disappeared, and later toward possible sexual relationships that Perry may have had with other women. He also questioned Perry about his and Janet's last wills and testaments, credit cards, life insurance policies and their dollar values, and beneficiaries. All in all, Perry's deposition consisted of over four hundred double-spaced pages of information that was gleaned from him during several hours of grueling questions from a man who, at times, seemed like the Grand Inquisitor, but whose methods were intended to bring out the inconsistencies in Perry's testimony and, hopefully, lead to the truth about what happened to Janet.

"When did you first talk to your father or see him after August fifteenth?" Jones asked.

"I don't recollect," Perry responded. "Relatively soon thereafter (Janet's disappearance), I would guess, probably within a few days."

"Was he in Mexico, to the best of your knowledge, on August fifteenth?"

"Yes."

"When did he come into the United States?"

"I don't recollect. I think it was probably—I think he arrived a couple days before Sammy's birthday party, which was on the twenty-fifth. So, my guess is, he came in sometime around the twentieth, maybe? Eighteenth? Twentieth? I don't remember."

"Why did he come?" Jones asked.

"Because I was distraught that my wife had run away, and he came up to help."

"Did you ask him to come?"

"Yes. Well, actually, no, I would—I rephrase that. He called up, was very concerned, volunteered to come up, and asked me if I would like him to come up. And I said, 'Yes. I really would like you to come up.'"

"Were you involved in an ongoing sexual relationship with anybody besides Janet as of August 15, 1996?" Jones asked.

"I refuse to answer your question," Perry responded somewhat testily. "I decline to."

"On what basis?"

"Again, none of your business. Irrelevant, intrusive, insensitive to the memory of my wife and to me. I decline to answer it. Take it to Judge Clement and we'll see if he wants me to answer it."

"And how is that insensitive to the memory of Janet to ask you that question?"

"None of your business."

"Are you presently involved in a sexual relationship on an ongoing basis with anyone?"

"Again, I refuse to answer that question."

"Let me say this," Jones said. "Such a person might well have information regarding his ongoing financial affairs and all the matters set out in relevance. . . . I'm entitled to know that—"

"And, again," Perry responded, "I really decline to answer it. I think you're vulgar and insensitive, and I will not answer that question."

"On August fifteenth, did you have a discussion with Janet about any relationship on your part? Of a sexual nature?"

"No."

"That subject never came up; is that correct?"

"Correct."

"Did you ever execute a will?" Jones asked during a later segment of the deposition.

"Yes, I have executed a will now," Perry responded.

"Okay. When did you execute a will?"

"I executed a will probably late September, early October. Mid-October. I don't remember exactly. I can find that out for you."

"Who prepared the will?"

"I did."

"What does it say?"

Lionel R. Barrett Jr., one of Perry's attorneys, interjected at that point.

"I am going to object," Barrett said, "strongly, to the relevancy as to the provisions of the will."

"Well, I don't mind answering it," Perry said. "In that period of time, Janet had been gone for quite a while. I was very concerned that if something happened to Janet, she was without a will. I'm without a will. So, I prepared a will, leaving everything to my children. Naming my brother as administrator, my sister or my brother as trustee for the trusts of my children, and naming my brother and his wife and my sister as alternate guardians of the children."

"Where was that will typed?" Jones asked.

"At my office."

"What office?"

"At my former law firm. Of Levine, Mattson, Orr, and Geracioti."

"Who typed it?"

"Me."

"On what computer did you type it?"

"My computer at my office."

"The one in your particular office?"

"Yeah, my computer."

"And where was it printed?"

"In my computer at my office."

"Do you have copies of that?"

"Yeah. I've got copies of my executed will. I believe Mr. Jackson has a copy of my executed will as administrator."

"Was that before September fifteenth?"

"No."

"After September fifteenth?"

"Yeah, I believe so. I had prepared multiple copies of wills for Janet and I both, prior to September fifteenth, but never was one executed."

"What credit cards do you have?" Jones asked a bit later.

"I have no credit cards in my name," Perry responded.

"What credit cards do you have use of?"

"I have the use of one Citibank card that my brother has gotten for me."

"In whose name is that card?"

"His."

"What do you mean your brother got it for you?"

"It's his. It's his credit card."

"Did he get it for you?"

"Yeah."

"When?"

"I don't know. Month ago."

"Why didn't you get a credit card in your own name?"

"Didn't make application for one."

"I didn't ask that. Why didn't you get one in your own name?"

"Chose not to."

"Mr. March," Jones asked during further questioning, "what life insurance was there on Janet's life, as of August 15, 1996?"

"To the best of my recollection," Perry replied, "there was a single term policy for two hundred fifty thousand dollars and that the agent is Janet's first cousin Mark—Michael Levine."

"When was that policy purchased?"

"Year, two years ago."

"Under what circumstances?"

"Janet and I discussed the possibility of what would I do if something happened to her, and vice versa. It was done in connection with our overall estate plan. She and I both agreed that I would need money to pay for a nanny or support a nanny or some alternative child care. And that's why we purchased the policy. Upon—also upon the recommendation of Mike Levine, who did the same for his wife."

"You said it was a part of your overall estate plan. Tell me what your overall estate plan was."

"We didn't have much of an estate plan at all."

"Well, that wasn't—"

"But that was the major issue," Perry interjected.

"I didn't ask if you had much," Jones said. "Let's try to get to the point today. What was your overall estate plan?"

"It was still in discussion. We hadn't firmly fixed on it."

"Tell me about the seven- or eight-hundred-thousand-dollar insurance on your life."

"Sure. I don't know exactly the total amount. I have a one-hundred-fifty-thousand-dollar whole life policy with the Metropolitan Federal—I can't remember the name of the policy. I bought it when I was at Bass, Berry, and Sims. Owen Kelley is the agent. It is a relatively expensive term policy. I mean whole life or universal life policy. I also had a term policy with them that I canceled when Mike Levine approached me to take over my insurance needs. I have two policies on my life, a—with Mike Levine, so I still have that policy with Mr.—no, it's Northwestern. I'm sorry. It's Northwestern. And I still have that policy on my life for one hundred fifty thousand dollars. I believe Janet is the beneficiary of that policy. I have a term policy with Mike Levine and Union Central, I believe, for one hundred fifty or one hundred seventy-five thousand dollars. Again—that might be—no, I'm sorry. That might be whole. That might be whole life as well. And I have about a—I think a five-hundred or a four-hundred-fifty-thousand-dollar term policy with him as well. So the aggregate number is in the seven-hundred-thousand-dollar range."

"Have you changed beneficiaries on those policies?" Jones asked.

"Yes. I changed on I believe the Union Cen, I believe, on the Mike Levine policies to fifty percent Sammy and fifty percent Tzipi, once this whole situation with Janet came about. I did not want money to go into an absentee's estate, since I'm currently in litigation over that right now, and I had no desire to have the Levines put their hooks into it. Or have—assert any control over it."

"Well, let me test a little of the truthfulness of that answer," Jones said.

"Uh-huh."

"Did you change the beneficiaries before or after you filed this litigation?"

"I don't know. All I know is when in my mind—"

"What do you mean you don't know?"

"I don't remember."

"Well, you just testified the reason you made the change was because of this litigation and to keep the money from going to an absentee's conservator."

"I think you heard incorrectly, or I spoke incorrectly," Perry said. "What I meant to say is, when the situation with Janet developed and she failed to return, and the situation looked as if it might be one that would go into litigation over assets, I determined that rather than put that asset and those assets into dispute, that I would make it very clear in the event of my death that those particular assets, constituting approximately seven hundred thousand dollars, would be directed to the benefit of my two children. Placed into the trust that I have created by will for the care of my two children."

"All right. So you have changed all of that—the beneficiary on all of your insurance—"

"I didn't do the Northwest."

"Why?"

"Janet is still the beneficiary there."

"Why haven't you changed that one?"

"I—I just didn't get around to it. It's a small policy in the back of my head. I don't really—actually, I probably just forgot about it."

"Now, who is the beneficiary on the policy on Janet's life?"

"To the best of my recollection, I am. Just as she was the beneficiary on my policies."

Chapter 12

Detective David Miller and his partner, Detective Tim Mason, continued running down lead after lead in their search to learn the truth about what had really happened to Janet March. Their investigation into the disappearance of Janet March had quickly become the most intensive and most talked-about case in nearly twenty years—since nine-year-old Marcia Trimble was abducted in February 1975 while selling Girl Scout cookies in Nashville's Green Hills neighborhood. Marcia's body had been found thirty-three days later in a garage, barely 150 yards from her home. She had been sexually assaulted by at least two people and strangled, and her killer(s) had robbed her of her cookie money. Although that case remains unsolved and still has a cold-case detective assigned to it, Miller and Mason were determined that the Janet March mystery would be solved.

As with most investigations of a purported serious crime, the detectives naturally focused some of their attention on Perry March's friends and acquaintances. Some of the people who knew Perry March characterized him as a man with high energy, a lawyer who was aggressive and determined to achieve his objectives. Almost everyone who knew him described him as highly intelligent and private, but those who did not think very highly of him described Perry as greedy, calculating, a schemer, and as someone not to be trusted.

"When he first told me Janet was missing, he had tears in his eyes," said former friend Elliot Greenberg. "Perry's very reserved. Typically, he won't exhibit that kind of behavior in public." It was clear that Perry had given the appearance that he was really broken up over Janet's disappearance, and Greenberg, as would many others, believed him.

Meanwhile, Perry appeared prepared to accept the fact that he would likely never see his wife again, or so it seemed to the people who knew him in Nashville; yet at times it seemed like he continued to maintain hope that she would turn up alive. His children often wondered what had happened to their mother and, he said, would ask questions about her.

"We don't know what happened to Mommy," Perry, by his own account, would tell his children. He said that no matter the outcome, whether she turned up alive or not, the children would survive.

"The longer we go, the less likely we are to hear from her," Perry was quoted as saying. "We can't hold out false hopes. I have to tell them the truth. People live through worse."

At one point in the investigation, Detectives Miller and Mason learned that Perry had replaced the tires on his Jeep Cherokee. He purchased the brand-new set of tires, the detectives learned, from Universal Tire in Nashville in August 1996, after Janet disappeared. When asked about it, he claimed that he replaced the tires because they were worn out. Naturally, the detectives wanted to know more—they contacted the management and employees at Universal Tire.

According to Robert Armstrong, the manager of the tire shop, the tires on Perry's Jeep had considerable tread left on them, approximately 50 percent, and Armstrong said he advised Perry that he did not need new tires. Perry apparently responded that he wanted a different brand of tires on his car. The detectives agreed with Armstrong's assessment that it seemed unusual for someone to replace perfectly good tires. The cops found themselves wondering whether Perry might have been concerned that tire impressions made in earth softened by the rainfall experienced in the Nashville area during the time of the massive search effort for Janet might prove incriminating, if found. Nonetheless, there was no law against purchasing a new set of tires, even when replacements weren't needed.

As Miller and Mason studied the evidence—what little there was—and again went over the details of the night Janet disappeared, they felt even more confident with the theory they had formulated regarding what had happened to Janet March on the evening of August 15, 1996. It was December, and nearly four months had elapsed since Janet had disappeared, and they needed to believe that they were making progress. Their theory and various scenarios that they had worked out earlier were, of course, discussed with writer Willy Stern, and would be reported in the *Nashville Scene* the following month as part of a major two-part series about the case.

To recap their theory and the various plausible scenarios in perhaps a bit more detail, according to the *Nashville Scene* article, Miller and Mason hypothesized that Perry and Janet had become embroiled in an argument on the evening of August 15 and that it had escalated to the point that Perry had lost it and had killed her, likely accidentally, with a karate blow of some sort. After all, he held a black belt in the martial art, and a blow delivered to just the right spot could kill a person almost instantly and not necessarily leave behind any blood evidence. They believed that at some point during the argument Janet had said something that had caused Perry to snap. Perhaps, they theorized, Janet had said that she wanted a divorce and had threatened to cut him off monetarily. After all, she had her own source of income, and her family was wealthy, too.

The cops also believed that Perry might have hidden his wife's body in their home's basement, or perhaps in the nearby woods that nearly encircled their property, only to retrieve it later, wrap it up in the rug that Marissa Moody claimed she had seen inside the March residence the following day, and then haul away the corpse and dispose of it—probably inside a Dumpster.

Had he first hauled her body to the woods in his Jeep Cherokee, only to later haul it away for disposal? If so, had it been the fear of leaving tire tracks or impressions that had prompted him to change the tires on that vehicle, even though they hadn't needed changing? Much of their theory was, of course, merely conjecture, and the only thing that had been confirmed at this point was the fact that Perry and Janet had had an argument—Perry had confirmed the argument while providing his deposition.

Since Miller and Mason's theories also looked at the telephone calls that Perry had made to his relatives and to the Levines the night of August 15, they realized only too late that they should have interviewed everyone he had called right away. As they went over that scenario again, the cops were even more adamant that the telephone calls may have been Perry's first attempts at covering up Janet's death. Perry, of course, had claimed that he merely called his brother and his sister to inform them that Janet had left him. According to the Willy Stern article, the detectives did not conduct timely interviews with any of the people Perry called that night. That fact, when combined with the fact that they had divulged considerable information to Stern, would soon return to bite them.

The detectives theorized that it was when Perry had finished talking to his sister, at 9:18 P.M., that he hid Janet's body, either in the woods or in the basement. They believe he then packed travel bags for Janet and placed them in her Volvo, which he drove to the Brixworth Apartments a few miles away. After parking her car in one of the spaces in the complex's parking lot, according to Miller and Mason's theory, and carefully placing her footwear on the driver's-side floor, he abandoned the Volvo and either jogged or rode a mountain bike back to his house on Blackberry Road, while Sammy and Tzipi continued to sleep in their upstairs bedrooms.

A witness would later tell the police that he had seen a man walking alongside a bicycle at 1:00 A.M. through the Brixworth Apartments complex about two weeks before Janet's car was found. The witness said that he hadn't realized until later that the man he had seen was Perry March.

The *Nashville Scene* reported that the local Volvo dealership that sold the car to Janet and Perry established that the Volvo 850 was designed to hold a typical mountain bike inside the vehicle. The detectives also believed that Perry created the so-called "to do" list on the home computer and printed it out before leaving for the Brixworth Apartments. They further believed that Perry had waited until around midnight to call the Levines so that he would have time to complete all of the aforementioned tasks in an attempt to cover up what had really happened that evening.

The detectives had apparently also mentioned that Perry's father, Arthur, and his brother, Ronald, were being looked at as "possible accomplices in the crime," according to the *Nashville Scene*. Both men, however, steadfastly maintained that they had no involvement in Janet's disappearance, and there was no evidence to indicate otherwise. In fact, even though Perry March had already been convicted in the court of public opinion regarding his wife's disappearance, there wasn't much that could link him to any wrongdoing at all.

Perhaps because of the lack of evidence in the case, Perry March continued to speak out publicly about how he had been wronged by the police, by his in-laws, and by the community over Janet's disappearance. At one point he compared himself to Richard Jewell, the Atlanta security guard who had been named by the FBI as the prime suspect in Atlanta's Centennial Olympic Park bombing. It had been three months before the authorities in Atlanta publicly cleared Jewell of the bombing.

Perry had convinced himself that he had been victimized. He had been ostracized by his former friends and colleagues, as well as much of the community. By this time his in-laws had taken steps to gain control of the Blackberry Road house, since they had provided the financing for it, and Perry was no longer able to keep up the mortgage payments. It seemed to Perry that his father-in-law had played a role in Perry's current hardships, including his sudden falling out of favor with the community and an inability to find work in Nashville. He said that he had also been accused of sexually abusing his children.

"Without a shred of evidence," Perry told the *Nashville*

Scene during an interview from his newly rented $3,000-a-month house in Wilmette, Illinois, a Chicago suburb, "the police and my in-laws have taken away my house, my livelihood, my community. They're trying to screw around with my son and daughter. I've been wrongly accused of sexually abusing my kids. My daughter has been subjected to a complete medical examination. But you'll see. I'll be vindicated. . . . I will not allow one misguided police officer, one vengeful man, and a few low-life journalists to destroy what I've taken years to build."

It was generally believed that Larry Levine had put out the word that he preferred his colleagues in the legal profession to remain silent about Perry March's difficulties, and some even said that Levine, a powerful and wealthy man in the community, had set out to destroy his son-in-law.

"When Larry is lucid, all he can talk about is destroying Perry," said a colleague, who did not want to be identified.

A former Vanderbilt University Law School classmate of Perry's recalled Perry as someone who held a passionate desire for monetary achievement, and lightheartedly referred to him as "the classmate most likely to be indicted for securities fraud." An avid tennis player, who spent many Sundays at the Whitworth Racquet Club challenging opponents in the active sport, Perry was characterized as an aggressive competitor who did not take losing lightly.

It seemed as if the entire Nashville community had turned its back on Perry March. Shunned at the Nashville nightclubs that he and Janet used to frequent, by December 1996, Perry March was lucky if he found a former acquaintance who was willing to even speak to him. It was one of the reasons, but not the only one, why Perry took the kids and his possessions and moved to the rented home in Illinois. He left all of Janet's clothing behind, including her wedding veil, hanging inside closets at the Blackberry Road home.

At one point the *Nashville Scene* enlisted the aid of a local psychiatrist, whom the newspaper asked to analyze portions of the anonymous letters that Perry had allegedly written to Leigh Reames while employed at Bass, Berry & Sims. The psychiatrist, who was assured anonymity by the newspaper, based his analysis of the letters on "informed speculation," without ever meeting Perry March. The psychiatrist was told, however, that Perry March was the person who had allegedly written the letters.

The psychiatrist characterized the person who wrote the letters as "antisocial," "manipulative," and considered the writer as an "unstable" person who had used "incredibly bad judgment." The psychiatrist said that the descriptions of sexual activity in the letters were "self-degrading," and always focused "on her orgasm."

"His orgasm is never mentioned," the psychiatrist said. "Is he impotent, or is he afraid of being impotent?"

The psychiatrist stated that the letters were "juvenile" in nature, and were something that "an eight- or nine-year-old" might write. Because the writer had gone on so about what "an excellent husband" he was, and spoke of how he had never been unfaithful to his wife before, the psychiatrist felt that this had been an attempt at making "an effort to prove this to himself."

"[He] appears to think that his wife is in the way of his having what he perceives as a satisfying relationship," the psychiatrist said. "Nobody who writes a letter like that could be an excellent spouse. It's okay to have fantasies like that, but don't act on them."

The psychiatrist said that the letters were written by someone who had displayed "significant narcissism.

Count the number of 'I's in the first letter. It's pretty impressive." The psychiatrist summed up his analysis by saying that the writer of those letters is "a very sick man," self-centered, and desirous of attention.

On December 11, 1996, an Illinois judge ordered Perry March to provide his in-laws regular visits with their grandchildren, Sammy and Tzipi. The judge also appointed a Chicago attorney to represent the welfare of the children. According to the ruling, the Levines would be allowed to visit their grandchildren for two hours that same evening; however, Perry was not at home when the Levines arrived. The Levines were told by a relative of Perry's that Perry and the children had gone away, out of state. The relative was not specific about where they had gone.

Not quite one month later, on January 16, 1997, following the appearance of "Part 1: A Good Thing Gone Bad" by Willy Stern, in the *Nashville Scene,* Detective David Miller was replaced as the lead investigator in the Janet March disappearance investigation.

It would be reported later that shortly after Perry March had moved to Chicago to try and make a fresh start, he purportedly told an acquaintance that he had been thinking about writing a book. He apparently said that what he had in mind would be a mystery, and that the story's main character was an attractive, dark-haired young woman. Perry allegedly said that the title of the book was *"Murder.com."*

Regardless of Perry March's actions up to this point, the police knew that they had no direct evidence that Perry had murdered Janet. Furthermore, just because there was a lack of evidence was not a reason to automatically presume that

Perry March had done a brilliant job of creating a cover-up. Being a bright lawyer, he was probably capable of masterminding such a plot, but it had to be considered that it was also possible that whatever had become of Janet March, Perry had had nothing to do with it. Without a body, the cops didn't know with any degree of certainty that Janet was even dead.

Chapter 13

Shortly after Detective David Miller was taken off the Janet March case in January 1997, veteran homicide detective Sergeant Pat Postiglione, forty-five, and Detective Bill Pridemore, forty-three, were assigned to the investigation to work alongside Detective Mickey Miller, forty, who would later make captain and become commander of the West Precinct. Both Postiglione and Pridemore had been involved in the Janet March case from its earliest days and had participated in some of the searches that had occurred at the Blackberry Road home. Although they were both members of the Metropolitan Nashville Police Department's Murder Squad, they would begin taking more active roles in the investigation from this point forward.

Postiglione, who was born and raised in Queens, New York, and spent much of his youth living and working in blue-collar Italian neighborhoods, had wanted to be a police officer for as long as he could remember. He applied to the NYPD, but was not hired because the waiting list was so long, and he did not know anyone who could help move him more quickly up the list. As a result, he worked in construction for a while, but never lost his interest in police work. For reasons that aren't clear, his interests lay in homicide.

"I'm not sure why," he told a reporter. "But I had a cousin who was murdered when I was young. If you have personal experience with murder, you see what the victims' families go through."

While vacationing in Nashville, Postiglione responded to a police officer recruitment ad there and applied. In 1980, as soon as he was notified that he had been hired, he relocated to Nashville and began his police career as a patrol officer. After only a few years with Metro, Postiglione made detective grade and moved into the homicide division in 1987. He has been working homicide, either as a detective in the homicide unit or as a detective in the somewhat elitist Murder Squad, ever since.

"Once you do it," Postiglione said, "it's hard to see yourself doing anything else. Some guys can't deal with the crime scenes, and that's okay. We're all affected by them. They stay with you, but if you can find justice for the victim and their family, it makes it worthwhile."

Detective Bill Pridemore, on the other hand, moved around a lot while growing up, because his stepfather was a military career man. At one point his family moved to Nashville, and he graduated from Stratford Comprehensive High School there. Shortly after high school, Pridemore went on to Volunteer State Community College, which was when he decided to take the test for the police academy. After being on a waiting list for about a year, he was finally accepted and began his police career as a patrol officer in 1976. He attributes his decision to make a career out of police work to his exposure to a military background from his stepfather's service years, and to the fact that a police officer once helped him recover his bike that had been stolen when he was a kid.

"A policeman was driving by and saw that I was upset," Pridemore recalled. "He put me in his car and we rode around and found my bike. It left a pretty big impression." It also left a pretty big motivation for Pridemore to want to help people who needed helping.

"I thought I would go to burglary," Pridemore said, recalling where he thought his police career would take him. "Homicide was a pretty coveted division. You find out real quick if you'll like homicide once you go on a couple of crime scenes."

Pridemore eventually went into homicide, and found that he liked the work that it entailed. The homicide division was where he and Postiglione got to know each other well as they worked together over the years. The Murder Squad, created in 1980 by Chief Joe Casey, would come to both Pridemore and Postiglione a little later, because the high quality of their work was quickly recognized. The distinction between the homicide division and the Murder Squad was simply that the homicide division investigated murders, suicides, and other violent crimes in which there was a known connection between the victim and the perpetrator, whereas the Murder Squad cases involved homicides in which there was no known connection. Murder Squad cases were considered the most difficult to solve.

"If a woman was found dead in an alley and you had no idea who did it," Postiglione recently said, "Murder Squad was called in."

Being asked to join the Murder Squad was a "big deal," Pridemore said. "You didn't ask to join Murder Squad. They looked at you to see if they thought you could do it.

And they asked the other guys on Murder Squad if they wanted you."

The Janet March case wasn't the first investigation that Pridemore and Postiglione have worked on together; there have been many, including serial killer Paul Reid. But the Janet March case was one of the most difficult ones, and was one of their cases of the longest running. They knew that it could be solved, but they equally knew that it would take some time.

"There were so many things that weren't right with his story and weren't right with him," Postiglione said of Perry March, "but he always thought he was the smartest guy in the room. . . ."

"If you look at one piece of evidence, you say, well, no," Pridemore said. "But put it all together and you feel like you might have a shot. It's a 'hip bone connected to the thighbone' kind of thing. . . ."

Progress through the remaining years of the century would be slow at best, nonexistent at worst, as each man assigned to the case worked diligently to determine the truth behind Janet March's disappearance. Many people, such as armchair detectives and mystery enthusiasts, bought into the scenario as described by Willy Stern in the *Nashville Scene* articles and were postulating, if not rehashing, the theory that Perry, a black belt in karate, had killed Janet, wrapped her up inside a large living-room rug, and disposed of her body. Whether that was what had actually happened was anybody's guess, but the detectives assigned to the case were determined to dog Perry March until the case broke—even if it meant the rest of their careers.

It was revealed by this time that Perry March had been

fired from his father-in-law's firm for allegedly embezzling funds. His once lofty career, in which he had specialized in tax law, was now suddenly in shambles, as was his personal life. One of his former clients had been indicted for money laundering and racketeering prior to Janet's disappearance, and there was speculation that he had helped another former client with tax evasion. A witness had purportedly told the authorities that he had seen Perry and the latter former client arguing in public shortly after Janet was last seen, which fueled speculation that Perry had blackmailed the former client into helping him dispose of Janet's body by burying her beneath a building owned by the former client. The theory was never proven, and the former client was never charged in any capacity in connection with Janet's case. It was merely one of many such red herrings that would crop up from time to time in the case.

Perry March was, naturally, feeling very unsettled by this time. Unable to find employment, first in Nashville and later in Chicago, Perry was becoming desperate for money. Steps had been taken by his in-laws to make certain that he couldn't get his hands on any of Janet's assets, and they had effectively taken the house on Blackberry Road away from him.

Because of the legal entanglements that were following him after Janet's disappearance, Perry found himself with minimal personal funds and virtually no way to tap into Janet's estate. As his life was being carefully scrutinized by the locals in Nashville, as well as by the police, he decided that he had to leave Nashville. He took the children and relocated to Illinois where he would be close to family members and where he thought he might stand a chance at making a fresh start. However, he soon found that the Levines, as well as the cops, dogged his every move.

On February 26, 1997, Mark Levine, Janet's brother, went before a state legislative committee that had begun to study ways that Tennessee's child custody laws could be overhauled. According to sources, Perry March would later say that the Levines had instigated the move while Mark was working as a summer intern in Senator Fred Thompson's office, prior to going off to law school at Harvard. Thompson, who sometimes moonlights as a Hollywood actor, would later run with the proposed legislation, along with Senator Bill Frist, one of the main stockholders of Hospital Corporation of America (HCA, Inc.), a multibillion-dollar Nashville-based hospital corporation, that would, if the law was enacted, assist grandparents in obtaining visitation rights, regardless of the parents' wishes. At this point the proposed legislation was still in its infancy, and would lie dormant for a while.

If things weren't going badly enough already for Perry March, his efforts to block his in-laws' sale of his Blackberry Road home would be rejected by a Nashville judge on March 19, 1997, when the judge approved a contract sale in the amount of $726,000 to a retired lawyer and his wife. Perry was, of course, further devastated by the judge's decision as his life continued to spiral downward. From that moment on, light of day would only appear in minor glimpses in Perry March's life.

In 1998, the Levines filed a petition seeking to summon forth a jury in the Tennessee Probate Court, in a wrongful-death action. Their goal, of course, was to find Perry March liable, in absentia (he was still in Illinois, and the legal action had occurred in Tennessee), of Janet's death. Perry chose, perhaps unwisely from a legal point of view, to avoid participating in the discovery process of the proceedings. As a result, on July 15, 1998, Davidson County probate judge Frank Clement Jr. ruled that Perry March had shown a "troubling and consistent pattern of contemptuous conduct," which had served to make it more difficult to resolve the issues with his in-laws over Janet's property. Clement had effectively gotten the ball rolling to push the Levines' wrongful-death lawsuit a step closer to becoming a reality and an ultimate success for the in-laws.

At some point during May 1999, Perry March moved to Ajijic, in the Mexican state of Jalisco, taking his father, Arthur March, up on an offer to help him out by allowing him to move in with him. Arthur, retired and alone, had moved to Ajijic and obtained a retirement home a few years earlier and felt right at home with the large population of other American retirees residing there. Ajijic, a beautiful lakeside town approximately thirty miles from Guadalajara, Mexico's second-largest city, seemed like a welcome change for Perry and the kids.

"I brought Perry down here because he didn't have any other place to go," Arthur March would later tell CBS News.

Part 2

MEXICO

Chapter 14

Idyllic in its natural setting along the northwestern shore of Lake Chapala, Mexico's largest freshwater lake, the small town of Ajijic boasts a wonderful climate for its approximately thirteen thousand inhabitants, about half of whom, like Arthur March, and now his son Perry, are expatriates. Most of the expatriate community in Ajijic is made up of American and Canadian retirees; there are also a few Europeans, as well as other nationalities. Many of the ex-pats moved there when they retired to escape the harsh winter weather "back home." Many wanted to take advantage of the lower cost of living and saw the small fishing village as a place where they could live out their golden years much more extravagantly on a retirement income that would not go nearly as far at home. Some just liked the peace and quiet of living in a desirable lakeside setting. Perry March liked it there because it placed some 1,500 miles between him and the problems he faced back home, and he saw *opportunity* there.

Like many parts of Mexico, Ajijic and the Lake Chapala area is home to an artist colony, which is culturally diverse in that it is comprised of Mexicans as well as non-Mexicans, and the fact that it is made up of artists who make souvenirs for tourists as well as artists who are painters and sculptors. There are several galleries located throughout the community, where the artists can exhibit their work. D. H. Lawrence lived there for a short time, and ended up writing about one of the local churches in his novel *The Plumed Serpent*. An oasis for tourists, Ajijic has something for every budget. There are plenty of hotels, restaurants, open-air cafés, ice-cream parlors, outdoor markets, cantinas, and sports activities for those who are sports-minded. One of the greatest pastimes is sitting at a lakeside bar, sipping a margarita while watching the ever-changing light as it glistens across the lake. To top it all off, the nicest homes in the area were those located inside gated communities. Perry March lived in a large spacious home in such a community. He and his father, according to those who knew them, preferred the cantinas, the nightlife, and cavorting with women when the urge struck.

Arthur was well-known around town. He had, after all, lived there long enough for the residents, barkeeps, and market owners to easily recognize the gruff-talking, sometimes crude man with the craggy face who was known to chase his tequila with beer. Rough-talking Arthur had managed to learn the language sufficiently to where it was not a barrier, and Perry, as he had done with Chinese, had soon claimed complete proficiency in the Spanish language.

Shortly after arriving in Ajijic, Perry met Carmen Rojas Solorio, a twenty-seven-year-old Mexican citizen with three children of her own from a previous marriage. Before much time elapsed, much less a courtship, Perry and his children had moved in with Carmen and they began a new life together. Perry enrolled the children in a nearby private bilingual school, and on the surface they seemed like one big happy family without a problem in the world.

Within a couple of weeks of his arrival in Mexico, Perry formed an alliance with a man named S. Samuel Chavez, a Mexican American who had received his education in the United States. Chavez claimed in promotional materials that he was a graduate of Purdue and the Indiana University School of Law. He also advertised that his specialty was dealing with immigration issues in a business relationship he had formed with a law firm in Guadalajara.

Perry March, soon after forming his association with Chavez, began claiming that their company was well connected to Mexican authorities, loosely translated as meaning that he had the ability to bribe government officials if needed. But in Mexico, who didn't? All it really took was the right amount of money for any given situation and—presto, like magic—the legal barriers or governmental red tape magically disappeared. As long as one greased the hands of the officials with money when they wanted it and didn't become high-maintenance for the government, a person like Perry March could do well for himself in Mexico.

Closer scrutiny later on revealed information that Chavez's license to practice law in the state of Indiana had been revoked because of felony convictions for providing false information on a credit application and on a bankruptcy filing. Further scrutiny showed that he had purportedly maintained an address in Nashville in the mid-1990s, giving some people reason to believe, but without concrete evidence to prove, that Perry and Chavez had known each other prior to Perry going to Mexico. Nonetheless Perry, shortly after his arrival in Ajijic, had been quick to form a partnership of sorts with Chavez, who at the time was operating a business as a bilingual legal consultant. Given

Mexico's nearly unfathomable legal structure, which is considered an abomination by most outsiders, Perry had very quickly realized the need for bilingual legal experts to help the many expatriates deal with visa and real estate issues which required them to become involved in Mexico's tangled and often unethical legal system. Such an opportunity seemed a natural fit for Perry, and Chavez already had the office space, where he had been running his own ventures at Plaza Bugambilias, part of a new business and shopping complex located in the town. Admittedly, it wasn't much—but it was a start for what Perry had in mind.

A short time after partnering with Chavez, Perry took out a full-page ad in the *Guadalajara Reporter,* a weekly English-language newspaper for that area, and announced his business venture with Chavez, according to an article that appeared in the *Nashville Scene.*

"Chavez & March," the ad read, "a private development and investment firm, wishes to announce a proposed significant investment in a state of the art clinc [*sic*] and emergency treatment facility." The two men reasoned that any kind of proposed modern local health-care facility would likely attract interest and, hopefully, investors who could see the advantage of how such a facility would enable many of the area's seniors to no longer have to make the hour-long drive into Guadalajara to obtain top-quality health care. According to the ad, the project would be called "PriMedical TM Medical Clinic Project," and it invited the public to "Meet the administrators & developers: S. Samuel Chavez, Esq. & Perry A. March, Esq., doctorates of law," on May 22, 1999.

The ad spelled out a project that would be financed by medical investors, mostly doctors; it was an international business venture that was set up as a Belize corporation.

Chavez and March were seeking investors who could fork over a minimum of $1,250,000. What seemed amazing, in retrospect, to anyone looking at the details of this case was not so much the level of ambition their project had as much as the speed in which Perry March had relocated to Mexico with his children, met a young woman and formed a romantic relationship with her, moved in with the woman, met up and formed a business alliance with someone he had either just met or had known in the past, thought up the business plan for the aforementioned ventures while opening up shop, and began holding public meetings—all in a period of less than a month!

Later that same month, on May 28, 1999, the Tennessee Supreme Court suspended Perry March's license to practice law while it looked into the allegations of fraud and embezzlement that were being made by his former employer. According to the charges being leveled at Perry by his father-in-law's law firm, it was also alleged that he had not provided records to a client despite the client's requests for them, and he had lied to prop up what was being described as an otherwise frivolous lawsuit. A year later, Perry March would be officially disbarred. Even before the disbarment occurred, he was unable to provide legal advice and services, at least legally, and he realized that he would have to find something else to do to make money. Being in Mexico, and with the large number of Americans living in Ajijic, Perry didn't think that he would have much difficulty finding a way to make a living down there.

His status as a lawyer hadn't seemed to matter much to him at the time. A short time after his license suspension, Perry and his partner placed another ad in the local newspaper under the helm of Chavez and March, Ltd., that read: "U.S. Doctorates of Law; Asset Protection Counseling;

Protect Yourself from Judgements [*sic*], Creditors, Government Impositions, Divorce, Disaster, Swindles and the Unforseen [*sic*]. Principals are Members of the American Bar Association Asset Protection Planning Subcommittee."

Chavez and March, Ltd., began to blossom. Although financial records showing just how much money their ventures had made, and who they had made it from, were held close to the vest, so to speak, no one, except for those who were involved in the day-to-day activities of their business dealings, namely Chavez and March, would know the company's bottom line, and they weren't talking. They were getting funding from somewhere, however, because by autumn of that year, 1999, the two men had added several new businesses to their "portfolio": C&M Development, C&M Insurance, Premier Properties (a real estate service), and Guardian Security Services, all of which were in addition to their PriMedical TM Medical Clinic and their Chavez and March, Ltd., Legal and Financial Services ventures. As their businesses grew, so did their need for additional office space. It wasn't long before their businesses had taken up most of the prime locations in the small business plaza, and they were able to purchase larger and classier advertisements in the local newspaper.

By the time the new year rolled around, Perry and his partner had come up with the idea of building a gated community for senior citizens. Plans for the development called for it to be a "full-service" community so that most of the residents' needs could be provided for within that community. They were planning to call it Misty Mountain Extended Care Community, and it was to be built within an already troubled subdivision called Chula Vista Norte, whose residents were dealing with a number of legal issues that were related to the subdivision.

Meanwhile, as Chavez and March, Ltd., counted its money and made plans to continue expansion into the new year, displeased and unhappy clients began making themselves heard throughout the community. Complaints ranged from fees that were too high, to poor service, to services that were paid for but never delivered. Some of the more aggressive complainers began looking into Chavez's and Perry March's backgrounds, and disseminated details of their seedy pasts by telling their friends, posting the information on the Internet, and by placing posters throughout the community in public places, all anonymously, of course. Perry and his father publicly dismissed the flying accusations as "bullshit," but business, nonetheless, began to dwindle. Before it was over, accusations toward Perry March and Chavez would include asset rip-offs that were tied to off-shore accounts and dummy corporations, which had been set up to dupe some of their unwitting older clients. It was not pretty even during the early stages of finding out what C&M was really all about, and it would get much uglier as more and more people learned that they had been swindled.

Things went even farther south for Perry when, on January 14, 2000, the judge in the wrongful-death lawsuit, which had been filed by the Levines, ruled that Janet March was dead and that Perry March was responsible for her death. The judge, Perry soon learned, had based his ruling on allegations that centered on Perry and Janet's troubled marriage, the details of which were touched on during Perry's November 1996 deposition, and on the fact that Perry had repeatedly refused to return to the United States to respond to questioning related to the lawsuit. If he had hated his in-laws before, he certainly held more hatred and animosity toward them now, after the judge's ruling.

Two months later, a probate court jury awarded the Levines $113.5 million in damages in their wrongful-death lawsuit and ordered Perry to pay the judgment.

After winning the wrongful-death lawsuit against Perry, Janet's mother and father were ready to step-up their efforts to gain grandparent visitation rights and, ultimately, they hoped, gain full custody of their daughter's children. Now that the momentum seemed to be in their favor, the Levines would use every legal means available to them to accomplish their goal of bringing Perry March to justice.

In March 2000, with Janet now formally declared dead by a court of law for the first time (she would be declared "legally" dead again two years later), Perry married Carmen Rojas Solorio and had a child with her.

"We're now the Brady Bunch," Perry later told CBS News. "We have three and three, exactly three boys and three girls. I love it here. I have a wonderful life, I have a wonderful house, I have a wonderful community around here, and this is where I want to live. . . . I've probably never seen them (the children) happier in their whole life than here."

"He's a great husband," Carmen said. "He's sweet. He's perfect. He's perfect for me."

But what had he told the children regarding the whereabouts of their mother?

"I've told the children the truth," Perry said, "that Mommy left home, we don't know what happened to her. It's very sad, but that's the truth."

Chapter 15

Perry March first realized, at least with a degree of certainty, that Larry and Carolyn Levine were serious about using the grandparent visitation order issued to them by an Illinois court when they suddenly showed up unannounced at the door of his palatial home in Ajijic one sunny day in May 2000. There had been changes to the Tennessee State Legal Code that gave grandparents who were residents of that state the right to pursue custody of grandchildren whose custodial parent(s) had been adjudged responsible in a wrongful-death lawsuit. There were people on both sides of the fence who believed that the Levines may have had some influence into the language of the new legislation. However, a big question on everyone's mind was how a Tennessee law could be applied in Illinois toward a person now residing in Mexico. Perry refused to allow his in-laws to see Sammy and Tzipi and, in the words of Perry's father, he "sent them on their way."

Perry later said that he had only heard of the visitation order when he was informed by a clerk in Cook County, Illinois, who confirmed that a copy of the court order was being sent to the U.S. State Department. He said that after he had verified the docket number, he went to federal court in Guadalajara, where he obtained an *amparo,* a legal device that is used for constitutional protection. In Perry's case the *amparo* was used to prevent the judge who had initially been approached by the Levines from implementing the visitation order.

The Levines, however, weren't about to give up that easily. Although Perry had turned them away, they would be back. And Perry would soon learn that when the Levines refiled the same Illinois-issued visitation order with a different judge and a new docket number was issued, the *amparo* that Perry had obtained was no longer valid.

A month later, on Wednesday, June 21, 2000, Perry March was going about his day-to-day business at his office in Ajijic when six Mexican immigration officials showed up at 9:00 A.M. and told him that there were problems with his immigration status. Although the men were unarmed, Perry recalled, only one of them had a badge and was wearing a uniform. In no uncertain terms, they informed him that he would have to accompany them to Guadalajara to straighten out his paperwork.

"They grabbed me under the arms and put me in a head-lock," Perry later recalled. "They lifted me by my ears, lifted me off my feet, and shoved me through my conference room doors."

After getting him outside, he said, they threw him into the back of an unmarked white van and sped away. The scene resembled something out of a thriller, with Perry bouncing around the back of a speeding van with several not-too-friendly-looking Mexicans at his side.

As Perry, dumbfounded and bewildered, was being

whisked off toward Guadalajara, Larry and Carolyn Levine, unbeknownst to Perry, were in Ajijic. They were accompanied by a local attorney, a Mexican judge, and several Mexican police officers, and they were heading for the school that Sammy and Tzipi attended. Perry would later learn that the Levines had somehow gained the assistance of the Mexican authorities to execute their legally questionable court-ordered grandparent visitation demand.

The judge, lawyer, cops, and the Levines were at the school for nearly an hour, arguing with school administrators about turning Sammy and Tzipi over to them for their court-sanctioned "visit." Finally, the Mexican officials were able to convince the school administrators to hand the children over to the Levines.

Meanwhile, Arthur March had heard what was going down with regard to the children and with Perry—Ajijic was, after all, a very small town and word often traveled very fast. Arthur acted quickly, jumped into his SUV, and arrived at the school only moments behind the Levines. In hot pursuit he chased them as they raced toward an airport, and at one point everyone stopped and had a face-to-face confrontation. Arthur allegedly pulled a gun on them, and told them that they would not get out of Mexico alive.

"I wasn't thinking rationally," Arthur later told a reporter. "But those are my grandkids!"

Following the heated exchange, the pursuit continued as the Levines continued toward the airport. They finally managed to elude Arthur, were able to get on a plane, and flew with the children to Nashville.

Perry, in the meantime, realized that the immigration officials were taking him toward the airport, but he wasn't sure why. Was he being deported? Thinking quickly, he finally mentioned the name of an immigration official that he suspected was behind his abduction. Upon hearing the official's name, the driver of the van pulled to the side of the road, stopped, got out, and began talking on his cellular telephone.

"Three minutes of conversation," Perry recalled, "he gets back into the van, turns around to me, and says, 'It's a terrible mistake. I'm sorry. Your paperwork is in order.'"

As soon as Perry was released by the immigration officials, he sped off toward the school. By the time he arrived there, his in-laws, along with his children, were already gone and flying toward Nashville.

"They are kidnappers," Perry said of the Levines. "It was all a big orchestration."

According to Perry, along with a CBS News report that ran later, the Levines purportedly had been forewarned by the FBI that Mexican immigration officials had planned to bring Perry March in for questioning and possible deportation that same morning.

The FBI, it was learned, apparently had Perry under surveillance in Mexico since his arrival. He was under a sealed indictment at the time for fraud at his father-in-law's law firm, and he was a murder suspect. The FBI can apparently watch anybody, since they have agents attached to embassies and consulates in countries all over the world, and they were monitoring Perry in case he had plans to leave Mexico and go to another country. The FBI agents that were watching Perry March were based at the American Consulate in Guadalajara, and the information that they were obviously reporting was somehow getting to someone in the Levines' camp. Ironically, Perry and his father knew about the sealed indictment from their own Mexican attorneys.

That particular day, June 21, the Levines were told, would be a good opportunity for them to attempt to exe-

cute their visitation court order. An operation like the one
that occurred would have taken some planning—it wasn't
as if the Levines could have received a spur-of-the-
moment telephone call to urge them to hop on a plane and
fly to Mexico. For such a plan to have been implemented
in the manner that it was, careful planning, observation,
and reporting had to have occurred.

Shortly after their arrival back in Nashville, the Levines
had to act fast because their court order, if allowed to
stand, only called for a thirty-nine-day visit. They quickly
began making plans to obtain permanent custody of
Sammy and Tzipi.

"This was a court order in which we were doing what the
court said we had a right to do," Larry Levine said later.

In many respects, whether their actions turned out to
be legal or illegal, who could blame the Levines? After all,
Sammy and Tzipi were the children of their only daughter,
now presumed dead—allegedly at the hands of her husband. Would any grandparent want to leave their grandchildren in the custody of the person who was suspected
of killing their mother?

Perry told the local media and anyone else who would
listen that the Levines had broken not only Mexican laws
but international treaties as well when they came and took
Sammy and Tzipi out of school and brought them back to
the United States with them. The Levines, Perry said, had
utilized high-level relationships in their efforts to win the
cooperation of the U.S. State Department and other U.S.
diplomatic connections in Mexico, which ultimately created a conspiracy that involved getting him deported, while
at the same time removing his children from his custody.

According to Perry, the visitation order from Cook
County Circuit Court in Illinois was in actuality a letter

rogatory, or a letter of request, a mechanism that one court or jurisdiction sometimes uses in which to request assistance from another, often a foreign court, in its effort to obtain desired information. According to Perry, such a letter can be used only for two purposes under the auspices of the Inter-American Convention, and that is "to serve notice, summonses, and subpoenas," or to otherwise collect evidence or information. A letter rogatory, Perry said, cannot be used for the purpose of coercion against people.

"This is an Illinois order," Perry said. "It's like Moscow issuing an order to grab John Doe in Ethiopia."

John Brennan Jr., an attorney in Guadalajara, who was consulted about the Mexican Federal Procedures Code, said that a hearing should have been required to determine the legitimacy of the order and whether it complied with Mexican law or not. The hearing, Brennan said, would also be used to allow the parties involved a chance to have their say about the matter. The procedure that is required to be followed, said Brennan, is called homologation, which means to approve, ratify, or otherwise officially confirm the issues stated in the letter. He said that a court official is required to convey the first notice.

"They can't do it," Perry said. "No court can allow another country to arrest or take property. . . . The concept of grandparent visitation does not exist in Mexico."

Perry indicated that he would file official complaints, known in Mexico as *denuncias,* against everyone who was involved in the action that allowed his children to be taken out of Mexico without his consent.

"I'll get my children back no matter what it takes," Perry said. "They will pay the price for kidnapping my kids."

Although Perry had initially believed that the Mexican immigration authorities had been involved in getting his children removed from Mexico, further investigation had convinced Perry that they had not, in fact, been involved.

"Following conversations my lawyers have had with people in immigration," Perry said, "we have concluded that there was no collusion regarding the removal of my children from Mexico by the immigration department here. Once the immigration department realized my kids were being taken out of school, they rushed my ass back to Ajijic at ninety-five miles an hour."

It was possible that the immigration authorities had been duped by part of a much larger "conspiracy" that had been born to have him removed from Mexico, Perry believed.

"The Levines had influence with Al Gore," Perry charged. "The State Department and the embassy asked (the Mexican government) to get me deported. Regular people would not get this kind of treatment."

Perry had been summoned by the immigration officials, in fact, to respond to a formal complaint alleging that he had been working in areas in which his immigration status did not allow him to work. After discussions the immigration officials had concluded that the complaint had not been proven and that the grounds to deport March did not exist at that time.

Additional background information about the visitation order showed that an Illinois judge had originally granted the Levines visitation rights with Sammy and Tzipi in December 1996. However, Perry had appealed the ruling; but the Levines' right to have visitation with their grandchildren was reinstated by a second ruling that had been issued in the early part of 1999.

Meanwhile, Perry, who didn't dare risk returning to the States for fear of being arrested on the allegations of embezzlement from his former employer, had managed to obtain privileges to contact his children by telephone.

"I've talked to them on the phone twice so far," he told a reporter for the *Guadalajara Reporter.* "My son was crying. He said he wants to go home, where I live. 'I want to come home, Daddy,'" he quoted his son as saying. "My daughter said, 'I wanna go home, Daddy.' They already both speak Spanish. This is home for them."

With the thought foremost on his mind that he might lose his children for good, Perry contacted Nashville lawyer John Herbison to help him in his quest to get his children returned to him. Herbison, who practices in criminal, constitutional, and civil rights law, agreed to help him. Born in Nashville in 1955, and admitted to the bar in 1987, Herbison was very familiar with the Levines and all of the controversy surrounding Perry March.

Herbison, the son of a former preacher, has been hailed in Nashville circles as a defender of free speech. By his own admission, the University of Tennessee Law School graduate likes "tangling with the government," and taking on difficult or challenging cases. With a reputation as a very good lawyer, Herbison has built much of his legal practice around defending adult businesses in Nashville and has represented clients who were involved in prostitution. Although Herbison once told a reporter that he doesn't utilize adult businesses himself because he is "not interested in it," he staunchly believes that people should be allowed to choose their own reading material. He has been known to refer to the city's vice unit as the "erection suppression" unit.

"There's a segment of the population, when it comes to matters of sex and sexuality, that is wound too tight,"

Herbison once said. "But there's a group of otherwise honorable politicians who pander to that crowd."

When all was said and done, Herbison seemed like the right match to take on Perry March's problems.

A onetime lawyer schooled at Vanderbilt, Perry March had managed to outsmart dozens of police authorities and judges throughout the states of Tennessee, Illinois, and, now, Mexico. Reduced to a somewhat transitory life, Perry had become an exile, with his children, Sammy and Tzipi, in tow. Perry March had found a place of safety in a small community, in Mexico, where he believed that he could still live like an American behind the barred windows of his lavish home, which he shared with his new wife and their "Brady Bunch" family.

However, as would be seen, that self-imposed "prison" was not good enough for some, namely Lawrence and Carolyn Levine.

Chapter 16

During the early part of July 2000, fearing that he would lose his children for good, Perry March announced that he had left his business, Chavez and March, Ltd., "by mutual agreement," so that he could dedicate more time and energy to finding a solution that would bring his children back to him.

"Sam and I have numerous projects, and things are cool between us," Perry said of his departure from the partnership. "I have to devote my full time and attention to getting my children back."

Chavez wished Perry March well, and told him that he hoped he was successful in regaining custody of his children. Chavez released a written statement to the *Guadalajara Reporter* in which he stated that he and Perry still had a few real estate projects that they were working on together.

In addition to finding a solution to get his children returned to him, Perry had other problems, among them a community that was quickly turning against him and labeling him as a swindler and a con artist. It was little wonder.

One of the more outspoken local residents, Esther

Solano, a political activist and Mexican citizen, had come out strongly several months earlier against Perry March and C&M Development and the other enterprises he was running with Chavez. Solano, along with U.S. citizen and ex-pat Joel Rasmussen, had taken it upon themselves to expose marauders, like Perry March, who had made it their business to prey on the expatriate community of Ajijic and the Lake Chapala area. Perry March and C&M Development weren't the only businesses that they had identified to focus on, but C&M and Perry March appeared to be getting the lion's share of the complaints. Some said that it was not only because he needed additional time to deal with the issue of his children, but also because things had gotten too hot to handle, that Perry had opted to leave most of his business ventures, which he had helped to create.

There were others in the community who assisted Solano and Rasmussen in their efforts, and together they collected documentation and built files, often sending copies of their information and testimonials to both Mexican and U.S. agencies with letters demanding that the various officials take action against the offenders that were ripping off the community. Solano went so far as to write letters to two successive Mexican presidents, demanding that they take action to protect the citizens from con artists and schemers, like Perry March. Some of the citizens began referring to Perry as a sociopath, and they advocated that Mexican officials should deport him.

Perry's father, Arthur, remained unflappable and lived in denial that any of the allegations being made against his son could be true. Instead, Arthur began telling his friends and anyone who would listen to him that Perry's problems were all being caused by his in-laws, the Levines. But word of mouth against Perry in Ajijic was strong, and so were the posts that citizens were putting on the Internet. At one point posters of Perry March began appearing all over the community, and were tacked on telephone poles.

The posters in question had been made up like a typical "Wanted Poster," but the ones being distributed were called "Un-Wanted" posters and depicted a grainy photo of Perry March at the top. In the photo that was being used, Perry sported a goatee and a mustache, and still had plenty of hair on top of his head. The verbiage that was used in the anonymous poster was brutal:

"How to Sexually Harass on the Jobsite, Steal from the Company You Work For, Defraud Your Clients, Kill Your Spouse and Hide the Body, Escape to Another Country, Pay Off Officials to Protect You, Marry Another Man's Wife and Take His Children (uses them as his shields), Open Several Scam Businesses, Rob the Elderly, Accuse and Threaten Those Who Attempt to Expose You, Live in a Large House with Swimming Pool without Paying Rent, Run Up Large Phone Bills and Don't Pay Them Either, Enjoy the Services of Maids and Gardeners, Gain Fame and Notoriety, Lie, Lie, and Lie Some More and. . . . Get Away With It All.

"Read the true story of this confirmed sociopath and his vile exploits. It's all there on the Internet and more. Check out these U.S. News services: www.tennesseean.com & www.nashvillescene.com. Soon to be a book. Perry "El Perrito" March and his team of con men are trying to transform this Mexican resort town, he's threatened to kill people, pays off the local authorities, perpetrates investment and land fraud, takes money from retirees, and has been disbarred as a lawyer in the U.S. His pistol packing windbag cohort father and he call themselves doctors

(doctors of chaos and sham for sure), and the outrage continues to this day. Do you 'know' them? If either has wronged you or approached you with a money scam please inform the FBI."

Of course none of the allegations in the anonymous "Un-Wanted" poster had been proven, but they nonetheless infuriated Perry and his father and were quite an embarrassment to Perry and his family in such a small community, where nearly everyone knows each other. But because no one knew who was responsible for tacking these posters up all over town, there was little that Perry could do except rip them down whenever he ran across one. And if anyone did know who was putting up the posters, it wasn't likely that they would give up the information.

Perry certainly made enemies wherever he went, and Mexico had not been an exception. Many of those who accused him of wrongdoing and running scams remained on the sidelines, silent, while others fought their battles in the name of seeing justice done. One person who came forward, however, had had enough and decided to take legal action against him for allegedly defrauding her out of more than $200,000. Gayle Cancienne, a woman in her mid-fifties, hired a legal adviser, Henri Loridans, to help her in her civil complaint against Perry.

When Gayle had first moved to Ajijic, life was great for her. During her first few years there, she would awake whenever she wanted, stroll along the narrow streets and stop at one of the several sidewalk cafés when the mood struck, and partake in one of her favorite pastimes—playing bridge—with several of the new friends that she had made. She was happy and contented—until she met Perry March. After that fateful day, however, her world was turned upside down.

According to information that Loridans provided to the news media, Perry was involved in the sales of Gayle's properties in the United States. He had set up corporations, holding companies, in Delaware, and in the country of Belize, to manage the properties she had owned, two of which were in New Orleans, her hometown, and the other in Kansas City, Missouri.

Initially, Gayle had expressed an interest in selling her properties and then depositing the proceeds into a Mexican bank, and would use the interest earned to pay her day-to-day living expenses. Several expatriates had made similar decisions and were living quite well as a result. However, enter Perry March, and Gayle's plans took a sudden departure along a different route—right into Perry's bank account.

Gayle had retained Perry's services by paying him an initial $15,000, and later paid him an additional $5,000 before she became aware that something very wrong had occurred.

He had apparently explained to her that the corporations could act as tax shelters to save money for her and would supposedly at the same time boost the value of her assets. Gayle charged that Perry, through his schemes, had allegedly attempted to pilfer the proceeds from the sales of her real estate holdings by assuming control of the corporations without informing her of his actions.

"Actually, he had opened the corporation for himself," Gayle said. "It's his corporation, not mine."

Apparently, Perry March had inserted himself as president of the corporation, and had named his father, Arthur March, as the sole shareholder of the Delaware corporation. On Perry's advice, Gayle signed documents that transferred her property to the Delaware corporation with the understanding that *she* would be the president and sole shareholder, not Perry and his dad.

Gayle later learned that Perry had sold one of her properties, a duplex, in New Orleans, but had failed to inform her of the sale.

"He sold it for one hundred eighty-one thousand dollars," she said, "because he wanted a quick sale." She said that the new owner sold the property a short time later for $252,000. Gayle claimed that she was never paid any of the proceeds.

"I'm pretty naive when it comes to business," she said. "I lived on the income of the rentals on the house. So, he took everything I had."

Although Gayle had filed a civil suit in a Mexican court, Loridans didn't believe that she would ever regain any of the money that she was claiming to have lost because of Perry's alleged actions.

"We feel certain that Perry's assets are protected or hidden . . . ," Loridans said.

After Perry's business dealings with Gayle had concluded, Gayle found that she was nearly flat broke. She had to go back to work, but was unable to make more than $2 per hour in Mexico. She held one full-time job and three part-time jobs, often working eighty hours a week or more.

"I'm getting too old for this kind of crap," Gayle said. "It's been horrible. I had to eat, for a long time, tortillas, beans, cactus, and eggs. Eggs are cheap."

Gayle Cancienne was forced to move out of the house she had purchased in Ajijic because she was unable to afford the expense of keeping it up, nor could she any longer afford to pay her utility bills. She moved into an inexpensive apartment located outside of town where she no longer had the basic conveniences of a telephone, computer, or a television, because she could not afford them. She also had to do without a washer and dryer in her new home.

"Who would expect this?" she asked. "Who would expect to be destitute? I don't see much hope for me in getting any money back. . . ."

According to Joel Rasmussen, many of the people allegedly victimized by Perry March had either been unable to gather sufficient evidence to bring forth charges against Perry and/or his partner, Chavez, and others had simply moved away. Many of the cases had proven very difficult to document, which had proven beneficial to Perry's freedom and well-being.

"They were careful not to leave incriminating paper trails," Rasmussen said. "Perry would hold on to the original paperwork, saying he needed it to make copies. Clients who tried to collect their documents and files often got nothing more than a brush-off. . . . It's inconceivable that so many people with no other common connection would cook up a conspiracy of this magnitude."

According to Esther Solano, many other people were afraid to come forward with details of their dealings with Perry March because, she claimed, they had been intimidated and embarrassed, or had been concerned that they might get into trouble for income tax evasion—better to let sleeping dogs lie, they believed.

"Some people knew that the way Perry March handled their investments was not legally aboveboard," Solano said.

Solano said that at one point someone had placed a dead cat on her doorstep. Although she didn't name anyone specifically as the culprit who may have placed it there, she believed, nonetheless, it had been done by someone as an unspoken threat to intimidate her into backing off from the crusade that she had been waging to expose Perry March's business dealings.

Although Perry and his father had been claiming that Rasmussen and Solano had been acting as instruments being manipulated by Larry and Carolyn Levine, the charges were without merit. Both Rasmussen and Solano denied the claims, and insisted that their motivation was simply to try and protect their community from parasites—like Perry March.

At one point a mysterious fire broke out at the C&M offices in which important records were supposedly lost or destroyed, and a short time later the Mexican insurance company that had taken care of their insurance needs stopped doing business with Perry March and Samuel Chavez.

At another point, prior to Perry leaving the C&M businesses, a Baptist preacher, Don Hauser, had jumped on the crusader bandwagon and had reportedly frightened off an important potential investor. Because of all the negative talk circulating throughout the community, several other potential investors had already backed away. But the investor discouraged by the Baptist preacher had been a big fish and would have been a substantial catch. As a result of the loss of the investor, Chavez filed a slander and defamation lawsuit against Hauser, who reportedly had responded with a countersuit. Hauser also reportedly had put out the word that he was seeking any clients unhappy over their business dealings with Samuel Chavez and/or Perry March, but his effort ended when he left Mexico.

In response to many of the accusations that had been leveled at C&M, Chavez published scathing remarks in a local weekly newspaper in which he referred to the expatriate community as "arrogant, misinformed, Alzheimered gringos." He also referred to them as "one foot in the gravers" and "gossipmongers," and ultimately laid blame to those who were complaining for the failure of C&M's businesses, particularly the PriMedical projects.

A short time later, Chavez became the apparent target of a drive-by shooting as he was taking his children to school one morning. Fortunately, no one was injured in the shooting. No one was ever identified, either, as the shooter.

Also, the headline coverage of the Levines' whisking their grandchildren out of Mexico didn't help matters for Perry March and C&M, Ltd. The fact that Perry had told a reporter that corrupt Mexican government officials had actively participated in assisting the Levines didn't improve matters, either. Perry's accusation prompted a public response from an official who said that Perry's statement could net him charges of criminal defamation. Nothing ever came of it, however, until weeks later when the government official who had made the public statement was replaced. It seemed that Perry had come away unscathed, again. Nonetheless, the locals, including the expatriate community, were relentless in their efforts to get Perry ousted from Mexico.

Whether in the United States or in Mexico, Perry March had become a center of controversy, motivating the media—for whatever reason—to continue to run articles on Perry's exploits, to which he frequently responded by telephone to the newspaper in question and to the reporters in particular, threatening to file suit over any given story. Perry's antagonistic, scolding telephone calls had become too much at one point for the *Guadalajara Colony Reporter*. It seemed that every time Perry called, he would upset people with his tirades. The newspaper finally had had enough and they began tagging the byline on their

Perry March stories as "Staff Reports." It would help keep the writer anonymous so that Perry would not know who to call to complain to and threaten with lawsuits.

Things also became worse for the business entities created by Perry March and Samuel Chavez, creating some local speculation that perhaps Perry had seen the failures coming and had bailed in July 2000 before the real damage occurred. Premiere Properties went belly-up, with its manager and real estate broker leaving town in the process. They also lost their Guardian Security manager, who took his family and returned to the United States. Much of the business plaza where C&M, Ltd., ran their businesses suddenly became vacant and were on the market again, and its owners were left holding unpaid rent bills that C&M had left behind.

Chavez remained in Ajijic for a few months after the businesses folded, then relocated to Guadalajara, where he opened up shop as a middleman handling international adoptions. Perry remained behind with his new family, living in his lavish rental home in the well-heeled subdivision of La Floresta, while he became more deeply occupied with his plans for the already-troubled Chula Vista Norte subdivision. There was also the café that he eventually wanted to open with his wife, Carmen, and he had begun thinking about starting up a new lakeside real estate project, or scheme, depending upon who was asked.

The Levines' thirty-nine-day court-ordered visitation officially ended on Sunday, July 30, 2000. Earlier that month, on July 3, the Levines had filed paperwork in Tennessee asking that Perry's parental rights be terminated, charging that Perry should lose custody because he had been found responsible for Janet's disappearance in a civil court. Nashville Juvenile Court granted the Levines temporary custody of the children until the parental-rights determination could be made. When Sammy and Tzipi were not returned to their father, according to the terms of the court order, Perry asked his Mexican lawyer to file a motion requesting that his children be returned to him immediately. He had also asked for further investigation into the manner in which his children had been removed from Mexico by the Levines, but a search of immigration records in Mexico failed to turn up any records of the children exiting the country.

"The Levines signed this order for thirty-nine days and they pissed on it," Perry said. "They're liars. . . . I have been cut off from my kids. August twenty-seventh was my son's birthday and they wouldn't let me speak to him. I don't even know where they are. People who have children will know what this feels like."

Perry's scenario could have been looked at another way—now he must at least have some semblance of how Larry and Carolyn Levine must have felt when their child, their only daughter, Janet, disappeared.

Chapter 17

As the summer of 2000 raced on, John Herbison, Perry March, and another attorney continued their search for the solution to getting Perry's children returned to him. After several weeks and hundreds of intensive research hours between them, their efforts were successful when they discovered an international treaty that addressed the problems associated with international child abductions. After studying the treaty intently, the three attorneys finally agreed that their remedy likely lay in the provisions of The Hague Convention on the Civil Aspects of International Child Abduction (aka the Hague Convention), and with the International Child Abduction Remedies Act (ICARA).

According to the Hague Convention preamble, the Hague Convention was adopted by the signatory nations "to protect children internationally from the harmful effects of their wrongful removal or retention and to establish procedures to ensure their prompt return to the State of their habitual residence, as well as to secure protection for rights of access."

Under the provisions of the ICARA, the lawyers learned,

a "petitioner must establish by a preponderance of the evidence that his children were wrongfully removed or retained in breach of his custody rights under the laws of the contracting state in which the children habitually resided before they were removed or retained," which, in Perry's case, was Jalisco State, Mexico. Once wrongful removal is shown, the children must be returned. However, a court is not bound to order return of the children if the respondents establish certain exceptions under the treaty. The ICARA requires that a respondent establish by clear and convincing evidence the *grave* risk of harm to the children if they are returned to the custodial parent from which they had been separated. Notwithstanding these exceptions, the treaty further provides that "the provisions of this chapter (pertaining to the return of the children) do not limit the power of a judicial or administrative authority to order the return of the child *at any time.*"

March, with the help of Herbison in Nashville and another attorney in Mexico, filed his "Petition for Return of Children" under the ICARA, on August 3, 2000, with the U.S. District Court in Nashville, Tennessee, asserting that they were wrongfully removed from their habitual residence in Mexico in violation of his custodial rights and the Hague Convention. In addition to the return of his children, March requested that the district court expedite matters; enter a provisional order directing the Levines to return his children pending a hearing, or alternatively, that the court grant him immediate rights of access, including telephone contact with the children and a schedule for the children to have time with him until a hearing could be held to decide the outcome; and that trial be set in advance of the children's school year, among other relief provisions.

The Levines filed a sworn "answer" on August 22, 2000. Among the numerous defenses that they had raised, the Levines had asserted that March should be "disentitled" from bringing his petition before the court under the "fugitive disentitlement doctrine." They also asserted that Mexico was not the habitual residence of the children, as required for the return of children under articles 3 and 12 of the Hague Convention. They further asserted exceptions to the return of the children under "articles 13(b) and 20" of the treaty, i.e., that return of the children to their father would present a *grave* risk of psychological and physical harm, as well as place them in an intolerable situation, and that the return of the children would "violate human rights and fundamental freedoms." In addition, the Levines asserted that "full faith and credit" were due to various state and Mexican court decisions under a variety of legal theories, including "abstention" or nonparticipation.

"We knew we might never see them again," Carolyn Levine said of her grandchildren, sobbing. "He told the children that their mother ran away and abandoned them. Her children grew up thinking that their mother abandoned them. But nobody loved them more than their mother."

In the meantime, on Friday, August 25, Perry March got at least part of what he had been seeking—arrest warrants naming Larry and Carolyn Levine, along with their son, Mark, on allegations related to "their probable criminal responsibility in committing the crime of abduction of minors."

On Wednesday, August 30, 2000, Perry March filed a motion asking for a summary judgment or partial summary judgment on the question of whether the Levines had wrongfully removed, or had wrongfully retained, the children under the ICARA. The next day, the Levines filed a motion to dismiss Perry's petition based on his inability to establish that Mexico was the children's habitual residence and on the fugitive disentitlement doctrine.

"The bottom line is," Perry said, "that this treaty says that you can't steal children and try to make custody determinations in the jurisdiction where you stole them to."

On Friday, September 1, 2000, the district court ruled that it would decide these pending motions prior to allowing any discovery. More than a month later, and after the court allowed a voluminous amount of evidence into the record in conjunction with the parties' briefs and independently sought information under the terms of the treaty, the district court entered a fifty-two-page opinion and an order in which it granted Perry March's petition and ordered the Levines to immediately return Sammy and Tzipi to him. Specifically, the district court held that Perry had met his burden of establishing wrongful retention. It further held that the Levines had not met their burden of showing exceptions to the return of the children under the treaty. In addition, the court declined to "disentitle" Perry from bringing forth his petition.

Without delay, the Levines obtained a stay from the court of appeals that was effective in preventing the children from being returned to Perry immediately. If the kids had been sent home immediately, the appeal would have become a moot issue, because the U.S. courts would lose jurisdiction of the children. And back and forth it went throughout much of the autumn and winter of 2000 and into the spring of 2001.

As part of the merits of their appeal, the Levines had argued that the district court erred when it declined to disentitle Perry March from pursuing his petition under the fugitive disentitlement doctrine based on various state court orders. The Levines also contended that the district court was in error when it refused to allow discovery or a hearing on the merits of their appeal prior to ruling on the petition, or "otherwise permit them to develop their affirmative defenses." They further argued that the district court erred when it granted the summary judgment in favor of Perry. Finally, in their response to March's response to their appeal and responding to March's cross-appeal, the Levines asserted that the abstention doctrine (that had been based on another case called *Younger*) was applicable to this case.

An abstention doctrine is sometimes used or applied so that a particular court of law can refuse to hear a particular case when it is apparent that hearing the case would infringe upon the authority of another court. Abstention doctrines are typically brought into play when the same or similar legal issues are brought in two different courts simultaneously. In *Younger v. Harris*, the case cited by the Levines, the United States Supreme Court held that United States federal courts were required to abstain from hearing any civil rights tort claims brought by a person who is currently being prosecuted for a matter arising from that claim.

On cross-appeal Perry argued, among other things, that the district court had erred when it failed to address his argument that the Levines had no standing to assert any defenses.

What it all boiled down to in the end was that Perry March, along with the attorneys that came to his rescue and used the Hague Convention as their legal tool, had beaten the Levines in that battle of the child custody war that each was waging. However, although a federal judge had ordered that Perry's children be returned to him, due to the stay that the Levines had obtained from the U.S. Court of Appeals, Perry would not see his children for another seven months. Finally a federal judge ordered the

Levines to return the children to Perry immediately, and they arrived in Mexico to be reunited with their father on Saturday, April 21, 2001.

The Levines, although they had no choice but to comply with the federal judge's order to return the children to their father, vowed to take the case to the U.S. Supreme Court—and they did—to appeal the federal judge's decision to return Sammy and Tzipi to Mexico. However, in January 2002, the Supreme Court declined to hear their appeal and thus ended this particular custody battle.

Chapter 18

Meanwhile, Evanston, Illinois author Wendy Goldman Rohm publicly announced that she had plans to write a book about Perry March's saga. She began putting the word out that she had already secured a book deal with Random House, according to published reports, and that her book, when finished, would set the record straight about the Perry March case.

"There have been inaccurate statements made on both sides," Rohm told the *Nashville Scene,* "but it does seem like there has been heavy misinformation coming from those who assume that Perry March murdered his wife. To date, there has not been even the slightest bit of evidence that he murdered his wife."

While it was true that the police had no physical evidence that Perry had murdered Janet, it was clear that Rohm's take on the story would show that Perry had been unjustly smeared by a news media that was being manipulated. The reporting, she said, "seems incredibly one-sided. I don't know if that's a function of reporters not

having access, but there has been lots of inaccurate reporting, judging by the facts I have collected."

Rohm, according to the *Nashville Scene* article, was not
familiar with the Willy Stern pieces that had appeared years
earlier in that paper, and the fact that Stern had had access
to Perry March, as well as the cops and numerous other
people, when he had written those articles. Although Rohm
claimed that her book would tell both sides of the story, her
statements to the *Nashville Scene* made it appear that she
was sympathetic to Perry's plight for reasons that were not
entirely clear.

Because Perry had been found civilly liable for Janet's
death, and although she believed the civil judgment to be
a sham, Rohm, hinting that Perry's civil rights had been violated, predicted that it would attract the attention of federal authorities and trigger a lawsuit against the state of
Tennessee.

"Based on information I have seen," Rohm said, "there
will be a massive federal suit against the state of Tennessee."

Rohm also opined that the powerful Levine family had
set out to destroy Perry's life, and it had been through their
actions that Perry could no longer find work in the States
to earn a living for himself and his kids. He had no choice
but to leave the country.

"As we speak," Rohm told the *Nashville Scene,* "they
are telling the kids, 'Your father killed your mother.'"

When asked how she came by that information, Rohm
indicated that she had interviewed people who had talked
with Sammy and Tzipi, but she did not name anyone
specifically. The Levines, upon hearing of Rohm's claims,
denied that they had made any such statements to the children, leaving Rohm's claims open to speculation that perhaps her interview subjects had consisted of Perry March

Victim Janet Levine
March.
*(AP photos/
The Tennessean)*

MISSING PERSON

METROPOLITAN NASHVILLE POLICE DEPARTMENT

Janet Gail Levine March is a female, white, 33 years old, DOB 02-20-63, 5'4", 104 lbs, brown hair, brown eyes, SS# 409-86-5820, TDL# 53097502, NCIC # M956251899. She has been missing since 08-15-96. There has been no family contact since that date. Victim's welfare and mental health are in question.

Victim is driving a 1996 Gray Volvo 850, 4 door, Tn Tag 844CBD

If located, contact Det. David Miller, Metropolitan Nashville Police Department, Homicide/Missing Person Unit 862-7546/862-7557.

Missing person poster issued by Metropolitan Nashville Police Department after Janet mysteriously "disappeared" from her home. *(Photo courtesy of the Metropolitan Nashville Police Department)*

Aerial view of Perry and Janet March's Forest Hills, Tennessee, home, which Janet designed, circa September, 1996.
*(AP Photo/*The Tennessean*)*

Nashville police and other officials search for Janet March's body on property adjacent to the home she shared with her husband and children before her disappearance. *(AP Photo/The Tennessean)*

Mike Carlton, left, Radnor Nature Area manager, and David Cain, Nashville Emergency Management, search for Janet March's body in Radnor Lake. *(AP Photo/*The Tennessean)

Nashville's Metro Police officers search for evidence that might lead to Janet March's body in the neighborhood near her home. *(AP Photo/*The Tennessean)

La Manzanilla, Mexico, a retirement community where many American expatriates reside, was one of many resort areas where Perry March and his father, Arthur, conducted business.
(Daniel Hallas)

Arthur March, Perry's father, talking to reporters at his home in Ajijic, Mexico.
(AP Photo/ The Tennessean)

UNWANTED

Perry March

How to Sexually Harass on the Jobsite, Steal from the Company You Work For, Defraud Your Clients, Kill Your Spouse and Hide the Body, Escape to Another Country, Pay Off Officials to Protect You, Marry Another Man's Wife and Take His Children (uses them as his shields), Open Several Scam Businesses, Rob the Elderly, Accuse and Threaten Those Who Attempt to Expose You, Live in a Large House with Swimming Pool without Paying Rent, Run Up Large Phone Bills and Don't Pay Them Either, Enjoy the Services of Maids and Gardeners, Gain Fame and Notoriety, Lie, Lie, and Lie Some More and . . . . Get Away With It All.

Read the true story of this confirmed sociopath and his vile exploits. Its all there on the internet and more. Check out these U.S. News services: www.tennesseean.com & www.nashvillescene.com. Soon to be a book. Perry "El Perrito" March and his team of con-men are trying to transform this Mexican resort town, he's threatened to kill people, pays off the local authorities, perpetrates investment and land fraud, takes money from retirees, and has been disbarred as a lawyer in the U.S. His pistol packing windbag cohort father and he call themselves doctors (doctors of chaos and sham for sure), and the outrage continues to this day. Do you 'know' them? If either has wronged you or approached you with a money scam please inform the FBI.

The Perry March "Unwanted" poster that was anonymously posted and distributed everywhere throughout Ajijic, Mexico at a time when residents wanted him to leave the area. *(Anonymous)*

A more youthful Perry March as he appeared in this April 1997 file photo. *(AP Photo/*The Tennessean*)*

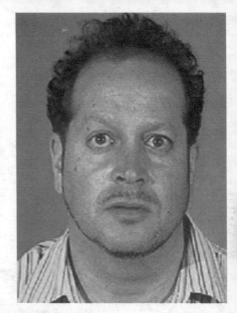

Perry March's booking mug shot taken April 8, 2005 following his arrest for the second-degree murder charge for his wife's death.
(Photo courtesy of the Metropolitan Nashville Police Department)

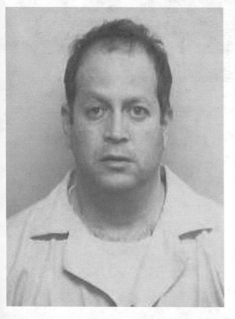

Perry March police photo taken October 8, 2005.
(Photo courtesy of the Metropolitan Nashville Police Department)

Nashville Police Chief Ronal Serpas, left, answering questions regarding the arrest of Perry March, during a press conference on Wednesday, August 3, 2005. *(AP photo)*

Perry March being escorted out of Metro Juvenile Court in Nashville following a custody hearing for his children after his return to Nashville following his deportation from Mexico.
(AP Photo/The Tennessean)

Perry March, right, talks with one of his attorneys, William Massey, during a bond hearing on September 22, 2005.
(AP Photo/The Tennessean)

Arthur March mug shot following his arrest for his alleged role in this very bizarre case. *(Photo courtesy of the Metropolitan Nashville Police Department)*

Arthur March appears at his arraignment hearing via video conference on Wednesday, January 17, 2006, in Nashville. The elder March told police that his son, Perry March, had confessed to killing his wife, Janet, and that he, Arthur, had helped his son hide her body in Kentucky. *(AP Photo/The Tennessean)*

Perry March schemed with fellow jail inmate Nathaniel Farris to murder his in-laws. *(Photo courtesy of the Metropolitan Nashville Police Department)*

Sergeant Pat Postiglione testifying for the prosecution at Perry March's second-degree murder trial.
(AP Photo/ The Tennessean)

Carolyn Levine, Janet's mother, holds a piece of evidence as she testifies for the prosecution during Perry March's second-degree murder trial.
(AP Photo/ The Tennessean)

Perry March talking with one of his attorneys, William Massey, during a break in his second-degree murder trial.
(*AP Photo*/The Tennessean)

Perry March, left, looks down at the table after being found guilty of second-degree murder in the death of his wife, Janet, on Thursday, August 17, 2006. At right are defense attorneys Lorna McClusky and Bill Massey. (*AP Photo*/The Tennessean)

Carolyn Levine, Janet's mother, hugs Deputy District Attorney General Tom Thurman following the jury's verdict. *(AP Photo/ The Tennessean)*

Detective Bill Pridemore, left, and Sergeant Pat Postiglione, center, receiving Investigators of the Year awards from Nashville Police Chief Ronal Serpas, right, in part for their work in helping to bring the Janet March investigation to a successful conclusion. *(Photo courtesy of the Metropolitan Nashville Police Department)*

and his new wife, Carmen. While she admitted that she had not spoken to the Levines, who have remained very selective about whom they talk to, she declined to acknowledge at that time that she had spoken with Perry.

Rohm later shared her opinion about Perry March with *Nashville Scene* reporter Matt Pulle: "I don't have any judgments on whether he is guilty or innocent, but to this day there has not been evidence gathered to accuse him of killing his wife. He has been accessible and has answered all my questions. There are some areas in our interviews that have worried me in terms of inconsistencies, but nothing solid enough to prove one way or another that he is guilty."

Chapter 19

As Perry March continued his involvement in the Chula Vista Norte subdivision, things began to look up for him again when, on March 17, 2003, with John Herbison as March's attorney, the Tennessee Court of Appeals overturned the $113.5 million wrongful-death verdict against him. The court of appeals ruling allowed Perry to thumb his nose at the Levines—for the time being.

Perry had other problems, however, with which he had to contend. Mexican immigration authorities refused his request to change his immigration status to that of permanent resident. He had been holding a visa that allowed him to work in Mexico as a financial consultant, but this, too, was canceled after numerous complaints had been filed against him regarding his business practices. Mexican officials also cited irregularities in his marriage to Carmen, and revealed that Perry's Mexican marriage certificate falsely claimed that his parents were Mexican citizens.

Perry followed up by going to the Civil Registry Office to have a correction statement to replace the false statement on his marriage certificate. The correction consisted of a handwritten attachment that read: "Licenciado Jose Enrique Banuelos Perez orders the clarification of this act in the sense that because of an error, the nationality of the mother and father of the spouse was given as Mexican when it should have been American."

"It was an administrative error," Perry said. "I didn't lie. Why would I say my parents are Mexican and then apply for a visa?"

Perry also filed an appeal pertaining to the revocation of his work visa.

"This suspends and nullifies the order until a final resolution is made," Perry said.

The matter then went to the immigration authorities in Mexico City, where a decision would be made, a decision that could take six months or more. Perry, however, took another opportunity to blame his problems on the Levines, who, he claimed, had worked their influence through Mexican attorney Rene Guzman—the source of some of the complaints about Perry's work ethics. Immigration official Jose Luis Gutierrez, however, refuted Perry's claims that influence from outside sources was to blame for his problems.

"I made the resolution (to cancel Perry's visa) without any pressure or fear, just based on what was in March's file," Gutierrez said. "There was no pressure put on me either for or against this man. I took the decision strictly by the book."

"I've won this case already," Perry said in cocky arrogance. "It's a stupid case."

However, it did not turn out that way. The immigration authorities turned down his appeal and ordered that he leave Mexico—he had ten days in which to do so. Perry, through an attorney, quickly filed an *amparo,* which is like an injunction. The *amparo* allowed Perry to remain in

Mexico for at least an additional four months. If the *amparo* is lifted or removed, Perry would have no further legal recourse to pursue regarding his immigration status. As long as he was not deported, a separate legal maneuver altogether, Perry could travel to another country and immediately return to Mexico on a tourist visa. However, under those circumstances he would no longer have the right to work in Mexico.

How could someone without a right to work earn a living in a foreign country, residing there, temporarily, as a tourist, even though married to a Mexican national? Maybe open a restaurant that a spouse, who did have the right to work because of being a Mexican national, could own and operate? It was entirely possible that that had been the line of reasoning behind Perry and Carmen's decision to open the Media Luna (Half-Moon) Bistro & Café, a family-operated establishment, that could act as a fallback source for money—should Perry lose his right to work in the event the *amparo* was lifted.

Perry and Carmen's café, however, by its mere existence, had created problems for its owners in part because of its location. The homeowners of the adjacent subdivision, La Floresta, where Perry and Carmen had moved their family into a rental owned by Jesus Madrigal, were not at all happy about a restaurant being located so near to their residences. Many in the community, such as Luis Ramirez, the La Floresta association's president, said that its presence there violated zoning regulations and should not be allowed inside the subdivision.

"We don't want businesses around here, because that's our rules," Ramirez said. "And it's a problem."

Ramirez claimed that the association had taken steps to close down the Media Luna. Because correspondence that the association and the government agency, in which it had filed its claim against the Media Luna and its owners, had not been responded to, Ramirez said, the association had no choice but to begin utilizing the court system to resolve their concerns about the restaurant. Ramirez claimed that it would take forty-five days to get a response from the court.

Carmen March argued that the government, if they closed the Media Luna, would have to close down other businesses within the subdivision as well. While she seemed to have a valid point, her argument gave one pause to consider that perhaps it really wasn't the restaurant's presence inside their community that bothered them so much, but was instead the fact that Perry March was attached to the running of the business. By this time he was being referred to by the locals as "El Perrito," or "the small dog." Nonetheless, despite the efforts of the locals to shut it down, the Media Luna would remain in business for at least another couple of years.

At one point, CBS News' *48 Hours* learned of the Perry March case and decided to cover it and devote the show's full hour to it. Correspondent Bill Lagattuta had taken a crew and gone to Mexico and filmed an hour-long story called "Where Is Mrs. March?" During the course of the story, which has by now aired a few times on television, Lagattuta takes the viewer through the events much as they had unfolded, inserting interview segments with Perry, Carmen, Arthur, Sammy, Tzipi, the Levines, Detective Mickey Miller, and others, including friends of Janet's, to respond to his questions between the narrative sequences and reenactments. It was during one such segment that Lagattuta asked Perry about why he had changed the tires on his Jeep, and Perry, eager as always to bullshit his way through a tough spot, told a lie. He had, of course, told lots of lies about the disappearance of his wife by this time, but this particular lie had been aired on national television for all to see. In order to understand his statement as a lie, one had to be familiar with the supposed "to do" list, which he claimed Janet had left him.

"It was on my list!" Perry said to Lagattuta. "The tires on the Jeep were bald. And she was worried the Jeep was going to be slipping in the rain, and all this other kind of stuff, and I was just knocking off the stuff on my list."

The fact of the matter was that changing the tires on his Jeep was not on the list, irrespective of who actually wrote the list. The lie was, of course, in two parts, the second of which was his statement that the tires were bald. It should be recalled that the manager of the tire store where Perry had taken his Jeep had told detectives that the tire tread was still very good, at least 50 percent, and that the tires had not needed changing at that time.

Another interesting response that Perry had made to one of Lagattuta's questions had to do with why he left the United States.

"I moved to Mexico because I needed to get the hell out of Dodge and start a new life, and get out of their (the Levines') clutches," Perry said.

It was an interesting use of the phrase, and was left up to the viewer how to interpret it. However, according to *Urban Dictionary,* to "get the hell out of Dodge" means to leave somewhere immediately, or to scram, and is a reference to Dodge City, Kansas, a location that was popularized in Western movies and particularly the television series *Gunsmoke,* in which the bad guy was often told to "get out of Dodge."

"He took our whole family from us," Carolyn Levine, crying, said to Lagattuta. "He took our daughter, he took our grandchildren, and he took himself, and he meant a great deal to us. But I didn't know him. I wouldn't trust him with anything today."

At one point Lagattuta asked Perry point-blank if he had killed his wife.

"The question is highly offensive to me," Perry responded. "The answer is no."

On Saturday, March 29, 2003, after having conversations with the Metro detectives in Nashville, Perry March's ex-partner, Samuel Chavez, handed over a computer hard drive that Perry had used in a laptop while working the various businesses with Chavez. While it was never mentioned again by the authorities, nor was it ever used in courtroom proceedings, the only people who know what was on that hard drive would be Perry March, Samuel Chavez, prosecutors in Nashville, and the Metro detectives. As a result, it can be said with certainty that the hard drive handed over by Chavez was not the one that had gone missing from Perry and Janet's home in Nashville. *That* hard drive was, after all, the only one that mattered to the case surrounding Janet's disappearance, as it would be able to establish whether Janet's "to do" list was written before or after the time that Perry told police that Janet had left the house.

The remaining months of 2003 were fairly uneventful in the grander scheme of things surrounding the Perry March soap opera that had been playing nearly every day south of the border since his arrival there, but the U.S. wheels of justice continued to turn, albeit slowly. The Levines naturally wanted justice, and they would not settle for less—no matter the cost. Despite the warnings from the court that the money in Janet's estate was being depleted quickly because of all the legal actions being filed by both sides, the Levines nonetheless began preparing another wrongful-death civil lawsuit against Perry March to replace the judgment that had been overturned in 2003 by a state appeals court.

As they had planned, the Levines went to court again, and on May 7, 2004, they managed to get their daughter declared legally dead for a second time. Then on October 20, 2004, Perry March was once again found responsible for Janet's death when he lost the Levines' wrongful-death suit in absentia, and the presiding judge ordered Perry to pay the Levines more than $6 million. Perry, of course, appealed the judgment.

Although Perry March didn't know it, Metro detectives Bill Pridemore and Pat Postiglione continued working behind the scenes to build their case against Perry. Because of the absence of Janet's body, they knew that they would have a tough time getting a jury to convict on charges of first-degree murder. As a result, after conferring with the district attorney's office, they felt that they had enough to make second-degree murder stick. There was also the concern that Mexico might not be willing to extradite Perry to the United States on a charge of first-degree murder, a charge that potentially carries a death penalty. That concern didn't exist on a second-degree murder charge, which has a potential penalty of fifteen to twenty-five years in prison.

On Tuesday, December 7, 2004, a Davidson County grand jury apparently agreed when they handed down a secret indictment against Perry March on charges of second-degree murder, abusing a corpse, and theft.

* * *

As 2005 rolled around, life hadn't gotten any better for Perry March in Mexico. He was still hated by the locals, and his life had been made all the more difficult because of his notoriety—it had become more difficult to find an unsuspecting sucker because so many people knew who he was, what he had been accused of in the States, and what many people had charged that he was doing in Mexico.

Later in the year, Perry and his family moved out of the lavish two-story, five-bedroom Spanish-style hacienda that he had been renting from Jesus Madrigal for the past four years. When they vacated the property, according to Madrigal, Perry owed seven months' rent and unpaid utility bills.

When Perry first moved into the hacienda with his family, Madrigal said, he paid the first year's rent in advance. The second year he paid slowly, in increments, but managed to keep the rent paid. By the third year it appeared that he could no longer afford the home, because he was frequently late with the payments.

"He would owe two months' rent, then pay the two months and then one month," Madrigal said. "Then it started to get more complicated. He would promise to pay, saying, 'I'll see you tomorrow,' or that he had to go to Guadalajara to get money."

Madrigal said that when Perry vacated the house, he owed roughly $10,000 in unpaid rent on the $1,100-a-month property. Madrigal said it appeared that Perry and his family had moved out quickly, because they had left some of their personal belongings behind. He wasn't sure where they had gone, but word got around

the community quickly that Perry had stiffed his land-
lord. His father, Arthur, however, didn't believe it.

"They moved, but they left the house owing money? I
doubt that," Arthur said. "I never heard anything about
that. To my knowledge, he doesn't owe any money. I didn't
hear that. You know, these people have stories."

Chapter 20

When eight armed Mexican officials surrounded the Luna Bistro & Café shortly after 7:30 A.M. on Wednesday, August 3, 2005, Perry March had a look of shocked surprise as they announced that he was being detained on a deportation order issued by the Mexican government. They forcefully and quickly escorted Perry out of the restaurant and into a waiting vehicle, one of a caravan of four cars, each with tinted windows, as Carmen watched, horrified and in stunned disbelief. With no further explanation, the vehicle carrying her husband and the armed men sped away and headed out of town, toward the airport in Guadalajara. The entire procedure of taking Perry out of the restaurant and placing him inside one of the waiting cars had taken less than three minutes.

Although Perry had no way of knowing it, the events of that morning had been in the planning stages for several months. First there had been the secret indictment, sealed, with everyone involved sworn to silence. The fact that very few people had any knowledge of the indictment made it easier for the just-as-secret negotiations to be conducted between top-level U.S. officials and their Mexican counterparts. The secret operation had been carried out swiftly and meticulously, right down to the thirty-mile drive from Ajijic to the airport in Guadalajara.

Upon their arrival at the airport, Perry March was handed off to a team of stone-faced, black-suited FBI agents, who escorted him through the terminal and boarded him on a flight to Los Angeles, accompanying him on the one-hour twenty-minute flight. Upon arrival at Los Angeles International Airport (LAX), Perry was taken to the Van Nuys Community Police Station, near Los Angeles, where he remained in federal custody while awaiting extradition from California to Tennessee. He was placed in a cell all to himself, and he would be allowed one visitor a day, with whom he could spend only fifteen minutes. He would also be allowed one telephone call per day.

Perry looked harried in his new surroundings as he awaited an unknown fate. Back in Ajijic, Carmen went to the local authorities and filed a kidnapping complaint over her husband's "abduction."

"Eight men grabbed him and covered his mouth," Carmen later told a television reporter. "Put him in a truck and took him away. So, when you know it's a policeman, you're like, 'Okay. I know where to go.' But, when you have no clue who it was, then it's bad, you know. I'm thinking the worst. We called the airport and I'm going to get a court order to see if they can give me that he was kidnapped. [I] filed and reported a kidnap."

She told the local prosecutor that the eight armed people who had taken Perry had not identified themselves as agents of the government, and they had not provided any written documentation to show why they had taken Perry. As far as she was concerned, they could have been anyone—even armed thugs with no connection to the government.

However, according to Jose Luis Gutierrez, the head of the Guadalajara Immigration Office, Perry had been deported for three primary violations of immigration statutes. The violations, said Gutierrez, involved Perry misrepresenting his address or place of residence on his paperwork. He had claimed that he lived at an address in Colima State, when, in fact, he resided in Ajijic. He had also stated on his immigration papers that he worked as a real estate agent, when, in fact, he acted as a legal representative for a real estate company. The third reason that Perry had been deported was that the immigration department had received numerous complaints from citizens who had accused him of unlawful and fraudulent activities and that he had allegedly made threats to people to strong arm his way into getting what he wanted.

"He lied to immigration," Gutierrez said.

As far as Sammy, fourteen, and Tzipi, eleven, were concerned, said Gutierrez, their authorization to remain in Mexico under their father's visa was no longer legitimate and they would have to be turned over to U.S. officials—as soon as they could be located. Their whereabouts were not immediately known, and Carmen wasn't talking except to say that they were safe.

Few people—with the exception of Carmen, the children, and Perry's father—were sad to see him deported. Esther Solano, for one, who had worked so diligently to bring about Perry's demise in Mexico, was pleased that he was gone. So were many others, people who had worked behind the scenes for years distributing Perry's "Un-Wanted" poster and a compact disc that detailed at least a dozen scams that Perry had allegedly committed and had caused his victims to lose amounts that mounted into the millions. No one knew where the money had gone, but many people suspected that it had been transferred into offshore accounts.

"Better late than never," said Solano. "Up to now, he has gotten everything he wanted, repeatedly thumbing his nose at the law."

Gayle Cancienne, employed at a veterinary clinic in Ajijic, was among those happy to see Perry deported and arrested.

"He robbed me actually, and took my property that was in the United States," Cancienne said. "I had homes that I owned in the United States that he talked me into putting into a corporation for tax purposes. He showed me papers [that] said I was president and sole owner of the corporation, when, in fact, it was his corporation. . . . I was delighted, yes. And I was surprised because it's been a long time. They were trying to indict him and extradite him, and I'm very glad."

Not everyone, however, held ill will toward Perry. Don Leach, who had business dealings with him, characterized Perry as a good father who had done a good job of raising his children.

"I knew them well," Leach said. "If they walked by now, they would go, 'Hi, Don, how are you?' They're great kids, and I've watched Perry parent. He's excellent. I felt bad for Perry because my experience with him has been very, very, very positive."

Perry's former partner, Samuel Chavez, after wishing Perry good luck when they had parted ways years earlier, now sang a different tune. Chavez said that he was "glad to hear that Mr. March was finally deported and that my efforts were not futile," and that his deportation should have occurred much sooner.

It would probably be an underst
lyn and Larry Levine were pleased
Perry's arrest.

"We've waited a long time for this,'
"We're not sad, let's put it that way. I'm sad fo
children."

They were also concerned about Sammy and T
whereabouts and well-being. The Levines had produced
document indicating that the children were to have been
turned over to the U.S. Consulate, which never occurred
because the children could not be located. Although
Carmen continued to say that the children were safe, the
FBI confirmed that Mexican law enforcement and immigration officials were looking for them.

A short time later, the Levines filed a motion in federal
court claiming that "Perry March or his agents are secret-
ing the children to hide them from Mexican authorities in
violation of Mexican law. . . . As the children's closest non-
incarcerated relatives in the United States, the Levines
would like to care for their grandchildren."

The mystery surrounding the children's whereabouts,
however, was short-lived. Carmen March came forward
with information that the children had been taken to
Chicago, where a judge had granted temporary custody of
them to Perry's brother, Ron. She said that they had been
with Ron for a few days, but indicated that she eventually
wanted them returned to Mexico.

Arthur March, as part of an interview he provided to
Nashville television station WTVF-Channel 5, claimed
that Perry and his family had been very happy living in
Mexico until the FBI showed up.

"The next thing I know, they kidnap my son," Arthur
said. "To say the least, I'm pissed."

S. and Mexican gov-
son's removal from
do so because of the

said. "First they kid-
federal court admitted
next thing I know, they

tatement to say that Caro-
when they learned of

Carolyn said.
our grand-

zipi's
a

Many people, when news of Perry's arrest and deportation began circulating in the news in the United States, began wondering what had changed in his case to warrant the sudden action by Mexican, U.S., and Tennessee authorities following so many years of apparent inaction. Although the Davidson County District Attorney's Office wasn't saying anything, there were sources who told Nashville media outlets that, even though the evidence was primarily circumstantial, there was an item of physical evidence found in the backseat of Perry's Jeep that, prosecutors might argue at trial, linked him to Janet's death. It was a strand of Janet's hair entwined with a carpet filament or fiber. If such evidence was to be admitted at trial, it could bolster the police theory that Perry had rolled up Janet's body inside a carpet for disposal.

"I wouldn't want to speculate about the significance of a person's own hair being found in one's own car," said attorney John Herbison, who would be on Perry's defense team. "If the government has brought those charges, it's now up to the government to prove the charges. Perry, all along, has emphatically denied having anything to do with Janet March's disappearance."

Herbison, meanwhile, had already begun receiving calls

from national news media outlets, including *Inside Edition,* FOX News, *Larry King Live, Good Morning America,* and *48 Hours.* Dealing with all of the calls, Herbison told the *Nashville Scene,* had been "pretty much a full-time job."

On Thursday, August 4, 2005, the day after Perry was booked into the Van Nuys Jail, John Herbison spoke with him by telephone. Following the conversation, Herbison said that Perry had decided to waive extradition to Tennessee and would formally do so in a Los Angeles court-room the following day.

"He's eager to return to Nashville, get this process under way, and get it in a forum where somebody has to finally bring forth evidence," Herbison said in his good ol' boy Nashville twang. "Because it hasn't happened yet. His accusers are going to have to bring forth something. Previously there's been a great reluctance to do that, but every court that's looked at evidence has ruled in Perry's favor."

During his court appearance on Friday, August 5, Perry, exhausted and unshaven, was represented by attorney Brett Fossett, a classmate of Perry's when the two of them had attended Vanderbilt University Law School years earlier. Fossett echoed Herbison's acknowledgment that Perry was ready to return to Nashville to have his day in court, so to speak.

"Anyone can see that this is a father who has been ripped away from his family without notice," Fossett said. "He was not a fugitive from justice; he was not given the opportunity to voluntarily appear in Nashville to face these charges. He was seized, and, I think, just as a human being, you can say he is concerned. Anyone would be in the same situation. Perry wants to get to trial as soon as possible so he can get home and see his family as soon as possible."

Jim Todd, an attorney who had worked in the district attorney's office for twelve years before opening his own practice, told a reporter that the second-degree murder case against Perry could be difficult to prove without the victim's body having ever been found.

"You have to prove in a homicide that someone was killed," Todd said. "Usually, you have the body, and a medical examiner comes in and testifies that the cause of death was homicide by asphyxiation or whatever. In this case you're going to have to prove the homicide first, before you can prove who committed it."

Despite the difficulty facing the district attorney's office in proving Perry's guilt without a body, Todd believed that the attorney chosen to prosecute the case, Davidson County deputy district attorney (DA) Tom Thurman, wouldn't have gone to the grand jury if he had not believed that he could win the case.

"Thurman crosses his *t*'s and dots his *i*'s. . . . ," Todd said. "It's going to be a good case."

Since it was their case, Postiglione and Pridemore would make the trip to Los Angeles to take custody of Perry March from the U.S. government. The two seasoned cops began making preparations for their four-and-a-half-hour flight to Los Angeles, looking forward—after all the time that had passed since Perry had left for Mexico—to having their prime suspect in Janet March's disappearance firmly within their grasp once again.

Part 3

BACK TO NASHVILLE

Chapter 21

On Friday, August 12, 2005, Sergeant Pat Postiglione and Detective Bill Pridemore, of the MNPD, picked up Perry March at the Los Angeles area jail, where he had been held for the past nine days, and escorted him in a rental car to Los Angeles International Airport for their flight back to Nashville. While en route to LAX, Perry told the detectives that he had spoken to an attorney, whom he identified as a friend from college. Noting that Perry seemed to be in a talkative mood, Postiglione told him that because he recognized him as a formerly licensed attorney that he would understand that he did not have to speak with them if he chose not to do so. The detectives claimed that they did not pressure Perry to speak to either of them, but indicated that they would obviously listen to any comments or questions that Perry may want to talk about.

While returning the car to the rental location, Perry expressed his appreciation for Postiglione's earlier remarks and indicated that he was ready to close this chapter of his life. According to what Postiglione later recounted, Perry said that he felt his attorneys would be contacting the police again soon. Not sure how to interpret what Perry had meant, Postiglione suspected that Perry's comments about his "attorneys contacting the police again soon" may have been a way to subtly steer the topic toward that of possibly making a deal. Postiglione, sensing that had been Perry's intention, responded by saying that "sometimes things happen that some people may perceive one way, when, in fact, it is something totally different."

Postiglione followed up his comments by using as an example "a moment of anger instantly regretted." He laid out a scenario of someone killing another person by accident as opposed to someone cold-bloodedly walking up behind another person and shooting them in the back of the head, and pointed out that there is a stark difference between the two.

While riding the shuttle bus from the car rental location to the Northwest Airlines terminal at LAX, the three men said little and engaged in only small talk. Upon boarding the aircraft, Perry took the window seat in coach class, Postiglione sat next to him in the middle seat, and Pridemore took the much-coveted aisle seat. Both Postiglione and Pridemore had decided before the flight that they would posture themselves by taking the position that they would not speak to Perry unless he spoke to them first.

Perry sat quietly for the first forty-five minutes of the flight, at which time he initiated a conversation with the detectives by asking about a newspaper photo of a woman at the 2004 Olympics in Athens, Greece. He said that the woman in the picture resembled Janet, and that he had sent a copy of the photograph to the prosecutor's office in Nashville. The photo had been taken from a film of the spectators watching the games, and he had claimed at the time he sent the photo to the prosecutor's office that Janet was in the crowd. The Levines, however, had examined the photo and had said that the woman in question was not their daughter—the woman in the picture looked considerably younger than Janet would have been in 2004. Postiglione told him that the lead had been investigated to the extent that they knew it was not Janet in the photo. Perry then suggested that Janet might be alive in Quebec, and began asking questions about the case and describing the evidence as circumstantial. He referred to the case as "the Janet incident."

"He wanted to know what we had, how strong the case was against him, whether we had direct or physical evidence," Postiglione said later, recalling the flight to Nashville.

Postiglione told Perry that they would not discuss the evidence with him, but Perry remained persistent and continued asking for more information. Among the things that he wanted to know were whether the police could establish whether Janet was dead, whether the civil suit had been the basis of him being charged with her death, and whether he was the only person indicted. While the conversation was occurring between Perry and Postiglione, Pridemore sat quietly reading a book about the Apostle Paul. When Perry asked him about the book, Pridemore told him that he was reading it for his Sunday-school class.

"Perry leans over and says, 'You know Paul was a Jew,'" Pridemore said, recalling the incident to a reporter for the *Nashville Scene*. "I told him I knew that. He said, 'You know, I'm a Jew.' Pat and I just looked at each other, and I told him I knew that, too. He said, 'When all this is over, I'd be happy to come to your Sunday-school class and talk about Paul.' When all this is over? The guy lives in his own little world."

During his conversations with the detectives, Perry adamantly denied any involvement in Janet's disappearance, but soon began to talk about a deal in which he would plead guilty and do five to seven years in prison. Postiglione told Perry that he could not speak for the district attorney's office, and explained to him that he had no authority to make a plea offer. Perry, seemingly absorbed with the prospect of making a deal, told Postiglione that he was excited to meet with Deputy DA Tom Thurman to begin discussing the possibility of making a deal, but insisted that Thurman would have to "be reasonable and honest" and "lay the cards on the table" regarding the strength of the case against him. He also said that he would plead guilty—even though he was not guilty—in order to avoid a thirty-year prison sentence. Perry added that if he did more than seven years in prison, he would lose his wife, Carmen, and he would not get to see the four-year-old he had with her grow up.

At one point during the flight, Perry asked Postiglione about the various prison types being operated in the state of Tennessee and whether or not he would be able to go to a minimum-security institution. He also asked questions about the different levels of murder, and presented a hypothetical scenario in which he questioned the possible outcome if a killing was an accident and whether it would still be considered second-degree murder if he admitted to an accident. Postiglione referred him back to his earlier statement in which he had said that such a determination could only be made by the district attorney.

At another point Perry told Postiglione that he could get an acquittal if his case went to trial because it only took one juror to hold out. Postiglione reminded the lawyer that a one-juror holdout would result in a hung jury, not an acquittal.

Perry also shared with Postiglione that his nearly week-and-a-half incarceration in the Los Angeles Jail had shown him a taste of prison life and that he now believed that he could serve five to seven years in prison. He said that he was going to "take the high road, do the right thing . . . be a man . . . and do his time" if he could reach an agreement with the district attorney's office. He also told the detective that he did not believe that he could get a fair trial in Nashville, and asked about prison visitation rules, such as whether children could visit him, whether he could have conjugal visits, and so on. He said that he did not expect to be placed inside a "Martha Stewart" type of prison, but would like to possibly get into a minimum- to medium-security facility.

Perry eventually turned the conversation toward sentencing, and he told Postiglione that prior to the "Janet incident," he was not involved in any other criminal activities. He told the detective that he "intensely" loved Janet, but did not respond when Postiglione told him that people sometimes hurt those they love during a moment of anger. A short time later, Perry asked the detective if they had a witness who saw him kill Janet, and why it took nine years to indict him. He also asked if there was any new evidence. Postiglione did not respond to those questions.

Following a short period of silence, Perry told Postiglione that Janet was not the angel that the media had portrayed her to be, and that he was not the monster. He turned the conversation at one point toward local Nashville television news reporter Larry Brinton, who has been reporting the news in Nashville for nearly a half-century, by saying that Brinton was on his "shit list" for traveling to Chicago and asking Perry's neighbors if they knew that the children's father had been charged with murdering their mother.

* * *

Brinton, it is interesting to note, had traveled to Mexico in 1999 to interview Perry and his family at their new home on behalf of the television station where he worked, WTVF-Channel 5. In the interview Sammy recounted details that he claimed he remembered on the night of August 15, 1996.

"I waved to her and she waved to me when she left," Sammy had said during the interview. "She told me that she'd be back soon. She came in and gave me my goodnight kiss. She took her bags, went downstairs, got in the car, and left." Sammy had also said during the interview that he remembered his mother had been wearing "her favorite white shirt and some brown velvet pants."

Sammy's statement to Brinton was markedly different from what he had told a psychologist three years earlier, shortly after his mother had disappeared. He had said that he was asleep when his mother left and that he could not recall anything about her going away.

Postiglione, as he reflected on Perry's comments about Brinton, recalled that Detective Miller had spoken with Sammy's kindergarten teacher at the private school, University School of Nashville, who had indicated that Sammy had been upset on the first day of school, August 26, 1996, eleven days after his mother disappeared, because he didn't know the whereabouts of his mother and had not said goodbye to her. He also recalled reading in the files about a domestic relations attorney in Chicago who had said that the last thing Sammy claimed to have been able to remember about his mother was a noisy argument between her and his father the night she disappeared. A child psychologist who'd had sessions with Sammy nearly thirty times would later say that Sammy had wanted to please his father and that the boy had "favored" him. It was conceivable that Sammy might be untruthful in order to cover up for his father; it was also possible that someone might have coached the boy about what to say at different times over the last several years.

Carolyn Levine would later tell the police that Sammy could not have seen his mother drive away from the house from his bedroom window because of its location in the house.

As the flight to Nashville continued, Perry became even more fixated on trying to work out a deal with the district attorney's office. He told Postiglione that not everyone who was representing him was looking out for his best interest and that he would be the best attorney in the room in that regard. He also mentioned that the cost of going to trial would be a good incentive for reaching some kind of plea agreement.

Postiglione explained to Perry that he would likely have to answer very specific questions that would be posed to him by the district attorney's office. Perry said that if he could work out a deal with Tom Thurman, he would answer all the questions completely and honestly and be "one hundred percent truthful." Postiglione later wrote in his report: "Judging by his words, demeanor, and body language, this appeared to be a departure from his earlier denial and more of a sign of resignation, which seemed to imply guilt."

Perry asked Postiglione if he was authorized to carry on a conversation like the one they were having. Postiglione explained to Perry that he was a police officer whose job entailed working on homicide cases—as such, he would listen to whatever Perry had to say. He also reminded Perry that he didn't have to speak with them at all, if he chose not to. He reiterated the fact that neither he nor his partner was authorized to speak on behalf of the district attorney's office and Deputy DA Thurman. Perry then wanted to know whether the district attorney's office valued Postiglione's opinion, to which he responded that they valued both his and Detective Pridemore's opinion. Perry stated that he wanted to be treated with respect by everyone involved— anything less, he said, would result in him wanting to go to trial, at which his attorneys would "bloody the Levines and Tom Thurman." Postiglione noted in his report that Perry had mentioned several times during the flight that he desired to now close this chapter of his life if a deal could be worked out so that he would have time left to spend with his family. Perry went so far, according to Postiglione, as to ask the detective to speak with Tom Thurman over the weekend about a possible plea agreement. He did not want to wait until Monday.

"This could have been taken care of nine years ago," Postiglione said.

Perry responded that he wished that he had taken care of it nine years ago.

"You know specifics about the case that I don't know," Perry said to Postiglione, "and I know specifics about this case that you don't know."

"I would be happy to discuss the specifics with you," Postiglione said.

"I bet you would," Perry responded.

At another point Perry began voicing his concern about the tremendous influence he believed the Levines had over the district attorney's office. He added that his ability to impeach some of the state's witnesses would help him decide whether he would agree to a deal or not, and he again mentioned the five-to-seven-year-sentence range that he earlier said he might be willing to serve in a plea bargain. Perry told the detective that a guilty plea would be easier on everyone involved and commented about the expense of having a trial, and said that a guilty plea would bring closure to Janet's family. After a moment of silent contemplation, Perry asked Postiglione if he knew whether a convicted felon could ever practice law again.

Perry then mentioned a newspaper article about a person who had reported seeing him with a dead dog, and insisted that the article was not only ridiculous but had been published to smear him. He told Postiglione that he had not wrapped Janet inside a rug, and he had not thrown her into a Dumpster or into an incinerator. Postiglione said that sometimes, hypothetically speaking, people will come forward with information to help their own predicament.

Perry asked Postiglione his opinion about whether or not he believed that Tom Thurman could help get his wife, Carmen, to Tennessee because she was not an American citizen. Perry indicated that he would tell her that he could be out of prison in five to seven years and ask her to wait for him. He said that he believed she would wait that long, but not likely any longer. He then gave Postiglione his word that he would seriously consider a plea if his conditions were met, and again stressed that he wanted Postiglione to ask Thurman if a plea arrangement was "doable."

"To be honest," Perry said, "I am scared shitless about this!"

Soon after landing at Nashville International Airport, Perry March was transported to the Criminal Justice Center in downtown Nashville, shortly after 10 P.M., where he was processed through night court. The charges of second-degree murder, abuse of a corpse, and evidence tampering were read to him. Perry said very little aside from indicating that he understood the charges. He was also informed that he would not be able to post bond—as if he could—until after his arraignment, which would not occur until the following week. Following the procedures of the night court, the Davidson County Sheriff's Department made every effort to bring Perry into the jail as quietly as possible. Noting that the jail inmates watch television, they were well aware of the new kid on the block by the time he arrived. For his own protection, Perry was at first placed in an isolated cell.

"A lot of times a new person to the system doesn't understand that they bring some sort of a trophy at times with their reputation, with their identity," Sheriff Daron Hall said. "Mr. March has had plenty of attention in the media, both now and over the years, and I think he will be, at least from the inmates' side of things, an attractive person for them to be involved with, so we don't want to put him in any danger from that standpoint or anyone else in any danger."

Sheriff Hall said that the isolation can be difficult for inmates like Perry March, and that it can also be dangerous.

"The first seventy-two hours are the most volatile time," Hall said. "Perry March fits the profile of inmates most likely to take their own lives—young, white, and rarely arrested. While he's not on suicide watch, he is under close supervision. He's in our protective unit, our most secure environment. Mostly, so we can evaluate his physical and mental status and know what we're dealing with."

Perry would be required to spend twenty-three hours a day inside his cell, with one hour out for recreation, show-

ers, and telephone calls. Perry kept himself busy the first
three days by meeting with attorney John Herbison, com-
piling a visitor list of people that he would agree to see,
and trying to call home, to Ajijic, to talk to his wife and his
father. However, he encountered difficulty getting through
on the Mexican phone lines, as is frequently the case when
trying to place a call from the United States to Mexico.

"Calling Mexico is different than, say, calling Antioch,
but we're making arrangements," Sheriff Hall said.

The following Wednesday, August 17, 2005, Perry
March, shackled at his feet but dressed in a dark business
suit instead of the typical jail-issued orange jumpsuit, was
brought before Davidson County Criminal Court judge
Steve Dozier. William Massey, a second attorney retained
by Perry, was with him.

"Perry simply wanted to appear looking as nice as he
could, without an orange jumpsuit and with a suit on,"
Massey said. Massey, president of the Tennessee Association of Criminal Defense Lawyers, has been practicing law
in Nashville for more than twenty years.

"It does appear to be an interesting case," Massey said,
"and we want to know what new evidence the government
has been able to come upon in the last nine years that
brings this matter to . . . open court."

Even though security appeared tight, photographers and
reporters seemed to be everywhere as Perry was led into
the courtroom, which was, at the moment, a media circus.

"Bring Mr. March up," Dozier commanded.

As Perry stood before the judge in the crowded courtroom, he provided his date of birth and Social Security
number to Dozier. After he entered a plea of not guilty to
each of the charges, he was led out of the courtroom
through the passageway for defendants. Prosecutors hadn't

provided any new information about the evidence against Perry, and his bail had been set at $3 million, an amount that he was not likely to be able to raise.

After leaving Judge Dozier's courtroom, Perry was escorted to juvenile court to continue a custody hearing regarding his children. The custody hearing had actually begun earlier that morning, but was in recess at the time of Perry's criminal hearing.

Sammy and Tzipi had been staying with Perry's brother, Ron. The purpose of the present hearing was to allow both sides to present their arguments as to who should be granted custody. The Levines' argument was that they should have custody due to the fact that Perry had been deported from Mexico and arrested for his wife's death.

"This is hard on Mr. March," Massey said. "It's hard enough facing charges from a secret meeting being brought against him. It's very hard facing those charges when you're also watching your children being taken away from you."

As many people had expected, a week later, on Friday, August 26, the juvenile court judge granted temporary custody of Perry's children to the Levines. Ron March, along with Perry's wife, Carmen, would likely appeal the judge's decision.

Perry March, through his attorneys, would later file a motion to exclude from evidence any and all statements that Postiglione and Pridemore alleged that he had made during their August 12 flight from Los Angeles to Nashville. Perry cited the Fifth, Sixth, and Fourteenth Amendments to the United States Constitution. He claimed that he was not given his Miranda warnings, that the detectives engaged in custodial interrogation or the functional equivalent of custodial interrogation after he had asserted his right to counsel, and that the discussion between himself and Postiglione had been in the context of Perry's attempt to ascertain what nontrial disposition of his charges might be possible and therefore should be excluded under Tennessee Rule of Evidence 408. After the court cited that his claims were basically without merit, Perry's motion to exclude evidence of his in-flight conversations with Postiglione and Pridemore would eventually be denied.

For the next several weeks, Perry March shared a section of the jail facility with sex offender Jeremy Paul Duffer, thirty-five, who was awaiting trial on a Tennessee indictment charging him with seven counts of child rape, four counts of aggravated sexual battery involving a child, and two counts of sexual exploitation of a minor. Duffer, who worked at a Nashville game store, had been involved in a sexual relationship for several months with a twelve-year-old boy whom he had befriended at the game store.

Also housed in the same section of the jail was Russell Nathaniel "Nate" Farris, twenty-eight, who was in jail on an arrest warrant charging him with aggravated assault that allegedly occurred in a domestic-related fight with his girlfriend. According to his thirty-seven-year-old girlfriend, Farris had been drinking and had taken a Xanax. On house arrest Farris had wanted to leave, but his girlfriend had advised him against it, at which time he purportedly became angry and grabbed her by the throat and pushed her against a wall. After he hit her in the face, she grabbed a kitchen knife to protect herself, but Farris had taken it away from her and held it to her throat, threatening to kill her if she called the police. Bald-headed Farris, with a goatee, mustache, and a tattoo of a question mark on the middle of his throat and another on the side of his neck, looked intimidating. He also had open cases in Davidson County Criminal Court on charges of attempted murder and aggravated robbery.

Perry and Farris had befriended each other shortly after Farris's arrival at the jail, and they began talking to each other regularly. Neither of them liked Duffer—who would? It wasn't long, however, as Perry and Farris became better acquainted, before Perry made another huge mistake in his life. If Farris could make bail, Perry wanted to know if he would murder the Levines for him in exchange for a monetary payment and a new life in Mexico. He told Farris that his plan would solve both of their problems, indicating that he would stand a better chance of not being convicted if the Levines were taken out of the picture. He also told Farris how good life can be in Mexico, and that his father would help Farris make the transition to his new country. Although Farris had initially agreed to Perry's proposition, he began to worry about what he might be getting himself involved in. Needing someone other than Perry to talk to about the murder plan, Farris called his mother, who, in turn, notified Larry and Carolyn Levine. The Levines then reported the plot to Tom Thurman.

"We didn't know who Nate Farris was," Thurman said. "We didn't know if maybe Perry had confessed to him, or if he was just another inmate trying to work a deal for himself. When he described it to us, we asked him if he thought he could get Perry to talk about it, so we could get it on tape. His response was that Perry never stopped talking about it."

Under the direction of the district attorney's office, Postiglione and Pridemore provided Farris with a digital recorder with which to record his conversations with Perry about Perry's plan to have the Levines murdered. Perry's "intense hatred" for the Levines would ultimately work against him.

Chapter 22

As Perry sat in his jail cell in Nashville, his wife, Carmen, remained his most staunch supporter. Described by those who knew her as a very decent and kind person, and as a person very much involved in her church, Carmen struggled to make ends meet for her and her children after Perry's sudden departure from Mexico. Perry's children had loved her, and had accepted her as their mother and not as their stepmother. In the few short years they had been together, Perry and Carmen's new family had become very tight-knit. Even though she needed the money, she continued to keep the Media Luna Bistro Café closed on Sundays, which, according to the locals, is the busiest day of the week for the restaurant trade in Ajijic, so that she and her employees could observe the day as one of worship and spend it with their families. With two children from a very troubled previous marriage, one from a prior relationship, and yet another from Perry March, it was all that Carmen could do to keep her and her family with a roof over their heads and food on their table. But she continued running the restaurant, and her perseverance became very admirable to those who knew her. A strong woman trying to succeed in a male-dominant society, where it was viewed that a woman's place was in her home, was certainly not an easy obstacle to overcome—but she continued trying, all the while in support of a husband whom she sincerely believed had been "kidnapped." Although it was difficult for outsiders to understand why, Carmen maintained that she loved Perry and would continue to stand by him. An attractive woman, Carmen had plenty of potential suitors, wealthier and of much better character than Perry, who had made it clear that they would like to have a chance with her—but she chose to remain faithful to Perry.

Why? many people asked. Perry, like he had done with the Levines when Janet had first gone missing—when he convinced them to wait two weeks before going to the police—was very persuasive in his ability to get others to see things his way or to do his bidding. It seemed possible, even likely, that Perry's actions in nearly everything he did were the product of a sociopathic mind at work. He certainly didn't display the actions of a man who had a conscience, at least not publicly.

Things did not seem to be any different as he sat in his Nashville jail cell and plotted his next moves.

"Hey, Perry? Perry? Perry?" Nate Farris called out from his cell adjacent to Perry's, on Thursday, October 6, 2005. Farris had the digital recording device that would be monitored by Detective Bill Pridemore and Sergeant Pat Postiglione.

"I'm so glad he's gone," Perry responded.

"Huh?" Farris asked.

"I'm so glad he's gone," Perry repeated.

He was referring to the fact that his neighbor, Jeremy Duffer, the sex offender, had made bail. Someone, a relative, had posted $90,000 for Duffer's release. Little had anyone known at the time that Duffer, confined to house arrest until trial, would skip bail and become a regular face on *America's Most Wanted* for the next several months.

"Man, I am too, but it's, it's crunch time," Farris replied.

"It's okay, wait till I come out . . . ," Perry said.

"Okay, I'm just gonna straighten up my bed and stuff."

"Nate," Perry called out. "Nate. Nate."

"Yeah, I'm listening."

"We gotta be real cool now, Nate."

"Yeah, I'm glad he's gone, too," Farris said, his mind still on Duffer's departure.

"Oh, man, it's a blessing."

"When Howard (a jail employee) told me (about Duffer leaving), I thought he was bullshittin'. Howard said, 'You know your buddy's gone.' I said, 'Who? Perry?' And he said, 'No, Duffer.' I said, 'Uh-uh . . . well, fuck, it really don't matter now. Hell, I'm you know, bonding out in the morning."

"Can I tell you something?" Perry asked.

"Yeah?"

"That's perfect."

"Hell, yeah."

"I'll come to the door," Perry said.

A short time later, Perry knocked on the wall to get Farris's attention.

"Are you able to talk?" Perry asked.

"Hell, yeah."

"I've been thinking," Perry said. "I thought you were gonna be gone today. I thought you were gonna come back and be gone this evening. . . . So, I was going to try to write all this in a . . . letter. It's so much better that we can just talk."

Perry spoke briefly about being taken to the classifications section of the jail facility, where he purportedly spoke to an administrator about Jeremy Duffer. He claimed that he told the administrator, who he also claimed was a friend of his, that Duffer was a "loony tune that you've got to get out of here." He said that he told his friend that "Nate is a good boy. Nate has done everything to keep from getting in trouble."

"Really?" Farris asked. He wanted to know which administrator was Perry's "friend."

"The long-haired fellow," Perry replied. "He's a case administrator of the jail. You didn't know this?"

"Uh-uh!" Farris responded.

"When I first got here, he came up and introduced himself," Perry said. "You know what he told me? He said, 'You know my wife, Cheri?' And I said, 'I do,'" Perry explained that she had worked for him when he was at Vanderbilt and on the Law Review. "You know what that is?" he asked Nate.

"Who?"

"Law Review?"

"No."

"Law Review is the top, top students in the . . . school."

"Really?"

"Yeah," Perry responded. "I was smart, and we'd write magazines. *The Vanderbilt Law Review,* it's a magazine and publisher, and we have a staff and everything, it's published. Anyway, his wife was my secretary."

"For real?"

"When I was [a] third-year law student, I was the editor of [it]. I was number one in the Law Review. . . . Anyway, so I was really nice to her and I did all kinds of great things for her. Anyway, he remembered me. So, he's gonna help me get the contact visits and everything. . . . Be [a] real quickie. Anyway, he said, 'Thank you, Perry, we're gonna get him out of there now.' Fifteen minutes later . . . a captain, a black captain, came up here, opened the door, and cleared Duffer's shit out. . . . They ambushed him."

"Well, good."

"Okay, we've got to talk about our situation," Perry said, now whispering and obviously changing the subject. Because of their whispering, some of what they said was inaudible. ". . . I'm one hundred and ten percent on board with everything we've talked about. I can't tell you how excited I am. Okay?"

"Yeah," Farris said.

"But I wanted to give you time to talk with me about hard facts. Okay?"

"I know, I know but, but . . . it's just, man, Perry, you know this is all I've been thinking about," Farris said as he deceived Perry. "You know, and especially now that I'm fixing to get out . . . it's just, it's, it's real heavy on my mind. . . ."

"Well, that's it," Perry said. "I'm set(ting) some rules . . . some perimeters [*sic*] now, right?"

"Yeah."

"Here's what I wanted to explain. Your witnesses may not show up in your cases, right?"

"Well, that's just one case," Farris said. "Even if my major cases get dismissed, Perry, I'm still looking at twenty, twenty-five years, and it's at eighty-five percent."

"Talk low," Perry said. "You're talking too loud."

"I didn't mean to do that," Farris said, his voice again at a whisper.

"I've got about a forty percent chance of walking," Perry said. "Forty."

"That's not good enough," Farris said.

"I agree . . . hear me all out," Perry said. "I'm not telling you anything different. . . . It won't be easy. . . . I'm just trying to explain to you what we have to deal with."

Farris continued to talk about his percentages of going back to prison, and he expressed to Perry how much he hated being in prison and he did not want to go back. Perry explained to Farris how he did not want Farris to get into any more trouble, particularly for him.

"So that is what I was trying to say," Perry said. "I mean it, okay?"

"I believe you, too, Perry," Farris replied. "I've never had no big brother, Perry. I've never had anybody outside of my family that I just really felt, you know, any real compassion for, man. And, Perry, just talkin' to you . . . I was kind of at ease with myself because I knew I could talk to you."

"We're gonna win," Perry said.

"I know we're gonna win, Perry. Look, like at first, I kinda doubted everything, but then just somethin' inside me was, like, you know, this is gonna come through, and, look, it's starting to happen. And, and, Perry, look, I'll tell you something, too. I've, I've done somethin' like this before."

Perry cut in and stopped Farris from talking.

"Hold on," Perry said. "Now, what we're gonna do is we're gonna get real smart right now."

Perry explained that he was going to step back and talk to someone else for a moment, and that he would return in a few minutes. Farris acknowledged his comments, and then could be heard speaking to someone else about an X-Men movie that was being viewed nearby.

"I feel like an X-Man," Farris said.

Moments later, Perry knocked on the wall again.

"All right, now listen," Perry said. "We got to make sure that we don't (inaudible) make it worse for yourself."

"Well, man, look, Perry. The only thing that can be worse for me is me going back to prison."

"Well, I know there's a couple of things that could be worse," Perry said. He reiterated how they had to play it smart so that none of what they were planning could come back on them. "I'd rather take a shot at forty percent . . . you know what I'm saying? Okay, even if I get convicted, I'll get fifteen years. I don't wanna die and neither do you. . . . Hey, trust me. Do you think I'd be talking to you if I had any doubt?"

"Oh, I know," Farris responded. "I'm gonna be takin' a great big step and you know . . . right now . . . I'm trusting you with my life."

Farris explained that he wasn't concerned about getting the job done, and reiterated that he could do it and said, again, that he had already done things like what they were planning. He wanted some assurances that "the colonel, your dad" would know who he was when he called him and that he would not deny knowing him and refuse to assist him after he finished the job that Perry wanted him to do.

"They don't know you right now, but they will," Perry said, referring to his father and anyone else who he planned to involve. "First of all, my dad is the totally coolest guy in the world. . . . If you showed up at my dad's door right now . . . my dad would . . . feed you like a king and take care of you the rest of your life."

"Yeah, but I don't want to go into it blind, Perry," Farris said.

"Well, you're not," Perry assured him.

"I'm serious about what I'm gonna do," Farris said. "I've . . . done it before, Perry. And you know, there's not a doubt in my mind that I'm gonna do this. . . . I've just got to know that, that once I do, that I've got a safe haven. That I've got somebody who's gonna know. . . . the money problem . . ."

"You're safe," Perry said.

"Are you sure?"

"Hundred percent."

Perry explained that he would talk to his dad, presumably about their plan, but for the moment the most important thing for Farris to do was to follow the ground rules that Perry had set up. Perry also said that once the deed had been done, that is, after the police had learned that the Levines had been killed, the police would be at Farris's door asking where he was at the time.

"We'll have to put together an alibi," Perry told him. "You have to stick to the plan and get it done. . . Safety and security are more important, you have to be very careful. . . ."

Perry advised Farris to remain low-key for a while following his release on bail, to go about life as he normally would, for approximately thirty to sixty days, before carrying out the plan. He kept driving home the point that Farris needed to be ready when the cops showed up at his door and began asking questions. When it came time to establish contact with Perry's dad, Arthur, Perry cautioned him that he had to be careful where he called from. He suggested that Farris use a cellular phone.

Perry explained that he would be contacting his father to fill him in on what was going to happen. He also said that Farris needed an alias, a code name that he could easily remember and use when speaking to Perry's father. They came up with the name "Bobby Givings," which had been the surname of a friend of Farris's from his childhood. Perry said that he would call his father within a day or two from an unmonitored telephone, which he claimed he could use, and would tell his dad that a "buddy," Bobby Givings, would be calling him. He said that he would instruct his father to take good care of Bobby.

"Well, look . . . let me ask you something," Farris said. "When this happens, when I get rid of these motherfuckers and I call your dad, he's gonna know . . . what happened. He's not gonna flip out, is he?"

"My dad has killed about three hundred people in his life," Perry said. "My dad was a Green Beret colonel."

Farris said that he wanted to speak to Perry's father before carrying out their plan, and suggested that perhaps they meet in Texas.

"My dad is a soldier, okay . . . ," Perry said. "He's at the end of his days. You know he's seventy-six. He wants nothing. He would give himself up for me in a blink of an eye. . . . That's where he is in his life. Okay, so here's the thing. If you want, you could even go down there first. He can't be leavin' Carmen to come up to Texas . . . because he's helpin' with the restaurant and the kids. . . . What you can do is just go down to Mexico first and meet him . . . if that doesn't violate your parole."

"Well, I'm not worried about that, you know," Farris replied. "Perry, look, what I'm worried about is . . . catching both of the Levines together, you know, 'cause I want to—"

"Without my kids around . . . ," Perry cut in.

"Exactly! Look, here's what I thought. I thought maybe, you know, go to that school. . . . Do they take the kids to school?"

"One of them does," Perry replied.

"Just one of them does?" Farris asked. "Is it her or him that takes them to school?"

"That I don't know," Perry said. After a moment he said: "Both of them do. . . ."

"Well, you know . . . I could just get her, you know, catch her going back into her house and I would wait there for him to get there."

"My kids would probably be there."

"Let me ask you one other thing . . . if I got to him and not her, would that still help you? Or would she still, you know, be a big—"

"Do it, you have to do it when they're both together for it to help me," Perry said.

"I've set [*sic*] on the side of houses and waited for people, okay?" Farris said. "It don't take but a second, Perry. . . . I want to do it in a way to get where I can get rid of 'em, you know, period . . . like they're just gone."

"There you go," Perry said.

"I'm gonna have to buy two cars, you know," Farris said. "I've got the money to get two cars, because one car's just gonna be for that sole purpose right there, you feel me? How am I gonna know where the hell they're at, you know?"

"Their house," Perry said. "I'm gonna give you their street address, okay?"

Perry proceeded to provide Farris with the Levines' home address. If giving him their house number and street name weren't enough, Perry provided detailed instructions on how to find the Levines' home, right down to the fact that it was a corner house off Highway 100, near a church called St. Henry's. He even included the fact that their house did not have a fence around it.

Because the Levines were getting their house renovated,

according to Perry, they had moved temporarily into an apartment.

"They will go to their house every day," Perry said. "One of them will go to the house every single day for lunch to see . . . how the house renovations are going."

Perry described the location of Larry Levine's office in Nashville, and explained that it was easy to find.

"I think he doesn't go to work a lot," Perry said. "I think he stays home with her during the daylight . . . which is perfect."

"Look here, Perry, if they're both in that house, if they answer that door, it's over," Farris said.

Perry cautioned Farris about leaving any form of evidence behind, and told Farris that he was leaving it up to him, the "pro."

"I might look like I'm . . . just some rugged bull or something . . . that'll kill somebody . . . but, Perry, like I've said, I've done this before."

"We don't need to be talkin' like that, let's just get back at it," Perry said.

"I'm just lettin' you know I am dead serious," Farris said. "Perry . . . here's what I want to happen. After these son of a bitches are gone, after I take care of them, they're gone, you get out, I want . . . within a year for us to have some kinda business down in Mexico."

"Within three months, I hope," Perry said. "Let me tell you something, deal with them. And when that happens, they're not gonna let me out immediately. . . . It's gonna be two months before . . . their case falls apart. . . . They might even try to go to trial on my case. . . . It goes from forty percent chance for me (walking), I go to ninety percent. . . . My lawyers think I've got a sixty, seventy percent chance of walkin' right now."

Chapter 23

"Perry, I don't give a fuck about no murder wrap," Farris said as he and Perry continued their jailhouse discussion about planning the murders of the Levines. "This is like my ultimate project. . . . The things you've told me, you know, like those express kidnappings we talked about . . . that's right up my alley. . . . I can do the footwork, Perry."

"You won't have to, I'll be with you," Perry said. "Here's the thing—I'm not a pussy, right?"

"I know you're not a pussy."

"Umm, I'm not . . . as tired, sick as I look, the way I look, right. . . . Trust me. I can whip someone's ass that easy. . . ."

Perhaps as an incentive to further whet Farris's appetite to carry out the mission of killing the Levines, and then later going to Mexico to live the high life and engage in "business" with Perry, Perry turned the conversation toward a wealthy family that supposedly resided in Puerto Vallarta. Philip Rolfe, he said, was a British citizen who, according to Perry, was a billionaire, and there were those in his household who, if kidnapped, would bring forth a hefty ransom from Rolfe.

"How much money do you think he's got in his house?" Farris asked.

"Not too much, but you don't need that," Perry said. "That's not the right way to do it. His daughter is a wacko, who he loves more than anything."

"How old is she?"

"About, I'd say, forty, and she has a daughter. [Rolfe's] grandkid. And Rolfe hired me to protect the daughter, and get the kids out of trouble. . . . He said, 'I don't care what it takes.' I'm just tellin' ya . . . givin' you an idea. . . . We could possibly do a Rolfe thing."

"Uh-huh," Farris grunted, feigning interest in Perry's kidnapping scheme.

"Three hundred thousand dollars without a blink of an eye."

"That would be great, Perry."

"In a day . . . easy . . . maybe more. . . ."

Perry gave Rolfe's daughter's name to Farris, as well as his granddaughter's, and said that he had been in the daughter's house a dozen times or more.

"I know . . . every entrance. I know exactly how to do everything, how they keep everything."

"Do they have a safe?" Farris asked.

"You don't need a safe," Perry responded. "Philip Rolfe is a safe. . . . Let me just tell you this. If I got a hold of [the daughter] . . . in that day he'd have your three hundred thousand in your hand."

Perry and Farris spoke of being partners, and Perry suggested that Farris not "do anything" until he had some "chillin' off" time once he made bail.

"Leave me here riding for thirty days or whatever,"

Perry said. "That gives you plenty of time to get what you need. . . . You take your time at it, you don't make any mistakes, you go carefully, you figure your reconnaissance. . . . Then thirty days, forty-five days later, you do what you need to do . . . you have to be ready to welcome Metro at your door 'cause they're gonna put it together."

"Well . . . they're not gonna think that I'm actually capable of, you know, probably doin' somethin' like this," Farris said.

"They're still gonna come and question you," Perry cautioned.

Perry advised that Farris live in such a manner that he would not raise suspicion that he was going to Mexico. He also advised against Farris leaving the country right away after the killings because, he said, it would cause the police to focus on Farris, and then himself. He said that the police would soon think of looking in Mexico for Farris if he was suddenly unavailable for questioning regarding the Levines' deaths.

The two conspirators talked at length about passwords that Farris could use to convince Perry's father that he was who he claimed to be, once he got to Mexico. They discussed using his dad's maid's name, a dog that his father had been fond of in his youth, and an uncle's name from East Chicago, among others. Farris continued to feign interest in the scheme, and played his deception to the hilt. Perry insisted that his father could be trusted.

"I trust my dad with my life," Perry said. "A hundred percent. Any day of the week. . . . Can I say something? If I'd call my dad, if I had a clear line, I'd say, 'Dad, come up here and shoot the Levines.' My dad would be up here and shoot the Levines."

"He'd shoot 'em hisself?" Farris asked.

"Yeah, my dad, when they kidnapped my kids . . . in 2001 . . . my dad got on the phone . . . four mercenaries . . . fuckin' mercenaries. They were gonna come in, kill the fuckin' Levines, grab my kids, and take 'em back to Mexico. . . . My dad would take care of you like a son."

Farris spoke of being able to get a gun, and Perry cautioned him again about not leaving any evidence behind. He also cautioned him about not doing anything that could connect Farris and Perry to the Levines' deaths.

Farris expressed concern about crossing the border into Mexico because, he said, he had never done that before. Perry explained to him how easy it was, that people walk back and forth between the United States and Mexico all day long. All he would need, Perry said, was the proper identification. Farris acknowledged that he knew how to obtain fake identification.

What would he tell the officials at the border, when he was ready to cross, what his business in Mexico would be?

"Tell 'em you wanna get pussy!" Perry said, laughing.

Perry cautioned Farris about the risks of trying to take drugs across the border, and suggested that he should do a test run at some point. Their conversation turned again toward which location, the apartment or the house, would be best to carry out the killings. Perry said that the apartment would be best, but he did not know the name of the complex or where it was located. Farris indicated that he could find out its location by following the Levines from their house.

"How would I go about getting rid of their bodies?" Farris asked.

"I don't know."

"I mean . . . should I just set 'em on fire after they're dead or somethin'? It's gonna be pretty scary for me to leave 'em there . . . say I've gotta put 'em in my car or somethin' and that's really gonna spook me. . . . You're not gonna get a fair trial," Farris said.

"I know. . . . When somethin' goes down (inaudible). . . . Within, within an hour the police (inaudible). . . ."

"Oh, I know they're, they're gonna come quick, but look, but, Perry, look . . ."

"Somebody without question, somebody is going to put us together," Perry said. "You've gotta be prepared for it."

"Look, let me tell you a story," Farris said. "One time me and this guy, we went and did a, a job. . . . We didn't kill nobody, but, you know, the person got their finger cut off and everything. Look here . . . when that happened, another person come to the house, they got in the house before we even knew anything. We started shootin' at each other. We take off runnin', we steal a car. . . . We're runnin' from these people shootin'. We know they just called the police. Look here, the car breaks down on Dickerson Road. . . . Look here, listen, listen, you know we had dope, money, we had, like, three guns. Okay, but the car broke down on Dickerson Road, about a half a block from the Circle K, which we call the cop shops. It's full of cops. I walked straight up in the store, police everywhere, I buy beer, I buy some cigarettes, a lighter, you know, like nothin' happened, you know."

"Face the fear," Perry said.

"You've got to, we've got to."

They spoke briefly about taking precautions with the evidence, particularly the kind left behind from firing a gun—gunpowder residue.

"Gun powder on your hands," Perry said.

"I know, look, you know, when you shoot a . . . handgun . . . but like, you know, there's ways around that type of stuff."

"Gloves," Perry said.

"Exactly, gloves, long sleeves, and look . . . I'm gonna get a silencer, too. They're expensive as hell to get, but I know I can get one. I can get all of that, and look the way that I go about gettin' me the gun and all this type stuff, I'm gonna get more than one gun, but, I mean, you know, as far as I know that you won't tell on me, Perry, and, look, let me assure you of something, Perry, if I got caught—"

"I don't wanna hear it. . . ."

"Well, but I mean we've got to look at everything."

"I don't wanna hear it. . . . We have everything under control. . . ."

"Well, look, I guarantee you I'm not gonna get caught," Farris assured Perry. "Okay. Look, when I do this, look it's gonna be so quick. . . . Here's what's in my head, here's what I want to do. I want to find out where they're stayin'at this apartment. . . . I'll wait till they go back in the house, if I can't find where this apartment is. Both of them there, knock on the door, *boom boom*. I don't touch nothin', nothin' . . . they're gone; you know what I'm sayin'? The only, you know, the only thing that my presence, the only thing if anybody else's presence being there is, is four bullets."

"What?"

"Four bullets."

"I don't know if they have video cameras in this apartment," Perry said.

"Look, don't worry about that, Perry. I wear wigs . . . gold plates that go over your teeth, you know. Look, I put on a ski mask, but before I put 'em on, look here, Perry; look here at me. From here to here, I paint it brown, put on a ski mask; you know I look like some black guy with gold teeth. Another thing, now look, take wigs, put 'em in a ponytail, put hats on like—"

"Maybe you can . . . when they're gettin' in a car or something," Perry suggested.

"Exactly. If I could catch 'em both gettin' into the car, it's over. . . . Perry, I don't plan on, I don't plan on gettin' caught, and look, Perry, I don't plan on going back to prison for these other charges I've got, either. What I plan on doing is, is—"

"Going to Mexico," Perry reminded him.

"Going to Mex, yeah exactly, going to Mexico with you and . . . Sammy . . . and . . . Zul?"

"Tzipi," Perry corrected him.

"Tzipi. I want us, you know, and . . . the dog, Snowball?"

"Yeah."

"Snowball and Diamond," Farris added, referring to Perry's dogs. "I want us on the, on the beach somewhere."

"We will be."

"I know we will be—"

"We will be. I just tell you on trusting, don't even have one shade of doubt about my dad. . . ."

"Look here, the reason why I'm not doubtin' your dad— for one, he's your dad; for two, he's your dad."

"I want you to know that we're like, like this," Perry said, indicating the closeness between him and his father.

Perry and Farris agreed that Arthur March would be the contact person in Mexico, and not Carmen. Perry also cautioned Farris against doing anything that would cause the police to look for him in Mexico.

"I know . . . I'm gonna tell you . . . where the police are gonna look. They're gonna look in East Nashville."

"Of course," Perry agreed.

"Well, you know, I don't even think that they will come

and question me. But if they do, well, look, look, what they're gonna be thinkin' is that this was, you know, they're gonna make up some story, 'Well, he, you know, his hit man from Singapore . . .'"

"They'll charge me with it," Perry said.

"But you'll beat it."

"I know."

"But look, you know, I don't think that they're gonna think about me, you know, they might come and question me and try to, well, you know, 'If you know anything about him,' and I'm gonna say, 'Hey, man, look, dude, I don't know much . . .' I'm gonna say, 'He was some fuckin' petty-ass lawyer or somethin'. I used to talk to him and he'd give me food.'"

"That's it," Perry agreed.

"You know what I'm sayin'? 'I'd talk to him because I wanted candy bars and envelopes and—'"

"And he wanted to know what prison looked like," Perry added. "You just call my dad up on Monday."

After some more small talk, Perry laid out the plan, or what he had envisioned as the plan, that Farris would follow in communicating with his dad. He said that his dad would be communicating via e-mail.

"He sends an e-mail to my sister, right?" Perry said.

"Okay."

"Then she prints and then sends it to me in regular mail," Perry said. "So, I get it, like, in three or four or five days right? In normal mail from Chicago, okay?"

"Okay."

"Here's the way we're gonna do it," Perry said. "I've got this old BMW down in Mexico. Just call it the BMW, okay? We're gonna have two stings, okay? We're gonna talk about them; sellin' the BMW . . . the BMW is gonna equate to our thing we're talking about here. It's gonna be the same thing . . . so, here's what you're gonna do. Once you establish a rapport with my dad, you're gonna have my dad send a message through an e-mail, which is, 'Bobby Givings is gonna buy the BMW.' Tell my dad, e-mail Perry and say Bobby Givings is gonna buy the BMW. Okay, now . . . that should be at least a few days before you do anything."

"Okay."

"So that way . . . you can say don't sell it. . . . And don't sell it, means don't do it.

"Okay."

"Or Bobby Givings can't find a way to buy the BMW now. He's gonna buy it next month . . . got it? When I get my dad's e-mail, I'll just call my sister and tell her that, and I can send my dad an e-mail that says tell, uh, you know, tell Mr. Givings that I'm not ready to sell it. . . . You get that part of it?"

"Yeah."

"Okay, that's real important," Perry said. "What makes my stomach hurt is when Bobby Givings buys the BMW . . . it's gonna be all over the news, it's gonna be all over the national news."

"You think, you think it'll be on national news?"

"Hundred percent."

Chapter 24

Pridemore and Postiglione found it amazing as they listened to the recorded conversations between Perry March and Nathaniel Farris that Perry could plan the cold-blooded murders of his children's grandparents and speak his children's names in the same breath. In their minds he could be nothing less than a scumbag.

"When we heard him talk about, 'Make sure you do it when the kids are not there,' we just found it incredible," Postiglione recalled.

"With his hatred of the Levines," Pridemore said, "he starts calculating how much better his case will be if they were gone."

"They were in discussions about killing the Levines five minutes into the first conversation," Postiglione said. "He thought he had Nate wrapped around his finger. The truth is, Nate had him wrapped around *his* finger."

"Look, Perry, the main thing is that you're here, okay. And, look, you know, I'm not, you know I'm not gonna run when I do it now," Farris said as he and Perry continued their jailhouse conversations.

"You can't," Perry responded. "You can't do anything that compromises (inaudible). . . ."

"I promise you that," Farris said. "But, look, you just promise me that once I do leave, that I'm gonna be okay in Mexico."

"You establish that yourself, with my dad—"

"Okay, yeah, yeah, exactly. I just, you know, I'm just . . . All I'm doin', Perry, is just reassuring myself; you know what I'm sayin'? Because . . ."

"No question in my mind. When I get out of jail and I (inaudible) set up in my restaurant, you're set up forever in business (inaudible). . . ."

Perry went over the plan again with Farris, reiterating the codes that they had set up, using the name Bobby Givings, the e-mail and telephone communications with Arthur March, and the "sale" of the old BMW Perry left behind in Mexico.

"My dad's the key," Perry said.

"Whenever you showed me the picture of him, I can see just, you know that, he kinda looks like the chief Indian or somethin', you know what I mean?"

"He's totally cool," Perry said.

At another point, after telling Farris to not draw attention to himself after completing the job, and to just let the police think that "Mexican hit men" or "guys from Singapore" had done the job, Perry raised a point of concern regarding his father.

"They'll investigate my dad," Perry said. "Where was my dad? Where was my brother? I'm glad I thought about it; when you talk with my dad, or my dad talks with you, and somethin' happens, they're gonna investigate my dad. The FBI's gonna be in Mexico and they're gonna check my dad's phone records, his bank accounts, and everything. . . . They'll lead 'em right back to you. . . ."

"Well, look, no, I thought about this. When I call your dad, I'm gonna call from a secure line. And what I mean by that is, like, it'll probably be . . . a cell phone out of New Jersey—"

"Okay, perfect. . . . Anytime, you make sure that he never calls on a phone that can be traced because they'll have phone records."

"Yeah, well, I don't want him callin' me," Farris said.

"I know, I know."

"The first time I call him, it's gonna be very brief. And, like, when I talk to him, I'm gonna let him know through some of these codes that, you just know, that I'm for real."

"And tell him he's gonna get a confirmation from Perry. . . . through Kathy . . . an e-mail . . . that Bobby Givings . . . is lookin' to buy the BMW."

"I'm gonna have ta write that down."

"Just think of the BMW."

"Kathy, okay, yeah, but see, like, I'll forget Kathy and all that shit. See that's one of the things I fear about, too, Perry, is me forgettin' little bitty things, 'cause when I call and, you know, I say the wrong thing and it spooks him, and he never talks to me again."

"The key for you is to be thinkin' about the trails of evidence," Perry said. "Think about everything you touch, everywhere you go. Video or recorded, there's links. We have to make sure there's zero links tying us and the reason we have to make sure there's zero links tying us is so that they're not thinking that you're in Mexico. Hold on."

There was a lengthy pause before Perry continued.

"We got to be careful (inaudible). I don't want to be (inaudible), fifty-fifty shot against second degree (inaudible) and then give that up and get nailed on the first degree," Perry said.

"That's not gonna happen, Perry," Farris said. "Perry, look here, before I would let that happen, I'd take my own life."

"No, I don't want you to do that. . . . You know, what I really want, I just want two years from now . . . living alone and havin' money and just relaxing and goofin' around and we can do jobs whenever we want. . . . That's what I really want. . . . I'm just gonna tell you, it's going to turn huge when something happens to them."

"But, look, ain't you gonna love it, though?"

"Uh-huh," Perry acknowledged.

"Think about it," Farris said, laughing. "I mean, really think about it."

"Oh, oh yeah, you know, there's no question," Perry responded, "as long as my kids are safe. . . . There's no question, but what I'm saying to you is that the day the DA is gonna come in for me like a fuckin', like a kissing dog did to a cat."

"Fuck him," Farris said. "Look here, Perry. He can, but he won't. You know what he's gonna do?"

"Nothin'."

"Exactly, nothin'," Farris agreed.

Perry expressed his relief again that Duffer was gone, that he had been moved to a different section of the jail or had been released, because it suddenly gave them a chance to talk without being overheard, to begin making plans to murder the Levines. Perry told Farris that Duffer's departure had been a "sign of God," and that he had been praying for a solution to his problem every night for the past three weeks, asking for God's help.

At another point in the conversation, Perry reminded Farris again about keeping his children safe when he killed the Levines. Farris brought up the issue of whether or not the Levines kept a safe in their house, and Perry told him that he didn't know whether they did or not. He did say, however, that he knew that they had an alarm system in the house—Sammy had told him about it.

"The kids will be at school and they'll both be home, and they'll both be working on my case," Perry said, relating a possible scenario to Farris about where the children would be when it came time for him to do his job. "Or they'll both be, you know, he'll come to the office for an hour or he'll come back at night again—"

"Hey, hey, wouldn't it be crazy if I caught 'em and they was workin' on the case?"

"Yeah," Perry responded.

"I'd take every bit of information they had," Farris said, referring to information that they had undoubtedly put together about Perry.

"Yeah."

"You hear me," Farris said. "Why, no, I wouldn't, either; I wouldn't touch that, but I will tear up the walls and everything, like I'm there looking for somethin' specific. I would take their rings and you know—"

"But I think there's plenty of opportunities when my kids aren't there," Perry said. "Carolyn stays at home all the time."

"Aw, well, look that's good," Farris said. "I'm not messed up with stayin' in the house with Carolyn for, you know, four or five hours waitin' on old Lawrence to come home."

"Yeah, but the problem is that her brother could come over. . . . My sister-in-law could be bringin' Tzipi . . . back."

"Yeah, you're right. Well, I'm not just gonna watch 'em for two or three days," Farris said. "You feel me? I'm gonna watch 'em a lot longer, you know, people have patterns, you know what I mean? And, like you know, too, we might get lucky, you know, like they might have a paper delivered and they come and get the paper. You know they walk out to get the paper, or, you know, they might have like when they come out to get the mail out of the mailbox, just anything. I'll find their patterns, and, you know, I'm just gonna have to time it right and it's not that hard."

"No, it's not," Perry agreed. "It's just havin' the balls and goin' and havin' good instinct."

"Look here, balls and that's it; balls and instinct," Farris said. "You know, listen to your gut."

"The thing you have to remember," Perry said, "is that you gotta clear the house of kids, make sure there's no kids there. . . . And then you have to wait for the opportunity of when they're together . . . and then you leave no trace of evidence!"

They talked briefly of making the murders look like they were the product of a burglary or a robbery, and spoke of somehow getting the fingerprints of another person onto the murder weapon, most likely a gun.

"Well, the idea of makin' it look like a burglary/robbery, that's good," Farris said.

"Exactly; you get a weapon or a club or crowbar held on to by somebody else," Perry said.

"Yeah."

"And leave it in the house."

"Yeah. Hell, look, hey, look here," Farris said. "I can, you know; look, I can go down to the projects with one of my guns . . . at any time there's seven or eight people, you know, hanging out selling dope. And, look, I can just walk up and say, 'Here, man, hold this while I go around here and talk to so and so,' and let them hold the pistol."

"And leave the gun in the house," Perry added.

"Exactly, leave that gun in the house."

"But make sure it's fired," Perry said.

"Oh yeah. Well, look, I can get 'em to fire it."

"What you do is, like, what you do is you think every-thing ahead, every step ahead, every step . . . ," Perry said. "No connection to me or you, see?"

Their conversation soon ended because of a visit from one of Perry's lawyers. When he was certain that Perry had left the area to go to a visitation room, Farris said the fol-lowing into the digital recording device:

"Perry just went to see his lawyer, but I'm gonna leave the tape recorder runnin' 'cause I don't wanna risk cuttin' it off and losin' everything that I've got so far. Also, this, uh, list with all these codes words on it, I wrote it in my writin', but I handed it to him, like two or three different times, to get him to check. Well, just to get his fingerprints on it."

Perry went to sleep that evening after meeting with his lawyer. He had taken some medication that he had ob-tained from the jail's infirmary, which would help him sleep, and therefore could not continue his conversations with Farris until the following morning. They would have approximately two hours to go over their plans again before Farris "made bail."

Early the next morning, after Perry's typical knocking on the wall to get Farris's attention, the two conspirators went over their plans to murder the Levines again, and Perry advised Farris to be careful with e-mail if he used it. He explained to Farris in detail how each computer leaves an Internet service provider (ISP) address that can be traced back to a locale and eventually to a specific computer. Because of this, he advised Farris to use a computer at an Internet café that was not located in Nashville or any-where near Nashville. Perry also revealed the excitement that he was feeling as a result of all the planning that he and Farris had done, and over their future plans together as "partners."

"Here, I'll tell you this," Perry said, "this is going to be fun. You know why?"

"Why?"

"I'm already figuring this. I'm already startin' to get a touch of this. We're gonna be fuckin' outrageous. When we're out, can you imagine the two of us havin' a fuckin' week on the beach to plan something? I'm so juiced for that, it gives me something totally to look forward to. Nate, can I tell you something? I'm telling you right now. That's my job."

"That's your job," Farris repeated.

"It's my . . . I think of this as my career," Perry said.

"Yeah, well, that's gonna be my career, too. You know, Perry, I can't work at McDonald's. . . ."

"I understand."

"You know what I mean."

"You understand our career. I'm not thinking about any-thing else," Perry said. "I'm thinking about my career."

"Well, what a career it'll be, too," Farris said. "I'd say what we'd make, like an average an hour, what a couple of grand an hour or—"

"An hour?"

"Yeah."

"Literally, for an hour of real work . . . we make twenty grand an hour."

"Twenty grand an hour," Farris repeated, laughing.

"Hey, Perry, none of our lawyers or . . . even the Levines make that much an hour."

"Especially when you only got to work two or three hours a month."

Following the discussion about their careers, Perry started in again on the importance of e-mail security, how computers work, and so forth. It was revealing, if not chilling, in that it depicted in his own words just how savvy he really was about the inner workings of a computer. It showed that someone with his knowledge would have little or no difficulty locating and removing a hard drive from the inside of a computer. The fact that Perry wanted to educate Farris on how to effectively delete e-mail from a computer—so that it couldn't be retrieved later—opened the door for Farris to be able to show Perry's father how to eradicate anything incriminating from his own computer when Farris met up with him in Mexico.

"When I take the trip down there," Farris said, "I can actually show him in person how to get rid of it."

"Yeah, while I think he knows how to delete, but it's a little bit more complicated than just wanting to delete," Perry said. "Just let me explain to you about computers. . . The hard disc is a round disc . . . on it, it puts information magnetically. . . . It shoots it and keeps it on there. What a computer does, when it wants to find something, it sends its little optical reader, and it finds that piece of information, and reads it. When you, quote, unquote, delete something from your computer . . . what it does is it takes away the code."

"So, it's still there," Farris said.

"It's still there," Perry agreed. "There's other programs that actually come in and write over it and it will erase it. . . . The difference between . . . what happens is when people delete normally . . . what they do is they force their machine to not be able to find something. . . . And then the machine can write over it again later. You have to scrub it."

"Because some other machine can come in and find it," Farris offered.

"Exactly."

"Okay."

"Hey, can I tell you something?" Perry asked.

"Yeah."

"This is crucial, crucial, for us . . . because a lot of what we're gonna do on our jobs . . . will be e-mail–related."

"In Mexico?" Farris asked. "You talkin' about—"

"Philip Rolfe. Remember that guy Rolfe, he's on his computer all day long with e-mail."

"And that's how we'll communicate with him?" Farris asked.

"Absolutely."

"That way, he never . . . hears a voice or nothing."

"Absolutely. . . . What to do and when to do it, and he'll do it; and then he'll have his little granddaughter back. . . . You see what I'm saying?"

"Yeah, and like . . . how you was explaining to me about the diamonds and stuff like that. I just wanna do that one time at least, too, because I want some diamonds."

"When it happens, you're gonna get on an airplane," Perry explained about the diamonds, a scheme that he had spoken to Farris about after they had first met. "You're going to fly to Amsterdam and you're gonna trade 'em in and put 'em in the bank."

"Do you think that would be safe for me going in to Amsterdam?" Farris asked.

"With a new passport. Can I tell you something? We're gonna totally be low-key . . . big-time . . . remember one thing. Pigs get fat, hogs get slaughtered."

"Pigs get fat, hogs get slaughtered," Farris repeated, laughing. "Huh, we're gonna be a couple of pigs."

"Low-key pigs," Perry corrected. "And for the next thirty days, you need to learn about the Internet . . . and e-mails. You need to look up and learn about Mexico and immigration. You'll see how easy it is. People just go whoring all day long (inaudible) . . . you need to remember . . . once the car gets, uh, sold—"

"Yeah?" Farris asked, laughing.

"They ain't gonna let me out for a long time," Perry said. "They're gonna try to keep me in here as long as they can, until they can figure out . . . The thing you need to know . . . I'm a fuckin' expert in Mexico. . . . I've got lawyers, I've got accounts . . . I speak Spanish. I'm an expert."

"Well, look . . . I pretty much figured that," Farris said. "That's why, like, when we talked, you know, a couple of weeks ago or whatever, we was talkin' about those kidnappings, that's why . . . I was sayin' . . . I would do the footwork and you could handle the other part."

"Oh, we're gonna both handle everything together."

"We're both gonna handle it together," Farris repeated, laughing. "Hey, Perry, the dynamic duo."

When Farris was taken out of the isolation unit a short time later, Perry March thought that he had made bond and had been released. In reality, Russell Nathaniel Farris was taken to a small room at the police station, where he soon began making supervised telephone calls to Arthur March in Mexico. While Perry sat in jail awaiting trial for murder, he believed that his new pal, Farris, would be keeping his promise by committing two additional murders.

Chapter 25

The first telephone call between Russell Nathaniel Farris and Arthur March occurred ahead of schedule on Wednesday, October 12, 2005. Farris was being supervised by Postiglione and Pridemore. He seemed a bit nervous at first, but soon fell right into the conversation as he did what the detectives had instructed him to do. After a few rings, Arthur March answered the telephone. Following is an edited transcript of that conversation:

March: (inaudible)

Farris: Hello? Hello?

March: Hello?

Farris: Is, uh, this the Colonel?

March: Yes.

Farris: Hey, uh, how you doin'? My name's Bobby Givings. Uh, has, uh, Perry March contacted you?

March: Yep.

Farris: Okay, uh . . .

March: Said I'm supposed to talk to you.

Farris: Yeah, uh, I—you know I waited a few days but, uh—well, first of all, uh, the phone I'm on it, it's okay for me to talk, what about the phone that you're on?

March: Uh-huh.

Farris: Okay.

March: I'm all right.

Farris: Okay. Uh, how you been doin'?

March: Well, you know.

Farris: Yeah. Uh . . .

March: It's tough, but it's tougher for him.

Farris: Yeah, I know, man, and I'm, I'm tryin'—I'm tryin' to help him out. Uh, has, has—uh, do you know about our agreement?

March: No, I'm sorry I don't know anything. He just said you'd call and I was supposed to listen and talk.

Farris: Yeah, well, uh, just, uh, what I'm just doin' now basically just, you know makin' contact with you. Uh, you know, 'cause I told him I would. Uh, I need you to . . .

March: Now where are you?

Farris: Okay, I'm, I'm on, uh, I'm actually at, uh, a friend's job of mine on a telemarketer phone. You know, I didn't want to use my home phone or nothin' like that, 'cause I didn't want it to be traced or anything.

March: Okay.

Farris: So . . .

March: Yeah, but you're in the States?

Farris: Oh yeah, yeah, yeah. I'm in Nashville.

March: Okay, well, I didn't know—well, I'm just tryin' to figure out where you are.

Farris: Okay. But, uh, what, uh, what I kinda want you to do is, uh—well, well, first of all just, just to let you know that I'm who I say I am uh, your, your maid's name is Marta, and, uh, uh, Paul's brother is Uncle Mike from East Chicago. Do, do you know what I'm talkin' about there?

March: Yep.

Farris: Okay.

March: Okay, we're on—you're on . . .

Farris: Okay, I'm just, you know—well, uh, what I need you to do is, uh, I want you to tell Perry, uh, however you, you'd get in contact with him that, uh, I've been lookin', I've been lookin' at some BMWs and, uh, I've not found the one that I want to buy, but, uh, you know, I've got my eye on a couple and I'm gettin' close to, to buyin' one. And, uh . . .

March: Okay.

Farris: He'll understand what you're talkin' about there. And uh, uh, I was thinkin' maybe, maybe here soon that I can, you know, somehow come and meet you just so I know, uh . . .

March: Okay, you got—you can also stay with me. I got a three-room house, so you're . . .

Farris: Oh, you—great . . .

March: . . . more than welcome.

Farris: Yeah, well, see that's, that's kind of what I was wantin', you know. You know, I just—I don't know how much you know about what's goin' on, but he did tell me that you was a real stand-up guy and that, uh, you know, I know, I know a little bit about you, and, uh, Perry, he's, he's a real great guy, and, uh, I got a lot of confidence and trust in Perry. And uh . . .

March: Well, how did you two get together? I, I'm, I'm . . .

Farris: Well, I was . . .

March: . . . well just, well just . . .

Farris: I was there, you know, I was—I just—I got out on bond. Perry helped me get out on bond. And, uh . . .

March: Oh. Well, see I didn't know that. Okay.

Farris: Yeah, we, uh, you know, uh, when they first brought Perry there, I—actually, I called, uh, I called, uh, your—I guess it's your, uh, son-in-law, Lee. I called him for him and . . .

March: Okay.

Farris: . . . and you know basically me and Perry, we just got to talkin' over there for—and, uh, I'm out on bond on a murder charge now. And, uh . . .

March: How'd you get out on a murder charge on bond?

Farris: Well, uh, I'm—I fortunately knew this girl. Her daddy owned a trucking company and, uh, Perry helped me, uh, talk to her, you know, convincin' her that I'm gonna marry her and love her, and, you know, just all this old bullshit. But, uh, I'm kinda stuck with her, you know, a little right now. That's why, you know like . . .

March: No, I just say to get—you play the cards the way they're dealt.

Farris: Exactly. And, uh, I'm tryin' to get us a royal flush now, if you know what I mean. But, uh . . .

March: Okay.

Farris: I'm, uh, I'm glad I got to talk to you.

March: Whatever I can do, you just let me know and it'll get done.

Farris: Okay, well, uh, you know, it is a couple of things that, that I'm gonna need a little bit of help with, just because like, like I . . .

March: All right, you just, just . . .

Farris: I don't, I don't want no middle man. I—you know what I'm sayin'? I, I don't, uh—the less people involved . . .

March: I . . .

Farris: . . . is, is, is . . .

March: The less—you just tell me what you want, how you want it done, and it'll get done.

Farris: Okay. Well, uh, well, is—are you sure that it, it's okay to talk on, on this line?

March: As far as I know. We, we had it checked about two weeks ago and it was . . .

Farris: Okay. Well, well, here's, here's . . .

March: But that's—you know, that doesn't mean it's, it's perfectly . . .

Farris: Yeah.

March: . . . safe now. I, I—you know, I'm bein' honest with you.

Farris: Okay, well, see you . . .

March: It should be. It's, uh, I don't think they're onto it, I'm getting a clear signal here.

Farris: Yeah.

March: And there's been no—no indication that it's not clear. And I, I can have it checked again if you want me to.

Farris: Well, well, how, how long would it take you to have it checked? 'Cause I'm in . . .

March: Uh, I can't do it tomorrow because of the religious holidays. I can have it done Friday.

Farris: Friday? Okay, well, I'll tell you what. Uh, you, uh, you, you have that done just, just so that—you know, I'm, I'm just tryin' to, to go over every . . .

March: I understand. Everybody to CYA.

Farris: Yeah. Exactly. And, uh, you, you do that and, uh, we'll talk some more, and, uh, Perry, Perry gave me an e-mail address. It's, it's, it's your e-mail address. Uh, do you think that it would . . .

March: I'll make sure he gave you the right one, 'cause I changed.

Farris: You, you changed?

March: To confuse—but I don't know if it worked. You know what I'm saying?

Farris: Okay, well . . .

March: It's *A-W-M*.

Farris: *A-W* . . .

March: *W-M*.

Farris: Okay.

March: At.

Farris: At.

March: Prodigy, *P-R-O-D-I-G-Y*.

Farris: Okay.

March: Dot net.

Farris: Okay.

March: Dot *MX*.

Farris: Dot *MX*?

March: Yeah, is that the one he gave you, or did he give you the Laguna?

Farris: Uh, he gave me the La—uh, Laguna.

March: Okay, this is the new one, so hopefully they're not—nobody's on this one yet.

Farris: Okay. Uh, and uh, I'll probably—I might— you know, I, I'm—I don't really know nothin' about no computers for one. I've never been on the Internet or whatever.

March: You and me too, I, you know, I'm uh . . .

Farris: I think that's a bunch of bullshit. I, I think they'd be able to trace computer logs easier than they would a phone call. You know what I mean?

March: Probably if they wanted us.

Farris: Yeah. But, uh, is, uh, Carmen doin' okay?

March: Well, yeah, she's, she's holdin' up. It's, it, uh—I'm there as much as I can be.

Farris: Yeah.

March: I'm there every morning.

Farris: Yeah.

March: And I'm trying to leave her a little bit, but she's, she's a tough broad and . . .

Farris: Yeah. Well, I . . .

March: She wants to do it herself.

Farris: Yeah.

March: And I have to stay on the—you know what I'm saying?

Farris: Yeah, I, I know things . . .

March: Do you . . .

Farris: . . . have been hard because of these Levine people, man, and, and, you know, it's time that all this shit is dealt and done with, if, you, you know . . .

March: Oh, well, listen.

Farris: Yeah.

March: You want to hear the latest?

Farris: Yeah, yeah, what's goin' on?

March: This one I'll tell you. You know the—that prosecutor that's after him, you know that one, that . . .

Farris: Uh . . .

March: . . . deputy prosecutor?

Farris: The, the—what, what's his name? Uh, I, I, I, you know, I know, I know . . .

March: I don't know what his name . . .

Farris: Yeah, I don't, either.

March: So, anyway. You know why they haven't had Perry, uh, before this? They tried to get him and they couldn't, and they, they could— 'cause they couldn't get anybody in the, in the, uh, prosecutor's office that would take the case.

Farris: Really?

March: Because they know there's no case.

Farris: Yeah.

March: So what they did, what the Levines did . . .

Farris: Um-hm.

March: . . . this guy was guaranteed, win, lose, draw, whatever.

Farris: Yeah.

March: He, he resigns when it's over and he's got a job on one of the big law firms in Nashville.

Farris: Well, hopefully—hopefully, he's not gonna win this case. If, if—look here, Colonel. If, if, if I've got anything to do with this, and, and right now, look here. I'll, I'll tell you what I've done so far. If, uh, you know, I, I, I know about what time, uh, Lawrence comes out of his house. You know, I know where he takes Zippy [*sic*] and Sammy to school at. And you know I, I've . . .

March: Did he tell you that—I think they're goin' to the school—well, you know, okay.

Farris: Yeah, I, I know exactly where . . .

March: I think it's the University . . .

Farris: Yeah, it's, it's out by Vanderbilt is where it's at.

March: Yeah, that's—it's part of it, it's called the University School.

Farris: Yeah. You know, and, uh, well, it's just like, uh, Monday mornin', uh, I don't know the wife's name, but that's who took 'em Monday mornin'. But, but, uh, Thursday— let's see, okay. No, let's see? It was Monday and Tuesday Lawrence took 'em to school, and then Wednesday, uh, this mornin' was, uh, the wife took 'em to school. So, you know, just, just . . .

March: Okay, they probably won't be goin' tomorrow, so you can lay back.

Farris: Yeah. Well, you know, I'm, I'm . . .

March: 'Cause tomorrow's a high holiday and they'll . . .

Farris: Yeah.

March: . . . that's one of the things they're gonna make sure that they're at the synagogue, because that's one of the things they, they said that we weren't doing here, giving them a good Jewish education, you know.

Farris: Yeah. Well, the—I, I think they're just, they're just full of shit and, you know, uh . . .

March: Well, they're—hey, hey, listen. Uh, this whole thing . . .

Farris: Uh-huh.

March: . . . is set up. They know they ain't got nothin' on Perry.

Farris: I know.

March: But this was sent to get the kids into their clutches.

Farris: Yeah. And that, you know, me and Perry . . .

March: Now are you on a, on a, on a phone, or you want me to call you? Are you having to pay for this?

Farris: Well, well, no. I'm on a—actually, my—I got a buddy who's on probation and, and like he's workin' at the five-star, uh, telecommunications thing out here on Forty-fourth and North Avenue. And, like, this phone that I'm on . . .

March: Oh. Okay, so . . .

Farris: You know, it's callin' all over the world.

March: So, so, you're all . . .

Farris: You know, but, but, like . . .

March: So, you're all right.

Farris: Yeah. And, like, I, I . . .

March: And Perry's been helping you. 'Cause he's good, let me tell you.

Farris: Yeah.

March: When he, when he's not—I don't know how, how steady he is right now because he's a little shook up.

Farris: Yeah, I know he is, and I'm . . .

March: He . . .

Farris: . . . I'm tryin' to help him out, but, uh, you know, it's just—I, I, I just, uh, I just need a couple of things to, to have . . .

March: (inaudible)

Farris: . . . this all wrapped up and that's . . .

March: Well, tell me what you need and I'll take care of it if I can, possibly.

Farris: Okay, well, uh, I, I—basically what, what I need from you and, and it, it might be kind of hard, but, it'd, it'd be the best way, I think, because, uh, I, I need a instrument, if you know what I'm—you know, if you know what I'm talkin' about, because . . .

March: I, I—there's no way I can get an instrument up north.

Farris: Yeah.

March: I'm in the barter . . .

Farris: Yeah.

March: And I . . .

Farris: Well, see, I, I can get one myself. But what that does is that the people I go to get it, you know, that, that, that's gonna leave a trail for me, if you, you know what I mean.

March: Yeah.

Farris: And, and, and . . .

March: The problem is that I'm down here . . .

Farris: Yeah.

March: . . . and I've got instruments . . .

Farris: Uh-huh.

March: But I can't—there's no way I can get 'em up, up, up to you, now I'm, I'm (inaudible). . . .

Farris: Well, like I've, I've got family that lives in Texas. I got a uncle that lives in Freeport, Texas. And like, uh, you know, me and Perry discussed it, you know, if, if everything went as planned that, that, that you know I, I . . .

March: Probably better off to purchase it in Freeport and then get it up there.

Farris: Yeah.

March: That would be the easiest and least traceable.

Farris: Yeah, well, see, like I, you know, I, I've got an uncle there, but you know, I—you know he don't know nothin' about, you know, anything like that. I'm just—you—basically what . . .

March: Well, I mean all he's gotta do—see Texas got pretty good laws there.

Farris: Yeah.

March: And he can walk in and if he's clean . . .

Farris: Um-hm.

March: . . . uh, whether it's, you know, you want the small size or the large economy size.

Farris: Yeah.

March: A large economy size is, uh, probably, uh, because hunting season coming up is probably your best bet.

Farris: Yeah.

March: I would use, uh, say a twelve.

Farris: A twelve?

March: Size twelve.

Farris: Well, well, well, see, I'll tell you where, uh, they're—they're not at home now. They, they're, they're, they're at this, like, condominium place. And, and, and, and it, you know, if, if, if, uh . . .

March: Uh, you mean they're not living on, uh . . .

Farris: They, they're not livin' on Vaughn's (Gap) Road.

March: It's just . . .

Farris: I, I went to Vaughn's (Gap) Road to that house. I went there myself. They're, uh . . .

March: Well, where are they livin'?

Farris: They're, they're livin' in, in . . .

March: See, I don't know. See, I don't know what's goin' on up there. You understand that?

Farris: Yeah. Well, well, see here, here's like— they're, they're doin' some kind of work at, at the house on Vaughn's (Gap) Road. Okay, I don't know what kinda work they're doin'. I think they're, like, redecoratin' the inside. And you know, I see drywall and shit.

March: Probably making room for the kids, because, see, they . . .

Farris: Probably so.

March: Then their kid, who's gay, in case you didn't know.

Farris: Nuh-uh. Oh yeah . . .

March: Yeah, one of these kids . . .

Farris: . . . I thought you were talkin' about their son in Washington or somethin'?

March: Well, he's there with 'em most of the time.

Farris: Okay, well, I, I haven't seen him yet. I haven't . . .

March: Okay. His name is Mark.

Farris: Okay.

March: He works for the only congressman that is gay.

Farris: (laughs)

March: And he's gay.

Farris: Yeah.

March: Now he's also on the side, his lover.

Farris: Really?

March: He's on the—he's on this guy's payroll—or the last my people told me, well, he—that's what he was doin'. I'm . . .

Farris: Okay.

March: Uh, that would be about a month, month and a half ago.

Farris: Okay. Well, uh . . .

March: So, that's—and he's usually with them whenever they make court opin . . . 'pinions and everything else.

Farris: Yeah.

March: 'Cause it's not a real job that he's got.

Farris: Okay.

March: So, watch your back and watch for him, 'cause he's the third party.

Farris: Okay.

March: He's, he's not dangerous.

Farris: Yeah.

March: But he's, he's with 'em.

Farris: Okay.

March: He'll be the guy that's walking to Larry's left, usually carrying some books or a folder.

Farris: Okay. Okay, that's, uh, yeah, that's, that's useful. Okay, uh, Colonel, look here, you, uh, you have that line checked again and I will get in touch with you Friday. And, and . . .

March: Okay. And do you want to give me a number or not?

Farris: Well . . .

March: In case I can get—well, I don't need you, you need me.

Farris: Yeah, yeah exactly.

March: So, okay . . .

Farris: Exactly.

March: . . . let's leave it at that.

Farris: Oh, okay. But I do want you to do one thing. Uh, you know Perry told me that uh, that, sometimes you e-mail your daughter and that she just downloads it and mails him a letter. Just tell Perry . . .

March: Yeah.

Farris: . . . that, uh, Bobby Givings contacted you about, about the BMW.

March: *G-I-B-B-O-N-S?*

Farris: Huh? Bobby.

March: *G-I-B-B* . . .

Farris: No, Givings, Givings. *G-I-V-I-N-G-S.*

March: Wait a minute. *G*—spell it.

Farris: Okay. *G-I-V-I-N-G-S.* First name . . .

March: *N*—Givings.

Farris: Yeah, Givings.

March: *G-I-V-I-N-G-S.*

Farris: Yes, sir.

March: Bobby.

Farris: Yeah, Bobby Givings.

March: I got it.

Farris: Okay, and just, just—that's just to let him know that, you know, things is goin' like they're supposed to go. And, um . . .

March: Well, I hope she'll have it tomorrow morning.

Farris: Okay.

March: I don't know how long it takes her to get things to . . .

Farris: Okay. And, uh . . .

March: . . . Perry, but it'll—this will be outta here tonight.

Farris: Okay, I'll be in touch with you Friday, Colonel. All right?

March: And I'll, and I'll, uh, take care of what I can at this end.

Farris: Okay, okay. Thank you.

March: Okay.

Farris: All right.

March: Thanks for calling.

Farris: Oh, no problem.

March: Bye-bye.

Farris: Bye.

[End of phone call]

Chapter 26

Two days later, on Friday, October 14, 2005, the second planned telephone call between Nate Farris and Arthur March occurred from the same jail facility. Obviously, the previously agreed upon jailhouse schedule had been accelerated. As with the first call, Pridemore and Postiglione were present. Postiglione provided a brief recorded statement prior to Farris placing the call. Following is an amended transcript of the lengthy call:

POSTIGLIONE: . . . thousand and five. The following is gonna be a telephone conversation between Russell Nathaniel Farris, also known as Bobby Givings. Uh, the time now is approximately four fifty-three P.M. The phone number dialed from the Criminal Justice Center is gonna be dialed to Mexico. Uh, this is be—uh, being done with the knowledge and cooperation of Russell Nathaniel Farris, he's a male, white. I'm Sergeant Pat Postiglione. Also present during this recorded conversation is going to be Detective Bill Pridemore, Assistant District Attorney, uh, Tom Thurman [*sic*], and

Assistant District Attorney Katie Miller. Also being contacted at the number given is gonna be Arthur March. This is a follow-up to the conversation that occurred on October twelfth, at approximately seventeen forty-five hours. This is gonna be second phone call made to the number that I've just given.

March: *Bueno.*

Farris: Hey. Hey, Colonel?

March: Hi.

Farris: Hey, this is Bobby, how you doin'?

March: Oh, fine. Everything's clear at this end.

Farris: It, it is? Great.

March: Yep.

Farris: Okay, uh, let me, let me go over . . .

March: Always be careful, though.

Farris: Yeah, exactly. Well I'm . . .

March: My guy said that, that he does not know of anybody that's got something here good. You understand?

Farris: Yeah.

March: He checked and he said that nothing.

Farris: Yeah. I checked about my uncle, too, and he, he was arrested for marijuana charges down there in Texas, so, you know, he can't do nothin' for me, either. But, uh . . .

March: Yeah, well, you know it's, it's got all of us that do things have problems.

Farris: Yeah. Well, uh, I've got a guy here that I can, you know, that I can get an instrument from, but, you know, it's just that, uh, you know, I want as less people involved as possible.

March: Your best bet, from my experience, is the black area of anywhere that you would look would be any for the—the cost is lower and the ability is cheaper.

Farris: Yeah.

March: But I would go to the black areas. And I'm sure you have some friends . . .

Farris: Yeah, I, I you know.

March: . . . or some, it, it's . . .

Farris: I've, you know, I can . . .

March: That's where I would go.

Farris: Yeah. Well, I mean, I could leave right now and go do that. It's just—it, it's a matter of people knowin'. You understand what I'm sayin'?

March: Yeah, but I mean there—the problem there is they don't know and you can, uh, with them it's an everyday sale.

Farris: Yeah, well, well, well, see . . .

March: Okay?

Farris: . . . here, here's what I kind of, you know, I was thinkin' that maybe if I did have to go that route, what I was gonna do is, uh, whenever I bought the gun, I was gonna try to get me a silencer, too. Because the way I'm gonna do this, you know, it's gonna have to be quick and quiet.

March: Well, I don't know how you plan to do it.

Farris: Yeah. But, uh . . .

March: But, uh, that, that'll be—that'll be more ex—that'll increase the cost . . .

Farris: Um-hm.

March: . . . and the, uh, the total operation by at least fifty percent.

Farris: Yeah. What, uh . . .

March: But I'm being honest with you.

Farris: Here's somethin' I wanted to tell you. Like, uh, if, uh, you know I was thinkin', you know, that you know, I, I probably will have to just locate one up here myself. But what I was gonna do, and, uh, I was gonna let a couple of people handle it. You know what I mean? And that way . . .

March: Yep.

Farris: And that way, you know . . .

March: If you go through se-several hands before it gets to you.

Farris: Yeah.

March: . . . that's a good way.

Farris: Yeah. And, you know, then, you know, of course I'm gonna have gloves on, and, you know, my fingerprints won't be on nothin'.

March: Yeah.

Farris: And, uh, you know . . .

March: Make sure that you, when you clean it . . .

Farris: Yeah, well, well, well, see this . . .

March: . . . you got your gloves.

Farris: . . . this is some of the stuff that I wanted to speak to you about. Because, I mean, Perry told me, you know, that you know, about your military background and, and, you know.

March: Okay, I, you know, I did Special Force time and . . .

Farris: Yeah.

March: . . . uh . . .

Farris: He's, he's told me . . .

March: . . . so . . .

Farris: . . . you know, a little, little bit about you, but, uh . . .

March: My suggestion is from the minute the product is got . . .

Farris: Um-hm.

March: . . . you wear thin surgeon's gloves.

Farris: Yeah. Okay, uh . . .

March: You do not take them off at all.

Farris: Okay, well, look, I want to run somethin' else by you. And, and . . .

March: Okay.

Farris: . . . and, I mean, I, I know that my end's clear, you said that yours is, too, so I'm pretty— I feel pretty good about this. Okay, uh, the, uh—Lawrence's wife, what I found out she does sometimes, it's not every time, but I mean the weather's been pretty good up here. When she comes back from, from takin' the kids to school, like this apartment—these condos that she's stayin' at, she, uh, she kinda walks around some. You know, like gettin' some exercise.

March: Uh-huh.

Farris: And, uh, like there's a lot of people joggin' out in this area. And, like, what I thought about doin' is, uh, I can get a car from a buddy of mine. And, you know, of course he don't know, you know, what I would do with it. And, uh, I found another car that's kind of similar to it and I was gonna switch the tags on the car.

March: That's—I was gonna say that's the first thing you do.

Farris: Yeah, okay. Then I was gonna . . .

March: And you have at least—my suggestion is three sets.

Farris: Yeah.

March: What it came with . . .

Farris: Uh-huh.

March: . . . one you use, and one you return it to.

Farris: Yeah, yeah, okay, and here's, you know, I've got a couple of joggin' suits with the hoods on 'em. And what I, you know, there's another apartment complex about six blocks

away from where they're stayin'. And I was
gonna maybe park the car there and just, you
know, kinda jog around the neighborhood,
you know, to, you know, and, uh . . .

March: Either, either that or park one and use a different one.

Farris: Yeah, I thought about that, too . . .

March: And then . . .

Farris: . . . but, but you know, for me to do that I
would have to, you know, somebody else
would have to take me to one of the drops
and I don't want to do that. But . . .

March: No, you don't have to do it that way. What
you do is you predrop one.

Farris: Okay.

March: And then at a later point, use the second
one . . .

Farris: Um-hm.

March: . . . or even a third . . .

Farris: Yeah.

March: . . . depending on—that, that's the easiest
piece of equipment you should be able to
come by with.

Farris: Yeah, that's, yeah, that's no problem. But,
uh . . .

March: And what I would do is use one, drop it
immediately, pick up the second one and if
(inaudible) even the third.

Farris: Yeah.

March: But that's the way I—I mean, I'm just giving you some advice.

Farris: Okay, well here's, here's, uh, here's somethin' else I wanted to run by you. Okay, when uh, when, everything's said and done, you know, I don't plan on leavin' right then. You know, I'm gonna lay back a little bit. You know I don't, I don't want 'em to . . .

March: Okay.

Farris: And, uh, but, but . . .

March: But you've always got a place here . . .

Farris: Okay.

March: . . . to relax.

Farris: Okay, well this, this is what I'm gettin' at. Uh, uh, how am I . . .

March: You can bring your friend with you.

Farris: No, I don't, I don't—I'm not bringin' nobody. The only pers—the only thing that I would bring with me would be my dog. You know I . . .

March: Okay. Well I got a Doberman, what do you got?

Farris: I got a pit bull.

March: Well, we can handle that, I've got a big yard.

Farris: Yeah. Okay, but here, here's somethin', too. Like, uh, you know, I've never been to Mexico and, uh, I mean, you know like, like . . .

March: Once you get here—once you get here, you got no problem.

Farris: Okay, well, well . . .

March: I handle everything.

Farris: Well, well see, I thought about, uh, takin' a
           bus there. Because I don't want to drive no
           car. But like . . .

March: Okay.

Farris: Where, where, where . . .

March: So, you get . . .

Farris: What, what . . .

March: You, you get a bus.

Farris: Uh-huh.

March: And you, and what you do is you just get it
           to Guadalajara.

Farris: I take—I can take a bus from Nashville to
           Guadalajara?

March: No, you have to change at the border.

Farris: Okay, I mean . . .

March: What you do is you walk across the border to
           the bus station. Anybody will show you
           where the bus station is.

Farris: Okay.

March: Get on a superbus—what they call a superbus.

Farris: Superbus?

March: And just sit there. It's a won—nice trip
           down, it's about, uh—the bus will take you
           twelve hours and it's got a TV, johns, every-
           thing. Don't worry about it.

Farris: Okay.

March: Don't use—if you can, bring it either in cash . . .

Farris: Yeah.

March: . . . or in a card that you, that cannot be traced to you.

Farris: Yeah, well, yeah, well, I'm, you know, of course, you know. Well, uh, here's something, too . . .

March: I mean, it should be made out to Mickey Mouse or Donald Duck . . .

Farris: Yeah, well . . .

March: . . . or something.

Farris: Well, uh, you know, I'm gonna have to get my instrument up here. It's probably gonna cost me just a little more than I figured.

March: All right, well, I can give you the cost of covering it and going here.

Farris: Yeah.

March: From the border on. I can't give you, uh, to there, okay, because I haven't been up there and I've been—I'm not an expert.

Farris: Okay.

March: Once you get to here, all you do to stay, if you include with me . . .

Farris: Uh-huh.

March: . . . you can do it for less than one, one K.

Farris: Okay.

March: And be here at least two to three weeks.

Farris: Yeah.

March: Now, if you want to bring that partner that, you know, helped you get out of whatever it was . . .

Farris: Yeah.

March: . . . you told me, perfectly all right. And you're an old friend and that'll be taken care [of].

Farris: Okay.

March: And uh, the only difference that that makes, it gives you cover.

Farris: Uh-huh.

March: But it doesn't allow you to play with, uh, the Mexes.

Farris: Yeah. Well, you know, Perry told me, you know, that that's one of the key things down there is not to fuck with the Mexicans down there.

March: All right, okay bring your own.

Farris: Uh-huh.

March: If the one we, you know, we talked about the last time . . .

Farris: Okay.

March: And you know, if she's willing, she also acts as a cover.

Farris: Okay.

March: Down here then, my people and I, we'll handle everything. Once you get onto that bus and get to Guadalajara . . .

Farris: Um-hm.

March: . . . you have my phone number.

Farris: Yeah.

March: I'll be there in—it'll take me from my—where I am right now to where you're gonna be, all you do is give me the name of the bus and I'll be there within forty-five minutes.

Farris: Okay. Well, uh, now I'm, I'm gonna have to—you know, there's still a few things that I'm gonna have to take care of.

March: I know. I don't want to know everything.

Farris: But I—uh, okay. You know, but, uh, I might, I might need some, uh, just a little bit of funds. And, and the reason why . . .

March: Well, uh, if you do that, try to do it—or after the—try to do it the last day of the month or one of the first three days.

Farris: Okay.

March: Up to that, I can help.

Farris: Okay, because we . . .

March: Always equip . . .

Farris: Because what I'm . . .

March: 'Cause the end of the month is a difficult time . . .

Farris: Okay.

March: . . . for me.

Farris: Okay. Because . . .

March: I live on an army pension and I (inaudible) get paid.

Farris: Well, I mean, you know, I wouldn't need, you know, not much at all just—because, like, you know, I'm gonna have to leave . . .

March: I can handle you and the friend. You understand?

Farris: Oh, okay, yeah, yeah, yeah. Well, look, I'll . . .

March: If you try to pull . . .

Farris: Do, do, uh, you got a pen?

March: Try to plan it that—to get here either in the last week or the first week or second week of the month. It—for me, it makes it easier 'cause I'm . . .

Farris: Yeah.

March: . . . I'm under control. You understand?

Farris: Yeah. Well, uh, you know, 'cause when I leave here, I'm gonna leave, you know, I'm gonna have to leave my momma with funds that I have, because, you know, my mom, she . . .

March: Okay, you're not gonna bring momma with you.

Farris: No, no, not at first. But, I mean, later on, maybe, because, like, uh . . .

March: Well, think about using momma as a cover.

Farris: Well I, I . . .

March: Because it's not expensive to have momma with you.

Farris: Okay, well, see, I don't want to involve my mom in any of this at first.

March: I don't, you know, I'm not talking [about] your real mom.

Farris: Okay.

March: I'm talkin' about the one that's got the hots.

Farris: (laughs) Okay, you . . .

March: No, no, I'm telling you she makes a good cover . . .

Farris: Uh-huh.

March: . . . because most people, and, uh, you know, you can send her back.

Farris: Yeah.

March: And you know, totally—explain to her you're gonna be here for a while or what—I'm not tellin' you what to do but . . .

Farris: Yeah.

March: Uh, do not overlook . . .

Farris: Well, I mean I, you know, any advice you give me is welcome because . . .

March: Well, my advice is consider—and you know the—you know who, who would—you—what we're talkin' about.

Farris: Uh-huh.

March: And you know better than I do and, uh, you gotta know—if you need—if you think you need cover, they're the best. Because you're with—and you're not messing with the Mexican.

Farris: Yeah.

March: You understand?

Farris: Yeah.

March: And, uh, I can handle it once either you—alone or with . . .

Farris: Okay.

March: . . . in, and you'll arrive here. You're in my custody and don't worry about it.

Farris: Yeah. Okay, well, um, you know, it's a few things I'm gonna have to check on, but, uh, I've got me a PO box under this Bobby Givings name. And, uh . . .

March: Okay.

Farris: . . . I'm gonna give you the PO box number. Uh, do you got a pen?

March: No, I'll go—I have to go in the other room. Hold on a minute.

Farris: Okay, okay.

March: And I'll be right back.

Farris: Okay. (long pause)

Chapter 27

A couple of minutes later, Arthur March returned from one of the other rooms in his house with the pen that he needed to write down Farris's, aka Bobby Givings's, information. Arthur then gave his mail address to Farris, too. From the way that the conversation was going, the detectives, as well as Tom Thurman, could see that Arthur March had swallowed the deception hook, line, and sinker. They would soon be realizing the fruits of their labor in a case that had taken nearly ten years to clear. Because of all the familial elements involved on both sides, the story seemed almost Shakespearean with its plots, egos, and complexities.

Farris: Well, uh, I guess I'll get back in contact with you, and, uh, maybe next week sometime, just to let you . . .

March: Whenever you need me. You know this time or a little later. I'm always here after seven.

Farris: Okay, after seven. 'Cause I'm gonna have to go—I'm gonna have to get . . .

March: And I'm here from seven at night to six-thirty in the morning.

Farris: Okay.

March: I leave the house at six thirty-five . . .

Farris: Okay.

March: . . . or six-forty.

Farris: 'Cause I'm gonna have to go and, uh, I'm gonna have to get started on gettin' this instrument. And, I hope I'm gonna be able to get me a silencer, 'cause I want everything to be as quiet as possible.

March: Well, you know, I . . .

Farris: You know.

March: I'm not tellin' you how to do your job.

Farris: Okay.

March: I'm your support and you've got—you're covered. Your ass—your ass is covered.

Farris: Okay. And, uh, what, uh—you know, I'm gonna keep up with this surveillance, and, uh, you know, I'm gonna find the best route possible. And what I want to do is, I'm gonna run it by you before I, you know, actually do it, just to get your . . .

March: Okay. The best way is to get to either Laredo . . .

Farris: Uh-huh.

March: . . . or that's the way I would come.

Farris: Okay.

March: I would go to San Antonio.

Farris: Yeah.

March: San Antonio to either Laredo or Brownsville, and then get to Guadalajara.

Farris: Okay.

March: If you go to Laredo or New Laredo, and you can walk across the border.

Farris: Yeah.

March: Uh, there'll be no sign of you leaving. You'll need—do you have a passport or some (inaudible)?

Farris: No, I don't have—I've never been out of the country. You know, I've . . .

March: All right, you need then, uh, either a driver's license or a birth certificate to get across.

Farris: Well, yeah, me and Perry, we discussed that part, and, uh . . .

March: Okay, well, he knows that as well as I do.

Farris: He's good. Perry's real good. But, he's told me that, you know, you was real good yourself. And, uh . . .

March: Well, I'm just old.

Farris: . . . you know it's, well . . .

March: And not as quick as I used to be, you understand?

Farris: No, not necessarily.

March: I'm seventy-eight, but I'm about in the physical shape of, uh, I would say fifty-five or sixty.

Farris: Probably me too.

March: (laughs)

Farris: But, uh, I'll, uh, you know, I'm really . . .

March: And I'm—once, once you get here . . .

Farris: Uh-huh.

March: And I can almost say once you get across the border and on that bus . . .

Farris: Uh-huh.

March: Uh, you're, you're in good shape. Just keep the little wife, you understand?

Farris: Yeah. I'm, I'm . . .

March: And if you bring her . . .

Farris: I'm lookin' forward to—I'm lookin' forward to comin' (inaudible).

March: You're here and you're covered.

Farris: Yeah. That, that, that's . . .

March: I got a three-bedroom house. You'll, you know, just be an old friend.

Farris: Well, you know, me and Perry, we talked about, you know, goin' into business, too, you know, once he's out. And, uh . . .

March: Well, once he's out, he probably could use you real well. We can . . .

Farris: Yeah.

March: You know, we'll—by bein' here with me, and from that point on . . .

Farris: Yeah.

March: . . . you know, you'll make your own decision.

Farris: Well, yeah, he, uh . . .

March: But, uh, you know, we, we can work you into the community.

Farris: But, uh, you know, I'm—this is, this is my shot of, of gettin' rid of my troubles, too, if you understand what I'm sayin'.

March: Okay, well, once you get across that border, we just have to—Perry'll tell you the best way to do, once you get to the border . . .

Farris: Yeah.

March: . . . how to get across . . .

Farris: How, how, how will . . .

March: . . . what you do.

Farris: How is Perry doin'? Is he okay?

March: Well, I talked to him today, he sounded a lot better.

Farris: Yeah.

March: Uh, and, uh . . .

Farris: But he, he does know that me and you've made contact, right?

March: Oh yeah.

Farris: Good.

March: Yeah, I talked to him this morning.

Farris: Good, I'm . . .

March: Talked to him at ten-thirty, to be exact.

Farris: Yeah, good.

March: Carmen and I talked to him, you know.

Farris: How's Carmen?

March: But I only, I only let him know that I had contact—that we had had contact.

Farris: Well, good. He—that, that's all you needed to let him know. He's . . .

March: That's right. And then, uh, you follow his instructions.

Farris: Uh-huh.

March: Because he's a lot smarter than I am. And I hate to admit it.

Farris: Yeah, well, I mean he, you know, he told me that, you know, if I had, you know, some problems with anything, that I could contact you and, you know, that, you know, he told me that, you know, first of all, he said the Colonel is a stand-up guy.

March: And I work for the Mexican Army, so I have some (inaudible).

Farris: Well, good. You know, that makes me feel better, too.

March: I've been workin' for 'em for twelve years, so.

Farris: Yeah. What uh . . .

March: See, the cover is there, once you get here.

Farris: Uh-huh. It's a—I heard there's a lot of good women down there and stuff?

March: No problems. I got more doctors than I know what to do with, because that's what I do for a livin'.

Farris: Really?

March: Yeah . . . you're bringin' dogs across.

Farris: Is the Doberman's name Onie?

March: Yeah.

Farris: (laughs) Okay.

March: Uh, if you bring a dog across, make sure you get the papers before you get to Mexico.

Farris: Oh, yeah, well, I have her papers. I have her papers.

March: Okay, make sure then that Perry says they're the right ones.

Farris: Okay. Uh, when do you think you'll hear from Perry again?

March: On Tuesday, ten-thirty in the morning.

Farris: Okay, well, if I haven't talked to you by then, just tell him that, uh . . .

March: That I'll hear from you sometime next week.

Farris: Yeah, and that, uh, that I've found the car that I wanted. And, uh, I'll probably be purchasin' it here soon.

March: Okay, you gonna take one or two out?

Farris: Excuse me?

March: Just one or the two?

Farris: Two. It's got to be two.

March: Okay. Okay.

Farris: Yeah. I'm not gonna . . .

March: You know, always watch for that kid.

Farris: Yeah. Well, well, well, see, I'm gonna—you know the thing about doin' that is, is, actually, I'm gonna have to do one at a time, but . . .

March: Yeah, that's right.

Farris: But, see I, I . . .

March: It's an abso . . . that's your best bet.

Farris: Yeah.

March: And the best time—I don't know his schedule now, 'cause it's been a long time earlier.

Farris: Well, I'm keepin' up with that.

March: 'Cause he's usually up and around real early.

Farris: Yeah, well, about seven-thirty.

March: But I don't know what they're doin' with the kids. You know, I know they're not . . .

Farris: Okay, well, they're takin' the kids to school every morning. And it's . . .

March: Well, that's—I think if they do that . . .

Farris: You know, it's, uh . . .

March: Uh, uh, you'd have to probably make it after that. They're . . .

Farris: Oh yeah, of course. Well, see, I'm gonna tell you this real quick before we go. What I planned on doin' is like the little joggin' thing I was tellin' you about? Uh . . .

March: Yeah.

Farris: I was just, you know, like two times this week, uh, the wife—I'm not, I don't even know her name. She . . .

March: Carolyn.

Farris: Okay, when, when she's . . .

March: Carolyn. She's the smart one.

Farris: Okay, well, I'm gonna—well, you know, she's not too smart, because what she does when she comes back, she walks around this place. And see what I'm . . .

March: Well, she doesn't—she thinks there is nobody gonna touch her.

Farris: Well, she's wrong.

March: And she has a built-in protection. Now, you should know that. Perry can explain it to you.

Farris: Uh-huh.

March: It's called the Jewish Mafia.

Farris: Yeah, well . . .

March: And she's the queen.

Farris: Well, I'm gonna tell you that, you know, they're dealin' with a little bit of power their-self. And, uh . . .

March: I know, but you have to understand . . .

Farris: Yeah.

March: They are very self-secure.

Farris: Uh-huh.

March: Because they, they do—they've got money.

Farris: Uh-huh.

March: They use it. And they only got one thing. They want those kids.

Farris: Yeah, well.

March: They could care less about Perry.

Farris: That's not gonna happen. They, they're, they might've won this little battle, but they're not gonna win this war. And, uh . . .

March: Well, we're excited to work on getting the kids and we'll start . . .

Farris: Well, that, that . . .

March: . . . by Tuesday.

Farris: Uh-huh.

March: Those (inaudible), the legalwise realization of getting my kids back is, uh, will be full-blown.

Farris: Okay, good. But, uh, but what I'm . . .

March: All right?

Farris: Okay, but what I was gonna say is that, uh, I'm just basically gonna force her in the house and, uh, I'm gonna, you know, do her there and I'm gonna wait on Mr. Lawrence to come back. And I'm actually gonna look him in the eye. You know.

March: Well, I don't know if he—once he gets out of the house, I mean, I don't know his schedule.

Farris: Yeah. Well, well, I don't, I don't know (inaudible).

March: (inaudible)

Farris: Well, see, I do know this. He's not workin' too much at his office. He's stayin' at this apartment a lot. But he does come and go. But I, you know, I'm not just . . .

March: I can't tell you because . . .

Farris: Yeah.

March: When I knew him and when I was with, uh, with him, he—around the house, and once it's morning, he worked at that house.

Farris: Yeah.

March: And he usually goes to Knoxville . . .

Farris: Um-hm.

March: . . . uh, once a week. Uh, to my knowledge, he's supposed to have some lady over there.

Farris: Yeah.

March: But I never followed it up, I mean, I never . . .

Farris: Yeah, well, I'm . . .

March: It wasn't my business.

Farris: You know, I'm not stickin' around too much, 'cause I don't want to get noticed out that way. But I mean . . .

March: Yeah. No, no, you're right. We're, we're . . .

Farris: So far, so good.

March: Now what they're—they got the kids in the condo with 'em?

Farris: Yeah. Yeah, the kids are stayin' there. Well, well, like, there's, uh, I think it's some type of community center, maybe, that they take the kids to a lot after school. And, and like . . .

March: See, I don't—is that the Jewish Community Center?

Farris: I—maybe so. I'm, I'm, you know, I, I don't . . .

March: Just check around. It's near . . .

Farris: Yeah.

March: It's near the—where their house used to be. It's within . . .

Farris: Yeah. Well, their house . . .

March: . . . eight or ten blocks.

Farris: There's some kinda work goin' on there, and,

uh, I know that Lawrence goes there once a day at least to, to, you know, I guess supervise what's goin' on. And I don't know, I don't know how much longer . . .

March: (inaudible)

Farris: . . . that this is gonna be goin' on, but, you know, they . . .

March: You know, I don't know.

Farris: He does have a pattern.

March: But keep your eye on your back.

Farris: Yes, sir.

March: Watch for the kid.

Farris: Yes, sir. Yeah.

March: Don't—I mean, he's a nothin'.

Farris: Uh-huh.

March: He's gay and he's never gonna bother you.

Farris: Yeah.

March: But he's there.

Farris: Okay. I, well, I still haven't seen him. I, you know, I've done a little bit of . . .

March: Make sure you reconnoiter, you know, the . . .

Farris: Yeah. Well, I've, I've . . .

March: . . . the opposition well.

Farris: I've done a little bit of checkin' since the last time I talked to you about this guy. And, uh, you know, I haven't been able to see a picture of him or nothin' like that, but I do know that he works out of someplace in Washington. You know.

March: That's the kid.

Farris: Yeah, yeah.

March: Yeah, he works for a congressman who's gay and he's [his] semi-lover.

Farris: (laughs)

March: You know they switch back and forth.

Farris: Yeah.

March: And I don't know what he's got in Nashville. It's been a long time.

Farris: Well, you know, hopefully he won't have (inaudible).

March: But he flits in and out. When they go to court, he's usually . . .

Farris: Okay.

March: . . . usually with . . .

Farris: Do you have any idea of when they go to court again?

March: Well, the next court date that I know of is the seventeenth.

Farris: Of this month?

March: But you'd have to check that with—no, November.

Farris: Okay, November. I, well—this should be done by then. You know.

March: Okay, but Perry can give you more of a schedule on that, 'cause I don't know exactly what's goin' on there.

Farris: Well, see, I've not had no contact with Perry since I've been out. And you know, I don't want no direct contact with him, because I don't want no trail leadin' me . . .

March: Okay.

Farris: . . . to him or anything like that. But, if somehow you could—you know, I—he's told me about, you know, you and him have little codes and stuff like that. If somehow you can get me just a little bit of information from him, you know, you know that, that . . .

March: Okay, what, what—when you get your plan worked out, then you go over any information you need, I'll see that I can get it to him.

Farris: Okay, great. Well, I'm gonna start workin' on this ASAP, and, uh, I'll be in contact with you.

March: Okay. And enjoy your freedom.

Farris: Yes, sir. I'll be in contact with you early next week.

March: Okay.

Farris: Okay, Colonel.

March: Good luck.

Farris: You too.

March: Good luck.

Farris: Okay, thank you.

Chapter 28

If Arthur March had not implicated himself in the conspiracy concocted by his son to murder the Levines in the first two telephone conversations with Farris through innuendo and direct statements, he certainly would during the course of the next three calls from the supposed hit man. Farris called him again under the same controlled conditions from the Criminal Justice Center in Nashville, on Thursday, October 20, 2005, with Postiglione and Pridemore overseeing the planned deception. After three or four rings, Arthur March answered the phone.

"Bueno," March said.

"Hey, Colonel?" Farris responded.

"Yeah."

"Hey, how you doin'? This is . . . Bobby."

"Oh, hi, Bob."

"How's everything goin'?"

"Well, so far as I know," Arthur trailed off. "How's it goin' on your end?"

"Everything's pretty much a go here. . . . Have you talked to Perry?"

"Yeah, I talked to him day before yesterday."

"Did you give him my message?"

"That I had talked to you? Yes."

"Is he okay with that?"

"Yeah."

"Good. Is . . . he doin' okay?"

"He seems to be. Seems to be up a little bit better and his lawyers keep tellin' him, I think they're giving him a lot of courage and . . ."

"Yeah."

"They don't have anything, so . . . it's just a matter of whatever. . . . How'd you do at your end?"

There was buzzing, an interference of some kind on the line, that interrupted their conversation for a moment or two.

"I've got me an instrument," Farris said when the telephone line cleared up. "I got me a silencer, too."

"Okay."

"Well, you know, the gun, it didn't cost much," Farris said. "The silencer cost me a little bit, but that's okay. . . ."

"Well, by the time you get down here, I'll be able to help you out a little financially," Arthur said.

"Yeah, well, I've done a little bit more surveillance and I'm about ready to do this."

"Okay," Arthur replied. "Just let me know when you get to Texas or when you get someplace on the bus."

"Oh, well . . ."

"You want a bus?"

"Well, see, I've checked on that, too, and, uh, like a Greyhound from Nashville to Laredo is like a hundred twenty-one bucks for the ticket. . . . Then I'd have to get on another bus from Laredo and go to Guadalajara."

"Once you get here, I can help you," Arthur said. "You understand?"

"Yeah . . . only thing I'm havin' a concern with is that when I get there . . . to Laredo . . . I'm kinda nervous about crossin' that border by myself."

"Well, you shouldn't have any trouble," Arthur assured him. "If you got, uh, either a passport or have a birth certificate."

"Yeah, well . . . I'm gonna get, you know, some old bogus-ass birth certificate."

"Okay. That's all you need . . . and you won't have any trouble. Just tell 'em you're a tourist goin' down to visit a friend in Ajijic."

"There ain't no way that . . . like maybe you or Carmen could meet me at the border or somethin'?" Farris asked.

"I don't think that would be a good idea, because I can't leave Carmen alone, that's my problem."

"Uh-huh."

"And I think if you just walk through . . . after you get off the bus, you just walk across the border . . . and get on the bus."

"Just get on the bus," Farris repeated.

"It's no problem," Arthur said. "They speak English, so don't worry about it. . . . You're gonna go to Guadalajara. Get on the evening bus so you can sleep on it overnight. . . . They're good buses, they got johns, everything on 'em."

"Yeah, well . . . the people I talked to at the bus station up here said it'd take like a day to get to Laredo."

"It's a twelve-to-fourteen-hour [bus ride] from Laredo to here."

"Well, I'll be comin' by myself, too."

"All you gotta do is get here. . . . You can call me from someplace in Mexico, at a bus stop, or you can call me when you get to Guadalajara and I'll be there at the bus station in thirty minutes."

"Thirty minutes? Okay. When would be a good time to call you . . . when I get to the bus station down there? Just anytime?"

"Anytime, like now. Anytime in the evening. I'm always home."

"I tried to call earlier, about five-thirty, maybe, and I didn't get—"

"I was at the restaurant, but normally I would be home. I'm always home at this time."

"Yeah."

"Well, good luck."

"I guess so . . . I guess everything . . ."

"Just call me . . . You can call me from the States, too, you know, and let me know . . . when you expect—and then I'll be lookin' for you."

"Yeah. Well . . . there's a couple things I want to go over with you, just to run by you . . . get your opinion about it. . . ."

"Yeah."

"Okay . . . what I plan on doin' is that . . . I've surveillanced everything and I pretty much know the routine. But it's just like some days it's the wife that . . . comes out and some days it's Lawrence."

"Yeah."

"But, see, Lawrence has been goin' to his office, you know, pretty much regularly this past week—"

"Okay, and watch. . . . Keep an eye out for the kid."

"I haven't seen the kid at all," Farris said.

"Well, he may be in Washington," Arthur said.

"I've already got a car parked . . . and I'm gonna leave . . . the car, leave my other car—"

"So will it be next week or the week after?" Arthur asked. "Is that what you're plannin'?"

"Yeah, I was tempted to do it earlier, today, but . . . it's a whole lot of traffic. . . . I want to do it maybe like on a Tuesday, or a Wednesday."

"That's fine," Arthur said. "That would be next Tuesday or Wednesday?"

"Yeah."

"That'd bring you in here . . . ," Arthur said, apparently thinking aloud as he trailed off. "And that's fine . . . see I get my money on the first, so we're, we're in hallelujah land."

"Yeah."

The voice of an operator suddenly came on the line.

"Somebody's on this line with us," Arthur said.

"Huh? Hello?" Farris asked.

"I think somebody's on this line. Did you hear that?"

"I'm gonna call you back, okay? Hello? Colonel?"

The line went dead, and Farris dialed Arthur's number again.

"What the hell was goin' on?" Farris asked.

"Well, we got cut off, and then you got caught up in the Mexican telephone system," Arthur said.

"I know it sounded somethin' like an operator," Farris said. "I didn't know what the hell it was in here."

"You'll get used to it . . . after you're here a week or so."

"It kinda spooked me a little bit," Farris said.

"It's not a bad system," Arthur explained about the Mexican telephone company. "It's just not good."

"Yeah . . . it kinda spooked me for a second . . . at first . . ."

"Now, now, don't worry about it. We were all right."

"Okay. Well, good . . . my heart was kinda racin', I didn't know what to—"

"No, no, no . . . just relax," Arthur said. "Everything else okay? Are the kids okay? Have you seen them?"

"I've seen 'em twice this week," Farris said. "You know, just . . . getting out of the car."

"They're still livin' . . . in that condo?"

"Yeah, they're livin' in a condo."

"At Hillmeade or someplace like that?"

"Yeah. It's not that far from the house. . . . It's pretty nice, actually. . . . What I was plannin' to do . . . just like I told you, I got me a silencer for my gun. But, uh, I'm . . . gonna try to catch the—hopefully, Lawrence—Lawrence will be gone to the office whenever she gets back. Sometimes she gets—"

An operator cut into the line again, and seemed to be attempting to put other calls through. Because of the interference from the operator, Arthur told Farris to call him back in three or four days.

"Okay, Colonel, I'll talk to you."

"And you'll know better [by then] what you're gonna do."

They were cut off again, but Farris called Arthur back to finish the conversation.

"Hey, Colonel? Damn, it's hard to hear you. I'm probably not gonna be able to use this phone again once I leave here tonight. . . . Probably the next time you hear from me, all this'll be said and done."

"Okay, I can hardly hear you," Arthur said.

"Yeah, I can hardly hear you, too."

"Give me a call tomorrow, okay?"

"Okay."

"'Cause I can't understand you."

"Okay," Farris said.

"Bye."

When the telephone call ended Farris, still in police custody, was taken back to the secret location where he was being held to await further instructions from Postiglione and Pridemore. To make the plan work, it was imperative that Perry believe that Farris was on the outside. If Perry got word from another inmate, or even a jailer, that Farris was still in jail, the game would be over.

While the telephone calls between Arthur and Farris had been going on, Perry languished in his jail cell, totally oblivious to the trap that was being set, and into which his father had leaped headfirst, from where there would be no returning. What seemed particularly amazing to many people at this point was Perry's unconscionable eagerness in getting his seventy-eight-year-old father, who was in ill health and who, he knew, would not turn him down in his quest to commit capital offenses, involved. It seemed even more amazing that his father, a man who retired as a high-ranking officer in the military and held a Ph.D., went along with Perry's sociopathy. Nonetheless, Perry continued meeting with his lawyers and gave the appearance that he truly believed he would win the cases against him, calling the murder case a "house of cards." Although he expressed the fact that he was not happy about being in jail, he said that he welcomed the opportunity to clear his name.

"The good thing for me in this case," Perry said, "is to finally put an end to accusations and allegations against me. I want a quick and fair trial."

When asked about the offer that Postiglione claimed

that Perry had made to him to plead guilty for a reduced sentence, Perry denied he had ever made such an offer to make a deal.

"I'm absolutely not interested in making a deal with anybody for something I did not do," Perry said. He again denied killing Janet.

"Nothing pleases me more than a final resolution to this," he said. "I look forward to trial and winning an acquittal. The police and DA had nine years and have spent money to build cases against me, a frame-up, that's what I'm fighting right now."

Meanwhile, prosecutors began publicly stating that they believed others may have helped Perry dispose of or hide Janet's body. They alleged that as many as three other people may have been involved, but declined to say how they had come up with the information to make the allegations. The district attorney's office named Paul Eichel, one of Perry's former clients, who, at one time, ran a few trendy nightclubs in Nashville. Eichel had retained Perry for his expertise as a corporate attorney. Eichel later pleaded guilty to money laundering. They had also named Morris Clinard, who died in 2000. Clinard was only connected to the case through Eichel, with whom he was acquainted.

Eichel adamantly denied to local news media outlets that he had helped dispose of Janet's body. Eichel insisted that throughout the years of the investigation into Janet's disappearance, he had always told the authorities the truth—that he had no idea regarding what had happened to Janet.

"The bad part about it is the DA and the detectives, when you tell them the truth, they don't like the answer you're giving—you're not cooperating with them."

Eichel said that he had asked Perry about Janet and what

had become of her, and Perry had always denied having killed her. Eichel told reporters that he had no idea whether Janet had been murdered or not, and that although he and Perry had a business relationship, they had never become friends.

"He never called me to go to dinner, never a drink, and then he's going to call me to move a body? That's ridiculous," Eichel said.

The third man that the district attorney's office named as a possible coconspirator was Arthur March. When asked by a news outlet if there was any truth to the allegations, Arthur denied having anything at all to do with Janet's disappearance.

"How could I dispose of a body when there is no body?" Arthur asked. "You're assuming. The court is assuming there's a body. They can't even prove she's dead. My comment is this: I wasn't even in the fuckin' country. I didn't get there till she had been gone a week. . . . I'm not sure she's dead. Nobody's proved to me she's dead . . . and I have very little faith in the judges in Nashville and Tennessee."

Arthur's tone seemed like he was daring the authorities to charge him with a crime in connection with Janet's disappearance, and did dare them to come after him. He said he would not return to the United States willingly.

"Well, I'm telling them if they fucking want to come down here and serve me, go ahead and see what happens."

Chapter 29

Russell Nathaniel Farris, under the assumed identity of Bobby Givings, did not call Arthur March back the next day, like he had said he would. In fact, he did not call him again until Tuesday, October 25, 2005, during one of the scheduled secret setup calls made in the presence of the authorities. Upon retrospect, many people later wondered why Arthur March had not been able to see through the sting—perhaps, like his son, he was so consumed with hatred for the Levines and with wanting them killed that he would have gone along with nearly anything presented to him. Whatever it was, Arthur March had swallowed the whole enchilada that "Bobby" had served him. Arthur picked up the phone on the second ring.

"Bueno."

"Colonel?" Farris asked. "Hey, how you doin'? This is Bobby."

"Hi, Bob."

"Look here, I got some good news for you," Farris said. "I will—I'll probably be with you tomorrow. . . . Everything looks good from up here, depending on the weather tomorrow . . . I'm gonna get this done. But, uh, I'm not gonna ride a bus. I'm gonna take a plane from here . . . to Houston. Then from Houston to Guadalajara."

"Okay," Arthur replied. "Now you got your birth certificate or identification with you?"

"Well, well . . . yeah . . . see, like, once I get to Guadalajara, Bobby Givings is gone. You know that's not my real name and I've got—"

"Okay, okay fine."

"I've got—"

"I don't want to know," Arthur said. "I'm around . . . this . . . number is available."

"Oh, okay. Well, look," Farris said. "If it rains tomorrow—it'll probably be delayed another day. But I've already checked, uh, Continental Airlines and the ticket's about three hundred fifty bucks. . . ."

"Okay," Arthur said. "And I'll have some money I can give you, actually a week from today."

"I can probably be in Guadalajara by five or six tomorrow. And once I get there . . . will you come pick me up?" Farris asked.

"Oh yeah. You just make the phone call. I'll be there. . . . Good luck . . . I'll see you tomorrow," Arthur said. It seemed like he wanted to end the conversation.

"I hope so. Just have me a cold beer on hand if you can."

"I got a whole refrigerator. Two sizes . . . the small economy and the large economy."

"Well, I hope everything will be good, and I—"

"Well, I hope you have your luck, buddy," Arthur cut in.

"Okay, and . . . just, just reassure me that . . . once I get there, everything . . ."

"Once you get there, you're home free," Arthur said.

"Okay, I just, you know . . . don't want no bullshit about this, 'cause—"

"You ain't got no bullshit," Arthur interjected. "You got a place to live and everything else is taken care of."

"Well, good, Colonel. Uh, be waitin' for a call tomorrow."

"Okay."

They each said good-bye, but Farris called back a minute or so later.

"There's a couple . . . of things I forgot," Farris said. "I just kind of jumped the gun. Do you know a certain place to pick me up there at the airport?"

"You just get to the airport," Arthur said. "When you come off, there's only one place you can come out. You come out through the international . . . I'll be there."

"What kind of car will you be drivin'?"

"Well, it'll be in the lot. I'm driving a Blazer. When you walk out, I'll be there. How will I recognize you?"

"I've got a slick bald head," Farris said. "And I've got a question mark tattoo on my throat. I'll wear a yellow shirt . . . that way you can see me from far."

"You got it. And you'll see me, I'll, uh—"

"I already know what you look like," Farris cut in. "I've seen a picture. . . . Perry showed me a picture of you."

"Well, I'll be there as you come out—you can't get lost."

"Have you talked to Perry?" Farris asked.

"Not about this."

"Oh, well, of course not. I mean, just . . . in general . . . have you talked to him?"

"I talked to him, uh, Friday."

"Is he okay?"

"Yeah, he's doin' better. Seems to be acclimating. . . . I hope tomorrow's a good one for him," Arthur said.

"Oh yeah . . . I'm pretty positive it will be good. I done

a walk-through today and I've got my car parked and I'm catchin' a bus in the mornin' to go out—"

"All right," Arthur interrupted. "I'm waitin' for you, buddy."

"Well, man, I'm lookin' forward to seein' you."

"We'll have some times. . . . Good luck."

Two days later, Thursday, October 27, 2005, Bobby Givings called Arthur March for the last time.

"Bueno," Arthur said.

"Colonel? Hey, this is Bobby. Look here. Everything's done, I'm in Houston right now and I will be in Guadalajara at about two-thirty. My flight number is twenty forty-six from Continental Airlines."

Arthur apparently took down the information, as he repeated it to Farris.

"Okay. There's nothin' on the com—on the computer on it," Arthur said.

"On the computer," Farris repeated. "Well, I'm in Houston now. . . . I'm leaving at, like, twelve."

"Yeah, but you finished the job up there?" Arthur asked.

"Yeah, uh, that's done. Every—everything's done."

"How come it's not on my computer?"

"I don't have a clue about the computer."

"Okay, I'll check the news later."

"Okay," Farris said, ending their final telephone conversation.

Investigators claimed that Arthur March drove to the airport in Guadalajara to pick up Farris, who, of course, was still in Nashville. However, the district attorney's office felt that they now had enough to move forward. Arthur, on the other hand, when later confronted after being tailed to the airport by an FBI agent, denied knowing anything regarding "what Perry did with this guy." Arthur was not arrested at that time.

The next day, Friday, October 28, a Davidson County grand jury indicted Perry and Arthur March on one count each of solicitation to commit murder and two counts each of conspiracy to commit murder. As Perry reeled in shock at the deception that had been carried out on him and his father while he sat in his Nashville jail cell, having previously brimmed with confidence that he had set things up so that he could beat the charges against him, Arthur, upon hearing about the indictments, again reiterated his previous sentiments about not returning to Nashville willingly. Confronted by officials from Nashville, he was informed that if he did not surrender, the extradition process would begin.

"I don't go peacefully," Arthur said. "I don't go like Perry. There'll be blood shed somewhere, whether it's theirs or mine. I'm a big boy. I take care of myself and carry my cane. That's all I do."

Arthur's "cane" purportedly acted as a sheath for a razor-sharp blade, approximately two feet long.

The paperwork necessary to begin extradition proceedings against Arthur March was promptly drafted and filed with the proper state, U.S., and Mexico governments, making it only a matter of time before Arthur would be in the hands of Nashville authorities. His days in Mexico were numbered.

Chapter 30

By the end of November 2005, the wheels of justice began turning a little faster as the district attorney's office announced that Perry March would be tried in three separate criminal proceedings. The first trial that was placed on the Davidson County Criminal Court docket was scheduled to begin on April 17, 2006, on a charge of felony theft, which stemmed from the embezzlement indictment for allegedly stealing an amount of money that ranged between $10,000 and $60,000 from Lawrence Levine's law firm while employed there. His second trial was scheduled for June 5, 2006, to face the charges against him for allegedly plotting to have the Levines murdered. During the third and final trial, scheduled for August 2006, Perry would face the charges of second-degree murder, abuse of a corpse, and evidence tampering surrounding the disappearance of his wife, Janet. As things continued to get hotter in the kitchen, Perry remained cool and confident that he would be acquitted when he had his day in court.

As November passed into December, there was much going on behind the scenes—although it wasn't all being

seen publicly, yet. Perry spent Christmas and New Year's
Day uneventfully inside his jail cell, with the exception of
his one-hour-a-day out to exercise, shower, and make telephone calls. It gave him plenty of time to ponder his fate
and, of course, to try and think up new schemes that might
help him escape justice. In the meantime, Perry had no idea
just how close the authorities were to arresting his father in
Mexico and the bizarre case continued to come together for
the authorities and to unravel for Perry and his father.

On Thursday, January 5, 2006, officers assigned to the
Instituto Nacional de Migracion (INM), the Mexican
equivalent of the INS in the United States, showed up
around 8:00 A.M. at the doughnut shop that Arthur was
known to frequent with his cronies almost on a daily basis.
Jose Luis Gutierrez, INM chief of that agency's Guadalajara office, explained that Arthur's FM-3 resident status
was revoked because of an official demand from the U.S.
Consulate based on Arthur's indictment in October for
his part in his son's scheme to have the Levines killed.
Under Mexico's immigration laws, the Mexican government can revoke a person's residency status if it was determined that the person in question has a seedy background.
In Arthur's case, the INM had determined that Arthur's indictment and arrest warrant were sufficient grounds to
revoke his residency and deport him. Gutierrez said that if
it turned out that Arthur was cleared of the charges against
him in the States, he would be welcome to return to
Mexico. The government, Gutierrez said, had waited until
an *amparo,* or injunction, that Arthur had obtained in a
separate proceeding that served to shield him from actions
by a number of Mexican agencies had expired before
agents showed up to take him into custody.

"We were prudent," Gutierrez said. "We were patient.

And I want all his friends to know that he was not kidnapped. He was subject to an expulsion procedure with all the rigors marked under law. He put up resistance and tried to attack one of the agents with a knife he pulled out of his belt buckle."

Mexican officials showed photos of a specially crafted, very sharp knife that had been fashioned into a part of the belt buckle Arthur had been wearing. In order to pull the knife, the person wearing it would have to release the belt connected to it first, then pull it out of the sheath that kept it hidden and which gave it the appearance of being a part of the belt itself. Because Arthur was known to have carried a cane that also served as a two-foot-long swordlike weapon, and was suspected of possessing firearms, Gutierrez's agents approached him with caution and disarmed him without any of the agents being harmed. Although Gutierrez's official position was that Arthur had put up a struggle, the descriptions of the incident provided by two men Arthur had been having coffee with contrasted significantly.

"There was no resistance," said one of Arthur's friends. "He is seventy-seven years old, having had a total hip replacement. He was approached from behind by two plainclothes personnel who immediately pulled his hands behind him, and he was handcuffed immediately."

The friend said that Arthur had gotten up from their table when the agents identified themselves and accompanied them to the front of the doughnut shop, where he was searched and handcuffed. Another friend provided a different account of how Arthur's arrest had occurred.

"March was walking toward his vehicle when he was jumped from the rear by three men in civilian clothes, and rapidly handcuffed," said the other friend who had also been with Arthur that morning. "The belt buckle knife takes two hands to open, and could not have taken place by a man with his hands behind his back."

When asked by a reporter to comment on why there were varying stories about the manner in which Arthur March had been arrested, Gutierrez dismissed the two men's claims.

"They are his friends," Gutierrez said.

Following a brief routine procedural hearing, which occurred at the INM offices at the Guadalajara Airport, Arthur was handed over to FBI agents, who placed him on a Continental Airlines afternoon flight to Houston, Texas. Upon his arrival in Houston, Arthur appeared before a judge prior to being placed in a jail medical facility because of his frailty and poor health. Fletcher Long, a lawyer from Nashville that Arthur had asked to represent him, indicated that Arthur would likely fight extradition to Tennessee. Long said that his client's detention and deportation had not been expected.

"Of course we haven't heard from our client," Long said. "We didn't see this coming."

Within days, however, Arthur decided against fighting extradition and agreed to return to Tennessee. On Friday, January 13, 2006, Arthur March was picked up at the Houston jail by two Tennessee police officers, who escorted him on a flight back to Nashville. At 10:30 P.M., he arrived at Nashville's Criminal Justice Center, the same facility where his son had been jailed since his arrest and deportation from Mexico several months earlier. He chose not to be processed through night court because of his inability to stand for lengthy periods of time, and instead consented to make his appearance via video while Postiglione presented the indictment to the night court judge. He pleaded innocent to the charges against him, which, if convicted of them, could net him twenty years in prison. Arthur, whose seventy-eighth birthday was only a day away, had expressed concerns about his health.

"He made it very clear in the press that he's on various medications," said Metro Jail spokesperson Carla Krocker, who indicated that his health would be closely monitored. "We wanted to ensure that we're prepared to receive him, but he'll be assessed like any other inmate for his classification and be held."

He was being held without bail until a bail hearing could be scheduled, but prosecutors, who considered him a flight risk, said it was unlikely that he would be immediately released. Although his lawyer had planned to ask that Arthur be released on his own recognizance because of his health issues, prosecutors indicated that such a move would not likely occur.

"We have every intention of asking the court to set a reasonable bond based on the health concerns of an elderly man with high blood pressure and heart problems, among other things," countered his lawyer, Fletcher Long.

At seventy-eight years old, and facing twenty years in prison, Arthur March didn't have to stew for very long in jail before he began thinking about making a deal. On Monday, February 6, 2006, barely three weeks after being jailed, Arthur, through his attorney, told authorities that he was ready to make a deal in return for a lighter sentence. When it had been formally agreed that Arthur would serve only eighteen months in a federal prison in exchange for pleading guilty to a charge of solicitation to commit murder and for agreeing to testify against his son, Arthur seemed ready to tell the authorities what they had long wanted to know.

Chapter 31

While meeting with Detectives Postiglione and Pridemore, Arthur March explained that his son Perry had admitted to him that he had killed Janet. Arthur, who would later be formally deposed over a two-day period, told the detectives that Perry had told him that on the night that Janet had disappeared, Perry and Janet had engaged in a major argument. At one point, he said, Janet had come at Perry with either a butcher knife or a kitchen knife, and that Perry had subsequently beat her to death with a wrench inside their Forest Hills home. Arthur told the cops that Perry had originally buried Janet's body himself, but he needed help moving it from its original location, because that area, he had learned, had become a construction site.

Arthur told the cops that four or five weeks later, he and Perry took Janet's body and drove it to a location near Bowling Green, Kentucky. According to Arthur, they checked into a Bowling Green motel. After checking in, Arthur left Perry at the motel room and drove Janet's corpse to a farmland area a short distance outside of town. After driving around for a while, he said, he came upon a brush pile, which he believed would likely be burned in the near future. He claimed that after parking the car, he placed Janet's body into the brush pile and returned to the motel.

While Arthur's story had proven interesting and had moved the police and prosecutors to a "very critical state" in the investigation, according to Metro police spokesperson Don Aaron, it had also raised a lot of questions.

Where was the blood evidence? If Janet had been struck on the head with a wrench, there would surely have been blood left behind. Dr. Corey Slovis, chairperson of the Department of Emergency Room Medicine at Vanderbilt University Medical Center, didn't necessarily believe there would have been a lot of blood.

"It is possible to have a life-ending injury without a significant amount of bleeding," Dr. Slovis told a *Tennessean* reporter. "It is also quite possible to have enough from ruptured blood vessels to have someone lose their entire blood volume."

Although it is difficult to clean up all of the blood left behind at a crime scene, even by those who use bleach and water, Perry had two weeks to look for trace evidence and, if found, to clean it, and then clean it again and again. On the other hand, if Janet hadn't lost much blood from her injuries, it was possible that there wasn't any blood evidence to worry about anyway.

Another question raised by Arthur's statements that some of the locals wondered about was how Perry March, having been named as a prime suspect in a high-profile missing-person case, had gotten out of town to dump his wife's body? Wouldn't the police have placed a tail on their prime suspect? Again, not necessarily.

"It is true that Perry March was named as a suspect in this case in search warrant documentation in mid-September of

1996," said Aaron. "But to assume or presume that a police officer was with Perry March every second of the day in August and September of 1996 would not be correct."

People also wondered why Perry and his dad would take the risk of moving Janet's body out of state, as well as the difficulty of moving a decomposing corpse. Had Perry somehow been able to preserve it for four or five weeks? If he had buried it, the decomposition would be severe, messy, and the odor horrendous.

And how could a sixty-eight-year-old man remove a rapidly decomposing corpse from the vehicle and carry it to the brush pile that he said he had found? Would Arthur have been in good enough shape almost ten years earlier to carry out such a feat? After all, when Janet disappeared, it had been reported that she was five feet four inches tall and weighed 104 pounds. While she wasn't large by any means, that much bulk and weight would be difficult, if not impossible, for an old man like Arthur to handle.

One of the biggest questions on everyone's minds, however, was whether anything that Arthur had told the police had even been truthful. There was, after all, the witness who claimed to have seen Perry March placing a rolled-up rug into a Dumpster shortly after Janet had disappeared. Had Arthur made up the story as part of yet another father-and-son scheme concocted to somehow help Perry's case by planting all of those seeds of doubt that had turned into questions? How might a jury react to such a scenario? No one, of course, had any way of knowing whether Arthur was telling the truth or not, or whether this was just another concocted ploy that Perry had worked out in his head. Due to a huge blunder by jail employees, he and his father had, after all, been allowed to have a face-to-face meeting a few days before Arthur had announced that he wanted to make a deal. Had they worked out such a plan at that time? The meeting between father and son had lasted about forty-five minutes, and had been approved by officials within the sheriff's department without the knowledge of the district attorney's office. The sheriff's department hadn't considered what kind of problems such a meeting might cause in a criminal case of such magnitude—they had only been concerned whether the visit would have been a security problem for the jail. When it had been determined that security would not be an issue, the visit was allowed.

"It was a visit," Davidson County sheriff Daron Hall said. "From our standpoint it presented no threat to either of them, nor did it present a threat to our institution. The visit was for forty-five minutes, it's not going to reoccur, and I don't believe that's enough time to mastermind ten-year-ago murder scenarios."

The sheriff said that the district attorney's office should have informed the jail staff that they did not want the father and son meeting with each other.

"We have never received a request from anyone not to allow it, either prior to the meeting or after it," Sheriff Hall said.

Deputy DA Tom Thurman, who had overseen the case from a prosecutorial standpoint since it began nearly ten years earlier, said that he had not been told of the meeting until after it had taken place. He said that because of the fact that Perry and Arthur were codefendants, their being allowed to visit "would give us concern."

"I wouldn't want to speculate on what they talked about or what impact it has on the case, because I really don't know," Thurman said.

"For nine years he says that Perry didn't have anything to do with Janet's death," said another local criminal defense attorney. "He has a meeting with Perry, and within a very short period of time, he's pleading guilty and telling the authorities that Perry killed his wife. . . . It's very suspect."

"Arthur has said what he needs to receive a shorter sentence rather than a longer sentence," one of Perry's attorneys, John Herbison, said. "Perry March and Arthur March are still father and son. They still love each other. They have very different accounts of what happened and what didn't happen. . . . Whatever Arthur does, we'll just respond to it at an appropriate time."

"If I'm Perry March's attorney," said a Nashville criminal defense attorney not connected to the case, "I'm skeptical of it (Arthur's deal) only because the government has the unique ability to offer something of value for a witness to testify. That would be like me offering some money to testify on my behalf. It's worth more than money. It's years of their life."

Could it also be possible that Arthur March had concocted the entire story on his own in order to shave several years off his own sentence? Had he come to the point where, after years of trying to help his son get through his legal troubles, he was finally fed up with having allowed himself to have been dragged into, used, and made a part of a plan that had ultimately cost him his freedom? At seventy-eight years old, Arthur knew that he would likely die in prison if he had to serve a long sentence. Was it finally time for him to go against his son in an "every man for himself" scenario?

"At this juncture I'm afraid any comment from me might jeopardize the work that I've done toward resolving the case on behalf of Arthur March," Arthur's lawyer, Fletcher Long, said.

Arthur's lawyer also said that he hoped his client

would not be required to help put his son in prison. Long said that Arthur was sorry for the part he played in Janet's disappearance.

"Maybe he won't have to, if his son pleas," Long said. "I think my client very much hopes that Perry will go ahead and plea. . . . I think Arthur March is guilty of loving his son."

Could Arthur's motivation in copping a plea have simply been a plan to pave the way for Perry to be able to get a plea deal as well? In other words, could Arthur's offer to testify against his son make Perry's case look all the more bleak for him than it already did? And would it be enough to prompt prosecutors—after all, Arthur's deal could have been made up as a reverse psychology of sorts against the prosecutors—to trick them, if you will, into opening the door to offer Perry a plea bargain by thinking he might take it when faced with his father's testimony? Such a plan, if that had been what it was, could have only been concocted by a sociopathic mind like Perry's. Admittedly, they were rolling the dice if that had been their scheme, but the father and son could have worked it out at their face-to-face meeting. True, it was only one of several possibilities, but given Perry's desire to manipulate the system, and to get one up on the prosecutors, made it seem possible, even plausible.

"It's got to be powerful," said U.S. Attorney Jim Vines, whose agency helped put together the case against Arthur March. "You have a father testifying that his son acknowledged that he killed the daughter-in-law."

"Arthur March has a strong incentive to please the prosecutors . . . ," Herbison said. He added that at trial the jurors would likely be informed that Arthur had cooperated with prosecutors, perhaps under pressure, in exchange for a lighter sentence in his case. Once the case made it to trial, Arthur's statements would be subject to cross-examination. "Perry understands the situation."

Although the father and son had pledged to each other during their jailhouse visit that neither would testify against the other, and both had agreed that they would "wear these orange jumpsuits as a badge of honor," Arthur apparently had decided, for whatever reason, to roll over on his son. The deal had been made, Arthur had pleaded guilty to a charge of solicitation to commit murder, and his statement had served as Arthur's first public acknowledgment that Perry had killed Janet. And if the sentencing judge agreed, he would only serve eighteen months instead of facing a sentence in which he surely would not survive.

At one point during Arthur's plea dealing, Postiglione and Pridemore checked him out of the Metro Jail and drove him to the Bowling Green, Kentucky, area in the hope that Arthur might be able to show them where he had supposedly dumped Janet's body. However, after spending nearly all day in the neighboring state, Arthur was unable to remember the exact location where he claimed he dumped his daughter-in-law's body.

Arthur March was moved to a federal detention facility following his plea agreement. He was scheduled to be sentenced on May 1, 2006.

Chapter 32

The deposition of Colonel Arthur Wayne March, as it came to be known, was taken over two days—April 10 to 11, 2006, a Monday and a Tuesday. Arthur's attorney, Fletcher Long, was present, as was his son Perry March. Tom Thurman and Katie Miller were present for the state, and attorneys William A. Massey, Lorna McClusky, and John Herbison appeared on behalf of Perry March. Following introductory remarks and the swearing in of Arthur March, the questioning began.

"State your name for the record, please, sir," Thurman instructed.

"Arthur Wayne March."

"And how old are you?"

"Seventy-eight."

"Do you go by Colonel, Mr., what do you like to be called?" Thurman asked.

"Well, I prefer to be called Colonel, except sometimes they call me Dr.," Arthur replied.

Thurman asked him if he was on any medication, and Arthur said that he was on "lots of it," taking seventeen pills each day for a medical condition that he thought had been congestive heart failure—except all the tests had come back negative. He failed to provide any other information about his medical condition at that time except to say that he had lost twenty-four pounds of excess fluid from his body. Thurman took him through a series of questions that established that Arthur was being held in a federal facility in Kentucky. Details of his family, children, educational background, and retirement from the army also were provided. After discussing the terms of his guilty plea, Thurman transitioned his questioning to the night that Janet disappeared.

"Do you recall when your daughter-in-law Janet March disappeared on August 15, 1996?" Thurman asked.

"Yes. I was in Mexico."

"Did you come to Nashville shortly after that?"

"I did."

"And why did you come to Nashville?"

"My son asked me to come up and help him with the children. He needed help."

"Do you know how many days after she disappeared before you were able to arrive here in Nashville?"

"I think it was three or four. I really don't—"

"Do you recall the day of September 17, 1996, when a search warrant was served on your apartment, as well as . . . the home of your son, Mr. March?" Thurman asked.

"Yes."

"Prior to that search warrant being served . . . did your son Perry March ask you to dispose of any items for him?"

"Yes, two items for the computer. One, I don't know what it was, and the other was the hard drive."

"And, did you do that for him?"

"Yes, I did."

"And how did you obtain these items?"

"Perry gave them to me."

"And what did you do with those items?"

"I—one that I don't know what the name on it was, I put into a disposable garbage box in a strip mall in front of a drugstore. And the other was the hard drive—I disposed of it by throwing it . . . in a wooded area relatively near the house."

In response to the questions being asked him, Arthur explained that he had disposed of the computer hard drive and the second computer item, which he wasn't familiar with, on two separate occasions because Perry had given the items to him on separate occasions. Arthur also explained how he had driven a rental truck loaded with furniture from Perry and Janet's house to the Chicago area the day after the search warrant had been served, September 18, which he had placed into storage in Hammond, Indiana, just outside of Chicago. He said that he had made the trip alone, and had taken a flight back to Nashville.

"Okay, did you ever travel back with your son Perry March?" Thurman asked.

"Yes."

"When was that?"

"That was . . . later."

"Later in September?"

"It could have been, yes."

"Now, how did you return from Chicago with your son Perry March?"

"Uh—we came back in his Volvo."

"On a trip back to Nashville . . . that time, did . . . you and your son stop and purchase anything?"

"Uh—we stopped . . . we bought . . . a shovel and I think the other item was Clorox, but I'm not sure."

Although Arthur said that he could not recall which state they were in when they stopped to purchase the shovel and the bleach, he said that the purchase had been made at a hardware store.

"When you arrived back in Nashville, did your son ask you to do something for him, to assist him in a—in a matter?" Thurman asked.

"A little later on, he asked me to help—uh, dispose of Janet's body."

"And how was he acting when he asked you to do that?"

"Little nervous."

"Did he say . . . why he wanted you . . . to help him dispose of her body?"

"Yes. He said where he placed the body was now being turned into a construction site and her body was placed right near the road that they were using to get to the construction site."

"Did you agree to assist him in disposing of the body?"

"Yes, I did."

"Where did you go from there, once you agreed to assist him?"

"Uh—we went in his car . . . up the highway . . . a fairly large, two-lane highway."

Arthur explained that it was perhaps a ten-minute drive to the location where the body was buried. He said that they parked the car, and Arthur got out of the car to retrieve the body.

"He told me where the body would be and I . . . got out of the car and went to get the body and he drove around."

"What instructions did he give you . . . about where the body was located?"

"Told me it was up this little road, ten to fifteen yards, and turn left and go in. It would be in the wooded section and I had a flashlight. He told me I should look on the ground and I would see where the body was."

"Did you follow his instructions?"

"Yes."

"Were you able to find—"

"Yes, with no problem."

Thurman asked Arthur to describe his observations when he found the body regarding its appearance.

"It was in this black . . . plastic bag. We call it a leaf bag up north . . . a large bag."

"Did it appear to have . . . any disturbance around where the body was located?"

"Yes, it looked . . . like there was some digging around . . . what proved to be the grave."

"Was the body buried to any extent?"

"It had dirt on top."

"And were you able to get the body in the trash bag, the leaf bag, out without digging yourself?"

"Yeah, but I pushed a little bit of the dirt off the top with my hands and then closed up the bag and pulled it down the hill. It was a slight hill where she had been placed. And I took it to the other side of the road that we came in on and I waited for Perry to come with his car. And then he stopped in front of me and took the bag and pulled it back into . . . the road. He opened the trunk to the car. We took . . . the body and put [it] in back of the Volvo."

"Now, you say you closed the bag back. Was the bag open?"

Arthur said that the bag had been partially open when he retrieved it.

"Did you actually look in it at the time?" Thurman asked.

"Not really. I saw some bones and I didn't really want to know what was going on."

"Okay. So, you secured the bag, took it down the hill. . . . Was it heavy for you to carry?"

"It was heavy, but it . . . was less than . . . somewhere between fifty and sixty, seventy pounds. It was under a hundred pounds."

"Okay. But you don't know the exact weight, obviously."

"No."

"But . . . you were able to . . . handle it . . . yourself?"

"Yes, I pulled it down, and it was a down slope."

"After the body was . . . put in the trunk . . . what did you do next?"

"We closed the trunk, got into the car, and went down to the highway. Perry was driving and we drove up north toward Chicago."

"Did you go all the way to Chicago after that?"

"No. When we got up past the Kentucky line . . . we found a motel . . . I don't know the name. It was Blue something or it was blue in color. That's all that sticks in my mind."

"What happened when you got to the hotel?"

"I got out of the car. Perry gave me some cash, went in and paid for the room, and that was it."

"Did you use your real name?"

"No."

"What happened after you got the room?"

"Uh, we went to the room, Perry laid down and said he was very tired. He gave me the keys to the car. I went back and got in the car, went back out to the highway, turned left, which was north, again, and started . . . to the other side of . . . Bowling Green."

"Do you recall what name you used when you registered?"

"No, I don't."

"Okay. So, you headed north to Bowling Green and then . . . describe what happened."

"After I got past where they made the . . . Corvette, I went . . . looking for a stream. We call it a creek. We [*sic*] found one. I turned. . . and I looked—had to stop a few times to see how deep the creek was. It wasn't very deep and I could not put the body in the creek. So, I got back in the car, turned around. . . went a little farther north, where I found another creek and it was the same thing. The creek was so low that there wasn't enough water to deposit the . . . the body. So, I started—I turned around, came back. It was just getting light at that time. And I drove up . . . pulled over to the side of the road, was parked on the left-hand side of the road. There was a big . . . pile of brush, I would call it. . . . I went and cleared away three . . . you might say they were holes (made in the brush pile). . . . In the first one I put the clothes that were in there on the top. That's when I saw the bones. I knew it was a body. In the next hole, I put Janet. I flipped out the—the body from the, uh, bag, the leaf bag, took the leaf bag and saw the clothes and put it in the third hole, closed all the holes up, went back, and that's when I saw a . . . car . . . not really a car—it was a school bus. And they came up to the crossroads, turned right and . . . went down. . . . I got into my car, went out to the highway to Sixty-Five, and turned right and went back to the motel, where Perry was."

"When you were disposing of the body, did you smell anything at that time?"

"No, I did not."

"Was the Clorox or the shovel ever used that was purchased . . . ?"

"Not to my knowledge."

"So . . . that same morning, did you then leave the hotel, and where did you go from there?"

"We went up north to Chicago."

"Did you tell Perry how you disposed of the body?"

"Well, I told him I put it in a creek with some water and nobody was to get to it. It was under the water, 'cause I didn't want to go through the whole thing with him. And to my knowledge, that's where he thought I put it."

"Did you ever discuss this again after that day?"

"Never."

"Did . . . you ever tell anybody about this prior to telling the police and prosecutors earlier this year?"

"No."

Arthur then explained under continued questioning how he helped the police in an attempt to find Janet's remains after nearly a decade had passed. Despite the earlier specificity when he explained where he had taken Janet's remains, he now explained that sometime during the last nine years or so, the highway had been widened by two additional lanes, making it impossible for him to locate the exact spot where he claimed he placed the body into the brush pile.

"Why did you agree to help your son . . . get rid of Janet March's body?"

"He's my son! He's my son."

Chapter 33

Arthur March was then cross-examined by Perry's attorney William Massey as the deposition continued. Massey took him through the typical formalities of general remarks about Arthur's age and general health and well-being. Arthur explained that he had good days as well as bad days with regard to his health. He said that his health problems were related primarily to his heart and high blood pressure, and now, since his "kidnapping" by "the Mexicans" when he was deported, he had problems with his right leg requiring him to use a cane to walk. Massey took him through details about his family, particularly his children in which it was described that Perry was the oldest of three, Ron was the middle child, and Kathy was the youngest, "the baby."

"Was your relationship with all your children good?" Massey asked.

"It's always been good, up until now," Arthur replied.

"Is it strained now?"

"From what I hear, it is. I don't know."

"What was your relationship with Janet March?"

"She was my daughter-in-law."

"Did you get along well with her?"

"Uh, yes and no."

Massey asked him to explain what he meant.

"Well, she was—the best way I can describe it, she was a typical JAP. . . ."

"And, by JAP, you mean?"

"Jewish American Princess. And . . . I was not comfortable with her. . . . I didn't think she . . . did anything with Perry. When she built the house, she went to her father when she wanted—anything she wanted. If she needed it, she went to her father. To my knowledge, Perry was . . . there for show purposes."

"Were you . . . in the presence of Perry and Janet a number of times?"

"Uh, yeah, I guess you'd say it was a number of times. It wasn't . . . a lot of times because—uh—only ate with Janet in her home three times in five years. She was not a cook and a homemaker."

"Was she friendly to you?"

"Yeah, she seemed to be. We both knew where we—she knew what I felt and I knew how she felt."

"And did you both respect that?"

"Yeah."

"Or, at least acknowledge that?"

"Well, I didn't acknowledge it. That was her feelings and she was used to being a JAP. And anything she wanted, she just had to whistle for it."

"Did she have a temper?"

"Oh yeah!"

"You say that very emphatically."

"Yes, she did."

"Why do you say that so emphatically?" Massey pressed.

"Well, I saw . . . her make Perry leave the house several times and she . . . was just used to getting her way and she was gonna have it."

Massey then took Arthur through a lengthy session of questions related to his plea agreement. At times Massey hammered home the difference between the actual sentencing guidelines and the amount of time that Arthur would likely receive as a result of his plea agreement. He fashioned his questions at times in a manner that seemed dedicated at discrediting Arthur's sworn testimony to call into question the strong motivation that a substantially reduced sentence could hold over someone in his shoes. Massey wanted to drive home the point that under the plea agreement, the government could withdraw it if it was deemed that Arthur had not cooperated with them.

"And if the government determines that you have not cooperated fully, that you've not been all the way truthful, then, they can prosecute you for perjury?" Massey asked.

"Now, Mr. Massey," Arthur said, "I'm a retired army officer. Congress granted me the right to be an officer and a gentleman. And, to remain that way, I have to tell the truth."

"I understand," Massey said. "But I have to ask you some questions about the plea agreement that you entered into with the government, okay? This isn't my agreement. It's an agreement that you entered into with the government and I have to ask you some questions about it. . . . I'll try to be as brief as I can about it, okay?"

"I know."

"I don't mean offense," Massey continued. "But the government in its sole discretion, they're the ones that get to decide. . . . If they decide that you haven't been truthful, they can prosecute you for perjury, you understand that?"

"I understand that."

"And they can charge you with other crimes—"

"Yes, I understand."

"Okay. And they can recommend a sentence up to that statutory maximum of twenty years."

"That's the way the ball bounces," Arthur replied.

"And, at seventy-eight years old, the odds are that you wouldn't make it out of prison; isn't that right, Colonel?"

"That's for damn sure. I almost didn't make it two weeks ago. . . ."

"So, again, it is in your best interest to tell the truth."

"Yes," Arthur replied.

Arthur explained that pleading guilty had been Perry's idea—Perry had asked his father to plead guilty, according to Arthur, because he had purportedly told his father that he was going to do the same thing.

"And that's why I did it," Arthur said. "I told the truth."

"I understand. It is correct to say that it is in your best interest to—"

"Tell the truth," Arthur said, finishing the sentence for Massey.

Massey took Arthur through the process of Perry arriving in Ajijic after he left the United States, and how Arthur had helped set him up. The questions and answers painted a picture of how Perry had met Chavez, and Carmen, and how Perry and Carmen had eventually opened the Media Luna restaurant. Arthur explained that its name means "half-moon" in Spanish.

"What type of restaurant is that?" Massey asked.

"It . . . started out as a bistro, and then became a full-time restaurant. . . . His wife ran the kitchen and he ran the front."

"Was he still working his consulting job at that time, or did he stop?"

"I—I assume he was. I did not know. I never asked Perry how he made his money."

"Do you have knowledge of any type of illegal activity Perry was engaging in in Mexico?"

"No."

"As far as you know . . . he worked at legitimate businesses?"

"That's right."

"Made honest money?"

"Honest, as far as I know."

Massey spent considerable time going over a timeline with Arthur that had been put together by the district attorney's office. Arthur ended up disputing much of the timeline to the point where it seemed questionable with regard to its accuracy. They eventually arrived back to the time when Perry had left Nashville to go to Chicago for Rosh Hashanah a few weeks after Janet disappeared.

"And you know that when Perry March returned to Nashville (after Rosh Hashanah) was when he told you that he needed help with Janet's body," Massey continued.

"That's—that's right," Arthur replied.

"And . . . you told him you would help him."

"Yeah, that's why I did it."

"And, I believe you said because he's your son."

"That's right."

"And that's the first that you had ever heard that Janet wasn't—hadn't just walked off or that she was in—uh—California," Massey said, reminding him of the initial story that had been circulated to explain Janet's sudden absence to her friends and acquaintances.

"No," Arthur disagreed. "That is the second time. The

first time . . . that Perry told me about it was at the house
when he asked me to clean up. . . . He was afraid there was
some bloodstains. That's the first time—so this, this was
the second time."

"All right, I see," Massey said.

"This was the convincer, 'cause when he told me the
first time . . . all I know [was] that she was dead," Arthur
said. "He never mentioned that he killed her, never. Perry
never mentioned that he killed Janet. He used the term 'accident.'"

"I want . . . to know in the timeline of when you arrived
in Nashville, when Perry first told you about . . . cleaning
the blood. . . . Is that the first time that he mentioned something to you about it when . . . he asked you to clean?"

"That's the first time he had . . . mentioned that Janet
was dead."

"What was that . . . conversation centered around? What
was he asking you to do?"

"He was asking me to check on the entranceway to the
kitchen for the—uh—if there were any bloodstains."

As Massey continued his line of questioning about the
bloodstains, he seemed intent on learning the precise location of where Perry had purportedly directed his father to
look for signs of blood. He also tried to extract from
Arthur's memory a more precise time frame of when Perry
and his father had the conversation about the cleanup, in
relation to when Perry had asked his father to help him dispose of Janet's body. Arthur claimed that he could not
recall precisely when those conversations had occurred,
but he believed that they had taken place within days of
each other, perhaps "within a week."

"When you say Perry asked you to help clean up, or
look for blood, what . . . exactly did he ask you to do?"

"Just clean the gravel around the entranceway," Arthur said. "There was a parking lot there, if anybody remembers. They used to park the car out there and then go into the kitchen with groceries or whatever the hell it was, and take it into the kitchen. And he said that I should check it and clean it up and see if there was any—anything, that he was afraid there might be some blood there. And that was the reason he told me that she was dead."

"So, directed your attention to outside in the—was it in the back or the side?"

"There—there's an entrance to the kitchen on the side," Arthur explained. "You pull the car in, park the car, get out of the car, and . . . you can go into the kitchen from there. That was the place he told me that there might be some blood."

"Is that close to the backyard or the side yard?"

"Well, I'm not sure that's considered a yard. That was a driveway . . . on that side by the kitchen. It was not considered—I didn't consider it—uh . . . a backyard. I considered it part of the driveway."

"Other than outside on this gravel, were you asked to look for the presence of blood anywhere else?"

"Not to my recollection."

Arthur also said that he had not found any blood to clean up.

"Do you remember . . . when Perry . . . told you . . . that he needed help disposing of the body? Do you remember what time of day it was that he told you, evening or morning, or—"

"No. It was—I think it was in the afternoon, but I'm not—I can't really give you a definite time, 'cause I don't . . . remember."

"Did you leave that same day to go to where the body was?"

"That night."

"That night," Massey repeated. "And you were in which vehicle?"

"The Volvo. He was driving . . . driving. I'm sorry."

Arthur said that he was "pretty convinced" that the location he led the police to was where the body had been hidden. He said that it had been covered with dirt, but indicated that it wasn't a lot of dirt because he could scrape it away with his hands. In response to questions about Janet's weight and height, Arthur said that she weighed about one hundred pounds and was nearly the same height as Perry. He said that she was not a heavy lady.

"Once you were able to locate this bag with her . . . you say her remains were in it, right? Then, did you pick the bag up?"

"I didn't pick it up with two hands," Arthur replied. "I brought it down . . . pulling it. I mean, I didn't lift it, 'cause it was a little . . . heavy. I don't even pick up a fifty-pound dog-food bag. . . ."

Massey entered into a round of questioning to try and more clearly ascertain the size of the leaf bag that held Janet's body, which, Arthur finally clarified, was the same thing as a garbage bag, but that it was a large bag. He said that it had not been double-bagged, but that her body had been placed inside a single black garbage bag, which he dragged down a small hill to the road, where Perry then met him with the car. He explained that Perry had helped him lift the bag containing Janet's body to place it in the Volvo's trunk. They also talked about Janet's weight when she was alive.

"Do you think she weighed a hundred pounds when she was alive?" Massey asked.

"I know I never lifted her, so I don't know," Arthur said. "I don't think she weighed more than a hundred pounds. She took very good care of her body."

"When you got the bag . . . when you went up . . . to the wooded area to find the body . . . did you look in it at the time?"

"No . . . it was, like, almost open, but it wasn't. And all I saw at that point was some bones and some clothing. And . . . I closed it back up and took it back down."

"Okay. And you said at that point you didn't . . . recall any kind of putrid smell or bad smell?"

"No."

As the deposition continued, Massey eventually turned his line of questioning toward whether or not Arthur felt that his family had been persecuted.

"Mr. March, did you ever feel that your family . . . unit were being persecuted?"

"By the Levines? Yes."

"What about by the police? Did you feel that the police were acting on behalf of the Levines?"

"They were just doing what the Levines wanted them to do, 'cause, as you know, Carolyn Levine is the queen of the Jewish Mafia in Tennessee and Nashville. And, she could . . . do whatever she wanted."

"What is the Jewish Mafia?"

"If you don't understand it, I can't explain it to you."

"I'm afraid I don't understand it."

"You know what a 'Mafia' is, the word means?" Arthur asked. "And you know what 'Jewish' means. And you don't understand those two words together?"

At one point Massey took Arthur through a lengthy

question-and-answer session regarding Nathaniel Farris, aka Bobby Givings, and the plans to kill the Levines that Perry and Farris had masterminded. Arthur testified that the plan to harm the Levines had been his—not Perry's.

"Perry never mentioned harming the Levines," Arthur said.

"Why did . . . you say this is 'my idea'?" Massey asked.

"Because it was."

"What was your idea?"

"That the easy way to get this was to take out the queen and no balls at all—her husband. . . . You said you didn't know what Jewish Mafia was, well, Carolyn was the queen. . . . And, uh—the reason she had so much power was she was the lady that distributed the money to—you have a hole in your judicial system, I'm sorry to say. The hole in your judicial system is that the judges at the lower level have to run for election. To get money to run for an election, they need money. They can't run for the office without getting money. And the Jewish Mafia was a big contributor, and the one who doled out the money was Carolyn. And that's where she got her power, and that's what Larry was building his on."

"I see."

"Now, do you understand what the Jewish Mafia is?"

"I understand what you're saying," Massey replied.

"Okay."

"Uh—Colonel, you said this was your idea to take them out?"

"Long before this happened."

"Had you ever followed up on that?"

"They were alive, weren't they?"

"Yeah. So, I take it you have not followed up on it?"

"No."

"But you had—let's just say ill feelings toward them?"

"Uh—I didn't like them."

"You didn't like them."

"They were liars. They were political animals who used her position with the Jewish Mafia and his position with the Democratic Party to get what they wanted when they needed it," Arthur said. "Otherwise, how did you control two judges who had no business even being in this case?"

Toward the end of the two-day deposition, Thurman, during redirect examination, asked Arthur the following question:

"There is no question that you intended for the Levines to be killed and hoped they'd be killed; is that correct?"

"Sure, several times," Arthur responded.

One of the major problems with Arthur's deposition was that of credibility. Arthur was known by a good number of people as a bullshit artist, a trait that was almost certainly passed along to his son Perry at birth. Even after the "bullshit artist" factor had been removed, Arthur's deposition still raised a few questions. One of the biggest questions, or problems, centered around his descriptions about the relocation and disposal of Janet's body, in which he had claimed that her body had been transported in "the Volvo."

Whether Perry and Janet had owned either one or two Volvos became important to the Perry March saga in that it could only be ascertained by this writer that they had owned only one, the vehicle in which Janet purportedly left home on the evening of August 15, 1996. If they had owned two such brand name vehicles, there would be no problem with Arthur's testimony regarding the name of the vehicle used in transporting Janet's body.

However, research indicated that they had owned only one Volvo, Janet's, and their other vehicle had been a Jeep Cherokee that Perry drove. So, here is the problem: It would have been impossible for Janet's body to have been transported in her own vehicle to the state of Kentucky during the time frame of mid-to-late September, which Arthur had laid out during his deposition. Her car, after all, had been found on September 7 at the Brixworth Apartments, and was impounded by the police and retained as evidence. In fact, if Janet's body had been transported to Kentucky in her own Volvo, it would have to have occurred prior to when it was found on September 7, in which case Arthur's testimony with regard to the time frame would be flawed.

It also seemed odd that Arthur would testify that there was no noticeable odor—despite Janet's body being in a plastic bag, placed in the outdoors in a shallow grave and exposed to the elements for several weeks after she was killed. The degree of decomposition would have been advanced, and the smell, or odor, of what was left of her putrid flesh and bodily fluids would likely have been gross. Had Arthur deliberately provided untruthful statements in his testimony? And if so, what had he hoped to accomplish?

At one point Dr. William Bass, who founded the Body Farm at the University of Tennessee where decomposition rates in human corpses are studied by researchers, was consulted by Davidson County authorities. Dr. Bass, who would also eventually provide sworn testimony, agreed that the condition of Janet's body would be much like that which Arthur had described. Bass stated that Janet's remains would have mostly decomposed and would likely be skeletonized after three weeks of exposure in temperatures consistent with the month of August. No mention of the putrid odors of a decomposing body wrapped inside a plastic bag, that likely would have been present, was made.

It was said by some who knew him personally after he was arrested and returned to Nashville, Arthur March no longer possessed all his mental faculties. If this characterization proved accurate, it could serve to further call into question the validity and importance of his deposition and the descriptions that he had provided of Janet's decomposing corpse. Arthur March was an enigma of sorts, and would remain that way until the day he died.

Chapter 34

Arthur March lived long enough to see his son Perry convicted three times in three separate trials over the next five months. He also granted *48 Hours* another interview, and was around to learn of a prestigious award that had been bestowed upon the two cops who had dogged him and his son for nearly a decade. Arthur's days were numbered, and at times it seemed like he knew it. During his last few months alive, Arthur frequently looked like death warmed over.

Prior to Perry's first case going to trial, Pat Postiglione and Bill Pridemore were named as the Metropolitan Police Department Investigators of the Year in an award ceremony presided over by Police Chief Ronal Serpas. The award was proudly provided to them for their relentless work over the past several years to bring closure to the Janet March case.

"The outstanding work on this case by Sergeant Postiglione and Detective Pridemore brought relief to Janet March's parents and hope to the families of other cold-case murder victims," Serpas said. "I am extremely proud of their efforts."

* * *

The first of Perry March's three criminal trials, each of which would be presided over by Davidson County Criminal Court judge Steve Dozier, was for his theft case for allegedly stealing money from his father-in-law's law firm, where he had worked. Prosecutor Tom Thurman wanted to try the theft case first, because if he could obtain a conviction in that case, he would be able to use that fact in an attempt to diminish Perry's credibility in the other two cases—particularly if Perry chose to testify in those cases.

The theft trial didn't take long. A jury was selected and sequestered on Monday, April 17, 2006, and by Wednesday, April 19, 2006, following only one hour of deliberations, it had convicted Perry March of stealing $23,000 from the law firm where he had worked.

"The theme of the case," said Ben Winters, one of the prosecutors, following the verdict, "was about betrayal. I mean, there wasn't a person that Mr. March dealt with that he didn't betray—from clients, to friends, to partners, to associates, and to in-laws."

The prosecution had played portions of Perry's 1996 videotaped deposition in which he could be seen and heard saying that he could not remember important details or simply refusing to answer the questions being asked.

"The most damaging thing in my mind was the deposition of Mr. March," said Ed Fowlkes, one of the attorneys representing Perry. "And it was damaging."

Jury selection for Perry's second trial, the murder-for-hire case, in which he faced charges of conspiracy to commit murder, got under way on Thursday, June 1, 2006.

Many local attorneys predicted at the outset that the recorded conversations between Perry and Nathaniel Farris, if played to the jury, could do him in at trial. Perry's defense attorneys were also looking to obtain records that would help discern the movements of Perry's former jail-house neighbor, alleged sex-offender Jeremy Duffer, who was still at large at the time of the trial after cutting off his ankle bracelet and skipping town. It wasn't likely that Duffer would be found in time to call as a witness, and it was uncertain what details, if any, might unfold if they learned his movements in the jail prior to his escape from house arrest later. Duffer's departure from the secure area of the jail, where he was held with Perry and Farris, had facilitated the conversations between the two that needed to occur if they were to plan the murders of the Levines.

Although Perry's attorneys had filed a notice of their possible intent to put on a defense of entrapment, local attorneys who were taking part in the soap opera, which was being trumpeted through a media circus, began publicly analyzing whether such a defense could be successful or not.

"Entrapment means that a law enforcement official, either directly or through another, induced or persuaded an otherwise unwilling person to commit a crime," said one of the local lawyers, a former prosecutor. "The key word(s) in entrapment is 'unwilling person.'"

Although Lawrence Levine had taken the stand to testify against Perry March, the chief witness against him was Nathaniel Farris, and the damning recordings of Perry's own voice plotting with Farris to murder the Levines. It took the jury of nine women and three men barely a week—and only six hours of deliberations over two days—to find Perry guilty on all counts. Their verdict was reached on Thursday, June 8, 2006.

* * *

On Thursday, June 22, 2006, Judge Steve Dozier ruled that a jury would be selected from outside of Nashville to hear the evidence and testimony of Perry March's second-degree murder trial. Dozier's decision was a response to a defense motion that had asked for a change of venue for the trial.

A month later, on July 24, the Tennessee Court of Appeals ruled to uphold the earlier temporary custody ruling in which the Levines had been granted custody of their grandchildren.

Three days later, Judge Dozier ruled that jurors at Perry March's murder trial would be allowed to hear that he had plotted to kill the Levines. Perry's lawyers had also argued that the statute of limitations had expired on the charges of tampering with evidence and abuse of a corpse and had asked that Judge Dozier throw out those charges. According to Tennessee statutes, prosecution must begin within two years after a person has been charged with abuse of a corpse and within four years for a charge of tampering with evidence. Prosecutors, however, had argued that the statute of limitations should be extended because of the fact that Perry had left the country. Judge Dozier agreed and allowed the disputed charges to stand.

Somewhere in between all of Dozier's rulings, Deputy DA Tom Thurman had told the judge that Arthur March was too ill to travel to Nashville from the federal facility where he was being housed at that time in Kentucky. Thurman also said that Arthur was too ill to testify against Perry, and asked that he be declared unavailable for the upcoming trial. Dozier granted Thurman's request, and it was decided that the jury would still be allowed to hear and view Arthur March's videotaped deposition. Dozier also ruled that the jury at Perry's murder trial would be allowed to know details of Perry's offer to Postiglione and Pridemore to plead guilty, and that they would also hear information in which he had told the cops that he was not really guilty and would only take a deal to avoid a long sentence.

Jury selection began on Monday, August 7, 2006, in Chattanooga, Tennessee, for Perry March's—third and final—trial. This one was for allegedly killing his wife, evidence tampering, and abuse of a corpse, as yet another media circus descended upon Nashville by news outlets from around the nation. Following an intense seven-hour process, six women and six men were selected after focusing on the question of whether they could convict someone of murder without a body. The jury consisted of nine white people and three African Americans. Four alternates were also selected. Afterward, they were transported by bus to Nashville, where they were sequestered at a location that was not made public.

As opening statements were under way on Wednesday, August 9, the drama of the Perry March saga intensified for a short while when members of Perry's defense team presented Tom Thurman a letter that had been received the prior afternoon from a person who claimed to have been a former lover of Janet March's who had purportedly carried on a relationship with her after she disappeared. The letter, which the defense claimed had been written by a convicted felon by the name of Barry Armstead, purportedly contained information that claimed Janet had taken sleeping pills and drank alcohol while depressed and had died. The letter writer had also claimed that he had disposed of Janet's body. The defense team asked for a delay in Perry's trial due to the appearance of the mysterious letter. Judge Dozier promptly denied the defense request for a continuance.

"A wacko could send an anonymous letter and delay every pending case in Nashville, if that were the criteria for a continuance," Dozier said.

Judge Dozier immediately sent for Armstead, who was incarcerated at the Riverbend Maximum Security Institution, for questioning. Riverbend is the prison that once held James Earl Ray and serial killer Paul Reid. The prosecution and defense teams later questioned Armstead about the letter. He denied that he had written it, and he refused to testify.

"We don't know where she went. We don't know if she's dead, and you know what? Neither do they," defense attorney Bill Massey said in his opening statement as he pointed toward the prosecution team. "Psychics, cadaver dogs, and inmates: that's what this case is about. How can you accuse murder when you don't know she's dead? How can you tamper with a corpse when you don't have a body? How do you tamper with evidence when there is none?"

The prosecution's opening statements outlined Perry and Janet's troubled marriage, and took the jury through a history that spanned ten years and culminated inside the Metro Jail, where Perry had masterminded a plan to kill Janet's parents. Tom Thurman said that Janet had planned to have a consultation with a divorce attorney, and had scheduled an appointment for August 16, 1996.

"That was an appointment that cost her, her life," Thurman said.

Prosecutors, as expected, put on a case of purely circumstantial evidence based on the facts of the case as they were known at the time. The jury heard testimony from Janet's mother, as well as from several of Janet's friends, in which they claimed that Perry had been both emotionally and psychologically abusive toward Janet. There was also testimony of marital problems, impending divorce, and Perry's sexually explicit letters to the paralegal.

As in his first two trials, it did not take long for the jury to decide Perry's fate. Perry had taken the witness stand long enough to say: "I choose not to testify." When all the evidence, circumstantial as it may have been, was laid out in a linear fashion for the jury to see, and when combined with testimony from a long list of witnesses from as far away as Mexico, the jury returned a verdict of guilty on all counts after barely two days of deliberations. As in his previous two trials, Perry showed little or no emotion when the verdict was returned on Thursday, August 17, 2006. Ten years and two days after Janet March disappeared without a trace, justice had finally found its way into Perry's life.

Afterward, Perry's attorneys vowed to appeal the verdict and indicated that they would ask for a new trial. As a matter of routine precaution, Perry was placed on a seventy-two-hour suicide watch in the special management unit of the Metro Jail.

On Wednesday, September 6, 2006, Judge Steve Dozier sentenced Perry March to fifty-six years in prison. One of Perry's attorneys, William Massey, said that he had expected a heavy sentence, and stressed that he looked forward to the next phase—appeals—and expressed confidence that the "system would vindicate him."

Arthur March's sentencing, which had been scheduled for May 1, had been postponed until after Perry's trials had occurred. His plea agreement had called for him to serve eighteen months in prison with a term of three years' probation. However, much to the surprise of Arthur and his attorney, Fletcher Long, the sentencing judge ignored the plea agreement and sentenced Arthur to five years in prison.

"I did not foresee this happening, and to say that we're devastated is probably a gross understatement," Long said of the sentencing judge's decision. Long said that had Arthur known that he would have been sentenced to five years instead of eighteen months, he would never have agreed to plead guilty. Long said that Arthur's sentence was equivalent to a death sentence, because he would never live long enough to gain his release.

Fletcher Long's prediction had been on the mark. Arthur March, after serving four months of his five-year sentence, died of respiratory failure on Thursday, December 21, 2006, at a federal medical facility in Fort Worth, Texas, where he had been transferred because of health concerns. He was buried three days later. Perry March was not allowed to attend his father's funeral.

As previously stated, Arthur March had granted *48 Hours* a final interview a few months before his death. According to the story by Bill Lagattuta, which aired on CBS in January 2007, Arthur March was no longer the same man that he had interviewed for the first time years earlier. No longer full of life, Arthur told Lagattuta that he never conspired with anyone to have the Levines killed.

"When you listen to those phone calls, it sure sounded like you were in on it," Lagattuta said.

"Well, it does," Arthur responded. "I have a big mouth. And I probably said some things I shouldn't have said."

"Did Perry tell you that he had killed Janet?" Lagattuta asked.

"Yes!" Arthur replied. "The only thing I did was help him remove the body from where he had buried it. . . . I picked it up, the body, and it was nighttime. I had one little flashlight. But I got it done."

He told Lagattuta the story of how he and Perry had driven Janet's body to Kentucky, where he had disposed of it in a brush pile, which he believed would later be set afire. At one point Lagattuta asked him how he could do such a thing to his daughter-in-law.

"Because at this point in time," Arthur responded, "she was not my daughter-in-law anymore. She was just a dead body. . . . It was over. I had taken care of the body in such a way that nobody would ever find it."

"He said he's following the creek all the way along," Postiglione told Lagattuta. "As he's driving back, he looks up, and lo and behold, there's this brush pile."

"And he takes parts of the body, disposes [them] in the brush pile," Pridemore added. "Drives back. Tells Perry, 'Don't worry about it. It's taken care of. Go back to sleep.' Perry just sleeps through this whole thing while his dad is out there disposing of his wife."

"His days are done in terms of Perry March, Perry March, Perry March," Postiglione said. "That's over. And now maybe the attention will be on Janet versus Perry. It was a satisfaction of knowing that finally some justice for Janet, so to speak, she's finally gonna get some justice."

"I'm sorry and sad that our grandchildren have had to live ten years without their mother and with the person who took her from them," Carolyn Levine said. "There's not a day that goes by that I don't think about my daughter. She had so many talents. She was a very caring, compassionate person. Every parent thinks their kid is special. But she really was."

* * *

As of this writing, Lawrence and Carolyn Levine still retained custody of their grandchildren, Sammy and Tzipi, providing them a well-balanced life, good education, and helping them as best they can to try and make some sense out of the horrific ordeal that had taken the life of their mother and had literally destroyed their family unit—twice. They are still battling Perry March in court for permanent custody of the children.

Russell Nathaniel Farris, still entangled in the grip of the Tennessee legal system, was released on 10 years' supervised probation on February 8, 2007, following a guilty plea to facilitation of aggravated robbery from a case that dated from February 2005. The assistance he provided in the Perry March case was a major reason that he received probation.

However, Farris's new-found freedom did not last long. Four days after his release, Farris was drug tested as part of his probation. He tested positive for cocaine. According to his attorney, Farris was supposed to turn himself in. When he didn't, a warrant was issued for his arrest on Valentine's Day, February 14, 2007.

A little more than two weeks later, the police located him in a seedy east Nashville motel where he was holed up with his ex-girlfriend. On Saturday, March 2, 2007, local police, accompanied by the U.S. Marshals and a Metro SWAT team, surrounded the motel at approximately 3 P.M. When confronted by the police, Farris refused to give up and a standoff began. The SWAT team had shown up at the scene because Farris apparently told officers that he was armed. Sgt. Pat Postiglione, as well as Farris's lawyer, Justin Johnson, and his mother stood by, occasionally pleading with him to give himself up.

Finally, six hours later, Farris surrendered. He was taken into custody and charged with violating his probation by using drugs and for causing an armed standoff with the police.

"He was a drug addict that got out on the street who had not had drugs for quite some time, and it was just a really powerful draw," said his attorney, Justin Johnson.

"In February I said the keys to the jail were in his own hands," said Davidson County Deputy DA Rob McGuire. "If he goes to prison he's turning the key. He blew it, in record time."

On Friday, March 30, 2007, Farris, in tears, pleaded guilty to the charges. He testified during the hearing that the day after his release from jail, he attended his brother's birthday party where he smoked marijuana that had been laced with cocaine. Davidson County Criminal Court Judge Cheryl Blackburn ordered Farris to begin serving the 10-year sentence that previously had been suspended due to probation. Because he was now known as a jail snitch, Farris would be placed on 23-hour lockdown for his own protection in the state prison system.

"Not only did he lose his freedom on the street," Johnson said, "he lost his freedom in jail."

While Farris was busy sorting out his legal problems with the authorities, Perry March began to have issues of his own. The local press cited that security concerns had arisen in early March 2007, prompting prison officials to transfer Perry from the Northwest Correctional Complex in Tiptonville, Tennessee, to the West Tennessee High Security Facility in Henning, Tennessee, where he was placed in isolation. According to his attorney, John

Herbison, Perry had purportedly received death threats from other inmates.

"Perry called his sister," Herbison told a *Tennessean* reporter, "and she was able to hear chanting in the background. . . ." Apparently a group of inmates were chanting, *Kill the fucking Jew.*

"It does seem odd," Herbison said, "because from the way Perry described it, he was doing well at Northwest prison."

For the next few weeks, prison officials remained tight-lipped about the transfer.

"All I can say is there were concerns of the security of the institution," said Dorinda Carter, a spokesperson for the Tennessee Department of Corrections. "There's still an investigation going on, so I can't say much more than that."

However, as news of Perry's transfer to the high-security prison trickled out, it was eventually revealed that he was moved because prison officials had uncovered an escape plot that involved him at the Northwest facility. According to the "plot," Perry was planning to somehow get transferred to a less secure prison so that he could escape. Instead, he was moved to a maximum security prison and placed in an isolation cell.

"We received information that (indicated) he was hoping to be moved to a minimum-security annex facility," Dorinda Carter told reporters. "If that happened, he was planning on escaping from that facility." Carter declined to say how prison officials learned of the alleged escape plot.

Perry March, due to his convictions, became one of 36,000 felons serving their sentences at various prisons in Tennessee. When he isn't filing petitions against the Levines in an attempt to regain custody of his children, he spends most of his days uneventfully.

Recently WSMV-Channel 4 in Nashville televised a number of interviews that their reporter, Dennis Ferrier, conducted with Janet's brother, Mark Levine, in November 2006. The interviews were well-received, particularly those shown in a two-part special, "Janet March's Untold Story," in January 2007. Ferrier had also been positioned to interview Perry March while Perry lived it up in Mexico and recently vocalized some of his experiences with him.

"I'll tell you what the deal is," Ferrier told a reporter for the *Nashville Scene*. "Perry March was the kind of guy you could sit by his pool and drink margaritas with as long as you kissed his butt and didn't ask too many tough questions. He would talk all day, and he would call you and take your phone calls," provided that he liked the questions that were being asked.

However, during that trip to Mexico, Ferrier had decided that he would go up against Perry, and instead of sympathizing with him, he would investigate the allegations of questionable business deals that were being made against him by his fellow expatriates and Mexicans alike. What Ferrier had discovered then was Perry's standard operating procedure of using "bullyboy threats against any local who would try to stand up to him." When Perry had learned what Ferrier had been up to, he became angry, and according to Ferrier, he had attacked Ferrier's cameraman and had broken the camera's viewfinder. Perry's parting words to Ferrier had been: "Eat shit and die."

"As I left, he kept demanding, 'Where are you staying? I need to know where you're staying,'" Ferrier said. "I don't think he wanted to send me a fruit basket."

Perry March will be eligible for parole in 2040.

MORE MUST-READ TRUE CRIME FROM
M. William Phelps